A Letter to the Reader

If you're thinking of starting your own business . . . if you've just started your own business . . . if you've been in business for a year or two . . . there're things you badly need to know. That's what this book is all about.

Things that'll make all the difference between your small business surviving . . . or going under. I'm talking about what *really* goes on, not what many people would like you to *think* goes on. Yet much of this vital information does not get talked about or written about, frankly and openly, because it would help business newcomers immensely–but only them. It would hurt the interests of everyone else out there, hustling and hyping their different brands of Small Business Snake Oil, to all those innocent, green, naive business neophytes, each with their tempting little nest eggs of start-up cash, ready to be spent.

So I wrote this book for the newcomers on the small business scene. It covers every "survival priority." It tells the truth, clearly and readably. Read it cover to cover. Reread it from time to time. And you will have a much better chance of being among the 30 percent who survive, rather than the 70 percent who don't.

The good news is that there's never been a better time to start and run your own business. For all sorts of encouraging reasons. This news gets a lot of upbeat, feel-good press coverage . . . but this is only part of the story. There's more news.

The old news is that it's always been pretty tough to do what you're planning to do, and it's no different today. It's a long, hard grind and you pay a high personal price. This old news doesn't get much media coverage; downbeat stuff doesn't sell newspapers, books or TV programs.

The bad news is that the Small Business sector has become a major "market segment" for Corporate and Professional America, hyping every product and service you can imagine, plus some you can't. So they're promoting Small Business like they sell body lotion–glamorizing it, romanticizing it, making it look trendy, quick and easy, oh so easy. This deceptive, self-serving hype never gets media coverage. Who wants to stomp on the toes of all those fat advertising clients with their multimillion-dollar budgets? Start believing the BS these folks throw out at you daily, that it's all easy and that success is just around the corner, and you're going to get your priorities all wrong, from the moment you start . . . and you'll soon join the 70 percent club of failures, just because your focus was wrong.

Forget about success. It comes when it comes, and not a moment sooner. It's in the hands of the gods. Concentrate on surviving . . . that way you'll still be around to enjoy the success, when the gods finally look your way.

So keep your attention tightly, constantly and single-mindedly focused on *surviving* through those tough first years. That's all that matters. The rest comes later. And I wish you the best of luck in your efforts. Luck always comes in handy.

About the Author

Tom Culley knows about beating the odds . . . and about running scared.

At age twenty-four, he was given a probationary admittance to the graduate MBA program at the Wharton School of the University of Pennsylvania . . . meaning: fail any course and you're out on your neck. This, because he never went to college, did not have an undergraduate degree and had finished the British equivalent of high school at the tender age of seventeen, to go to work in a small family insurance business in Rio de Janeiro.

So he ran scared.

After only sixteen months at graduate school, he surprised everyone, himself included, by graduating in first place in the Wharton MBA class of '65, with honors society stuff, the works. He is the only businessman in the U.S. ever to have placed first in his class at a top graduate business school, without first having gone to college. He explains this extraordinary achievement rationally: *fear motivates, absolute fear motivates absolutely.*

So he beat the odds, first time around.

Bursting with self-confidence, he then started an entrepreneurial supermarket venture in Brazil, with a fellow Wharton MBA. Four years later, the business went spectacularly bust, from too rapid expansion.

The second time around, the odds were tougher.

So much for MBAs. Welcome to the real world of small business.

From there, Tom Culley built a most unusual, diversified professional career, spanning both the corporate and the entrepreneurial worlds.

In Big Business, as a McKinsey & Co. consultant in the U.S. and Europe, and as an international corporate executive with Nestlé and other major companies. In Small Business, as an entrepreneurial workout artist, start-up operator and hands-on manager, in a diversity of small and medium-sized businesses in both Brazil and the U.S.

Finally, he took a professional "sabbatical" to concentrate on writing a comprehensive book he felt was sorely needed in the entrepreneurial field: a book explaining the hard realities of small business life to newcomers, to help them beat the odds against survival.

Tom Culley's book had been steadily incubating for many years, as he learned from his own business successes (and failures) and observed up close the struggles of small business owners . . . and the needless early demise of many of them. Always wondering why it was so hard to find an honest book about small business, which tells the unvarnished truth to those who so badly need to know it.

He self-published the first edition of *Beating the Odds in Small Business* in South Florida, where its grassroots success attracted the attention of Simon & Schuster, now the publisher of this new edition of his original book.

Tom Culley now lives in Connecticut, where he and his partner run their own business . . . named, naturally enough, *Small Business Matters, Inc.*

BEATING THE ODDS IN SMALL BUSINESS

Tom Culley

A Fireside Book
Published by Simon & Schuster

FIRESIDE
Rockefeller Center
1230 Avenue of the Americas
New York, New York 10020

First Fireside Edition 1998.

FIRESIDE and colophon are registered trademarks
of Simon & Schuster Inc.

Beating the Odds in Small Business is a
trademark of Small Business Matters Inc.

Designed by Tom Culley with Katy Riegel

Manufactured in the United States of America

10 9 8 7 6 5 4 3 2 1

Library of Congress Cataloging-in-Publication Data
Culley, Tom.
    Beating the odds in small business / Tom Culley.
        p.   cm.
    Includes index.
    ISBN 0-684-84183-5
    1. Small business--Management.   2. Success in business.
I. Title.
HD62.7.C85   1998   97-36427
658.02'2--dc21   CIP

ISBN 0-684-84183-5

Permissions

The quotes and excerpts in this book, from the newspapers and national magazines indicated in each quote side panel, are reprinted from various issues by kind permission of the respective publishers:

- *The Wall Street Journal* © 1994/96 by Dow Jones & Company, Inc. All rights reserved.
- *The New York Times* © 1994/96 by The New York Times Company. All rights reserved.
- *The Miami Herald* © 1994/96 by The Miami Herald. All rights reserved.
- *Business Week* © 1994/96 by The McGraw-Hill Companies. All rights reserved.
- *Fortune* © 1994/96 by Time Inc. All rights reserved.
- *Time* © 1994/96 by Time Inc. All rights reserved.
- *Esquire* © 1994/96 by The Hearst Corporation. All rights reserved.
- *Inc.* magazine © 1996/97 by Inc. All rights reserved.

The author thanks each of these publishers for their understanding and support of this book and its aims.

In Thanks

There are those special people who helped keep me going, when cold, hard reason was telling me to throw in the towel, you conceited fool.

No long, boring lists of names . . . they know who they are.

Thanks, to each and all of you. Yet a special, sweeping doff of the cap is due . . .

to Fred Hills, my editor, who bet on a dark horse with long legs,

to Keith and Kristin Lyon, my business partners and friends, for support over and beyond,

to Amy Wade, my sister, for transatlantic help, encouragement and much more,

to Liam Brown, a supporter and fan, for contagious conviction in what the future holds.

In Dedication

To my father, another Tom Culley, from another world and long gone era, who nevertheless would have gotten one delighted chuckle out of all of this, had he been around to read it, out beside the river on the swing chair in the morning sun.

There's got to be a library up there.

About Legal Disclaimers

In microscopic type, buried among those little notes that publishers love to place in the first pages of their books, I was told I should put this kind of save-my-precious-butt boilerplate disclaimer:

> This publication is designed to provide accurate and authoritative information in regard to the subject matter covered. It is sold with the understanding that the publisher is not engaged in rendering legal, accounting, or other professional service. If legal advice or other expert assistance is required, the services of a competent professional person should be sought.
>
> *—From the declaration of principles jointly adopted by a committee of the American Bar Association and a committee of publishers*

In translation, here's what those illustrious committee members are telling me I should tell you (with a nasty "or else" hidden in there somewhere): Look, folks, I don't really know too much about what I'm talking about. In fact, I don't really think my advice is much good at all. Come to think of it, don't even know why I wrote this book. So please don't sue me, if you make some idiotic, bone-headed mistake in running your own small business and you (and your lawyer) want to pin the blame on someone else, because it's not my fault either, see, because basically I'm just a rank amateur. What you should have done all along is not read my book, let alone buy it, but instead go talk to someone who really is competent like . . . *now would you believe this?* . . . a lawyer, an accountant or other "professional person."

For a professional fee, natch. One that might turn out to be pretty horrendously heavy for your small business's very limited financial resources. But hey, pal, us professionals have gotta stick together, gotta help each other turn a fast buck, any which way. That's what committee members are all about.

That's also one small part of what this book's all about.

Check out Chapter 13. I have my own point of view on these jokers.

Only personal opinions, you understand. Nothing you could ever sue me for. After all, what do I know?

So here's my amended version of that boilerplate disclaimer:

> This publication is designed to provide you with honest advice from the real world of business. Like everything else in this imperfect world, this book can't be perfect but you're getting my best shot and my hardest work for your money. Everything in this book represents only my opinions, from a lifetime of real-world experience. They're the best opinions I've got to give, but they don't come with a five-year money-back warranty. If you think my advice ain't worth diddly squat, that's your opinion and you're entitled to it. Go take your spending money elsewhere and buy yourself some trendy guru book, with the right disclaimer (in real small type). See how much good that's gonna do you. This book is sold with the understanding that the author is not engaged in rendering legal, accounting, astronautical, biophysical, theological, zoological, medical, psychiatric or all and any other professional service of any shape, size or form. You name it, I'm not engaged in it, don't do it, never did. So there. And, by the way, I still think this is the best book of its kind around, bar none. But that's only my opinion, you understand. What do I know?
>
> *—From my declaration of my own principles*

CONTENTS

Warning Label

Lest There Be Misunderstandings:

This Isn't a Management Theory Book . . .
It's About Running Your Own Business, Is All

Success = Easy; Survival = Hard

Words paint pictures in your mind.

Almost everything you hear or read or see these days about small business, your own business, home business, new ventures and entrepreneurial activities, comes plastered all over with that glitzy word *success*. Why? Because the word almost makes a promise by itself. It paints pictures of instant gratification, of goodies you richly deserve and are going to grab very soon, of something that may take a little work but is, somehow or other, *quick and easy*.

Success = Easy.

The hustlers flashing you this seductive *S* word use it only because they want to sell you something. A whole lot of somethings. They want you to hand over your wallet and lay open your checkbook. They want you to start your own business, not because they have your best interests at heart, but so that you will spend your money and buy whatever services or products or deals or dreams they are hyping. Right away, while you are still wet behind the ears and still have some start-up capital to spend. What happens to you a little later on, once you've spent it all, is not something these Good Samaritans stay awake at nights worrying about. You don't have to be a marketing genius to know that salespeople close sales by making you promises you'd love to believe.

And you'd love to believe the promise of success, wouldn't you?

Sorry, folks. Wrong *S* word.

Success, when and if it comes, comes much later. Only after you've overcome many obstacles and shed your fair share of blood, sweat and tears.

The right *S* word is *survival.* Not a cosy, comforting word; a cold, unforgiving word, which conjures up images of suffering and struggle. The moment you hear the word *survival,* a little voice inside warns: uh-oh, this means *hard.* Not a word that is going to entice you to race off and plunge heedlessly into a new business venture. Not a word that those marketing folks like to use. Even if it is the correct and honest word to use . . . in fact, the only word to use.

This book is about survival. It is not about success. I wish you all the success in the world. But what I will teach you is survival. Success is the fun part, and that you will be able to handle on your own . . . if you've made it through the survival stage.

Survival is the operative word for what matters in starting and running your own small business. If everything I have to tell you in this book makes you run screaming for the exit, the way I see it is I've done you a big favor. If it makes you grit your teeth, mutter, *I thought there was a catch here somewhere but now at least I know what it is,* yet still persist in your small business plans, then this book will have been one of your better investments.

> Depend on it, Sir, when a man knows he is to be hanged in a fortnight, it concentrates his mind wonderfully.
> —Dr. Samuel Johnson, 19 September 1777

Survival = Hard.

Hard but possible, hard but doable. If you have the right focus.

So They're Telling You It's Easy?

Small business newcomers would naturally like to believe that business is easy, and that there are shortcuts to success. There are a whole bunch of predators out there, who make a living fostering such illusions. You'll read about them, shortly. They won't appreciate my book. But then, this book's for you, not them.

There's no way around it. Small business is tough. Hard work. Long hours. Serious problems. Heavy responsibilities. Self-discipline. Self-criticism. Worries. Sacrifices. Detail work. Persistence. No self-indulgence. No ego trips. You're very much on your own. It's tough . . . it's hard . . . it's lonely.

> Most people suffer from what I call the Doris Day School of Management. They think life is a bubble bath. Well, it's not.
> —Michael Feuer, head of OfficeMax, quoted in *Fortune*

Qualifications? Only two, really (apart from the essential personality and character traits you need to endure all that tough stuff). One is common sense–a whole lot of common sense. Another is a substantial dose of smarts–street smarts, not academic smarts. With those two qualifications, you can get started in small business just as well as anyone else. From there on, it's on-the-job learning, which is up to you and you alone.

No, you really don't need a stack of technical qualifications, academic achievements and big-time business experience. In fact, businesspeople with impressive credentials don't seem to do any better in small business than the credentially deprived. If you're looking for a job, sure, that's what you'll need, prettily presented in a shiny résumé.

But no one's going to interview you for your small business job. You have to interview yourself. If you do it right, it'll be the toughest job interview you'll ever have. You have to look hard in the mirror, ask yourself the toughest questions and give yourself the straightest answers. Painful but essential. Otherwise, you'll only be fooling yourself. You'll pay for that self-deception, sooner than you'd expect.

So what's the big problem?

It's that the majority of new small businesses do not survive. They close down in their first year or two. Go belly-up. Kaput.

Why?

Because the newcomers don't understand the jungle they're stepping into. Not from stupidity but because they happily swallow the sweet-smelling success snake oil the hustlers and the gurus are hyping out there and they buy their "rose garden" vision of small business.

Because they do all the unimportant, unnecessary, unwise and time-consuming things they are told trendy modern managers must do, instead of those basic, dreary, boring, critical, essential tasks that might save their entrepreneurial asses.

As a result, they make too many mistakes, early on . . . and fail. New small businesses are babies. They're frail and fragile in their first years. A couple of bad mistakes is all it takes to wipe them out. Older, established businesses make their share of mistakes too, but they have more resilience and greater staying power. They're tougher. They've learned their survival skills. They've built up their defenses.

You may want to believe that small business should be like high school, where you get a chance to learn from your mistakes and gradually develop your skills. Not be dragged out into the schoolyard and summarily shot, the first time you get the answer wrong. But small business isn't a school. It's a jungle where you are fighting from Day One to survive.

> The opportunities to make a killing, and make it fast, are spectacular in small business. So are the opportunities to lose everything. The big goof that leads to a lost merit raise in corporate America, can lead to a lost *company* in small business.
>
> –The Wall Street Journal

So Is It Worth the Effort?

Survival in small business is all about focus, not about brilliance. Focus on reality. Focus on dangers. Focus on opportunities. Hard-nosed focus, always. You've heard the many stories of successful businesspeople who started from nowhere, with only average abilities and intelligence. No geniuses here. Often the only thing that separated these successful entrepreneurs from the failures is that they had no illusions about the harsh realities of business, from Day One. They got their focus straight, right off. They concentrated on the basic tasks that would guarantee their survival. They did the right things, from the start.

Now here's the good news, before you decide you have just bought the Business Book from Hell.

Yes, it's worth it. It's worth the tough parts and the rough times and the scary risks. In spades. The rewards of being your own boss, running your own small business, are immeasurably greater than being some corporation's employee. Especially in today's miserable, neurotic, downsized, restructured, reengineered corporate world. It's not just the opportunity of being better off financially–possibly much better off, if you're lucky. It's the extraordinary satisfaction of working for yourself. That's the ultimate in "job satisfaction." Satisfying yourself, not some impersonal corporation or bozo boss.

The Dealers in Success Snake Oil

But it's hard and that should come as no surprise; it's no big secret.

So you'd at least expect that business books and entrepreneurial magazines, seminars, workshops and what-have-you would treat the subject respectfully and dead serious, focusing on survival instruction. Like being trained in piloting, parachuting, mountain climbing or scuba diving. Where the instructors are honest, they feel responsible for their students' well-being, and their message is:

"Get this basic stuff straight, pal, take it seriously, learn it carefully and use it always. Or you're toast."

Fairly logical, right? But that just ain't the way things work in the Wonderful World of Entrepreneurial Preparation.

There's a whole thriving industry out there, selling a whole different rose-tinted vision of small business heaven, through books, magazines, newpapers, TV and radio talk shows, videotapes, audiotapes, courses, seminars, advertisements, you name it.

There's a whole lot of hogwash out there. Dangerous, misleading, dishonest hogwash. Hogwash that points you in the wrong direction. Hogwash that sets you up for a fall. Hogwash that sells you "business opportunities" that you need like a hole in the head. Hogwash that sells you business stuff you don't need and business services you can do without.

What isn't hogwash is often just repainted, reupholstered and retuned basic business common sense. What there is of value usually applies only to the problems of mid- and large-size corporations, with their complex organizational and managerial problems and their inefficient, ingrained corporate cultures.

That is an entirely different world from the small business world you're planning to live in and survive in. You'll have plenty of problems, for sure, but of a whole different kind.

Turn to the business gurus, and you'll be fed an endless stream of the latest organizational theories and newest management fads, trendy buzzwords and fashionable slogans, motivational seminars and touchy-feely workshops and politically correct agendas.

Their messages are relentlessly upbeat . . . just follow the advice, little children, change your attitudes, get in touch with your Inner Child, try the Seven Healthful Management Systems of This, follow the Twenty-nine Successful Business Steps of That, adopt the One Hundred Personal Hygiene Habits of Top Corporate Chieftains and, bingo, you'll be a successful entrepreneur quicker than you can say Deepak Chopra, Stephen Covey, Tom Peters or Anthony Robbins. Everything'll work out just fine.

It won't. Believe me. Not with that kind of advice, it won't.

IGNORE THE PSYCHICS AND STICK WITH WHAT YOU FIND MEANINGFUL

The search for deeper meaning in one's career goes on. Consider these nuggets from the American Management Association's recent conference . . .

All people are spiritual and all work is sacred, said [an executive coach]. She suggested, among other things, that people take time out each day to "concentrate" –i.e., meditate or pray. Eventually . . . we can make the workplace "a sanctuary that is purified from the corrupting influences in the world." . . .

[Another executive coach] described how she develops a "perfect life vision" for clients by asking them to describe a time when they felt fully utilized and to imagine how they would spend their time if there weren't work, family or money considerations.

Certainly, finding work you consider meaningful is important. But I wonder what planet some of these people come from. Certainly not this messy, imperfect orb, where careers are often embroiled in office politics, tough tradeoffs and grim economic realities, and work, family or money are nearly always considerations. Instead of a sense of spirituality or perfection, I recommend a sense of purpose and a sense of humor.

–Hal Lancaster, *The Wall Street Journal*

It will only increase the probability of failure, by giving you bum steers, hokey advice, a highly distorted view of the real business world and unwarranted optimism. But this stuff is all so well packaged, so smoothly marketed, so sexy, that many readers don't see it for what it really is: fluff, pure fluff.

So they overlook the harsh realities of the real business world they are entering. They don't learn the sometimes unattractive, often dreary and usually plodding "business basics" that might just possibly be the key to their survival in their own businesses.

Overdosing on Advice

Like intelligent dieting or healthy living, there is only so much good, practical, solid advice that can be given about business. Beyond that, it's just a waste of time and money.

In small business, you really need to know two things: the realities of your situation (Are there thunderclouds out there? Is the weather clearing?) and the operating basics (How do you pilot the damn thing and land it safely?). Beyond that, success or failure is strictly a matter of your own competence, hard work, skill, talent, common sense, intelligence . . . and plain, old-fashioned dumb luck, good or bad.

But the folks who make their living hustling management "advice" have to keep inventing new angles, new theories and new miracle solutions. To keep selling those books, magazines, videos, seminars, workshops and consulting services, naturally.

Now that's no big deal in the diet and health businesses. It's part of the game and no real harm is done. So you blew twenty bucks on a glossy book touting the latest miracle diet and it didn't work. You're still twenty pounds overweight. But no real damage was done . . . except maybe to your pride and motivation. You learned something, even if it wasn't what you intended. On to the next diet, on to the next book.

It works that way in Big Business, where every few years top management switches gears to the latest, most fashionable organizational or management theory. Gotta stay current, gotta keep trendy.

> **ON THE BRIGHT SIDE, HE'S BEEN LOSING WEIGHT STEADILY SINCE**
> Stuart Berger, the author of *Dr. Berger's Immune Power Diet,* died at forty weighing nearly four hundred pounds.
> —*Esquire*

> Just as reading diet books is a substitute for losing weight, reading management books is a substitute for good management.
> —Professor Terrence Deal, Vanderbilt University, quoted by Eric Schonfeld, *Fortune*

But it doesn't work that way in Small Business.

You can't screw around in Small Business. You can't keep switching priorities and directions. You can't change management methods and business procedures the way you change your clothes. Most small businesspeople have only one shot at getting it right and very little time in which to do it. Small business is a constant battle for survival. The time, effort, attention and money you can end up devoting to the latest, trendiest management fads, business fashions and organizational theories is all time, effort, attention and money diverted from your small business's priorities.

Which can tip the balance between survival or failure. And most businesspeople who fail don't or can't go around for a second try. You can get blown away, financially and emotionally.

It isn't funny, it isn't a game and it just isn't right that so much irrelevant, misleading "advice" is hyped as the Shining Path to Easy Success, to people embarking on one of the more serious ventures in their short lives.

So pay no attention to all that trendy advice and those feel-good philosophies. Just remember:

Survival comes first. Concentrate all your initial efforts on surviving in the jungle. You can have fun with success when you're out of the woods.

Grasping Reality

The single biggest problem facing people starting out in small business is this: they don't correctly and fully comprehend what is really going on in the world they are about to enter. How can you get off to a good start if you haven't gotten it straight to begin with? Especially if time is not on your side, due to the natural vulnerability of new businesses and the narrow time frame you have to get your act together.

So, as the Grinch Who Stole Your Small Business Christmas, I must first straighten out this little problem of rosy perceptions and unreasonable expectations. There won't be much point in giving you detailed advice if we haven't reached a clear, common understanding on what the realities are all about. We have to be talking about the same jungle, the same dangers and the same opportunities.

Check it out for yourself. Go talk to anyone, friend or family, who's been in their own small business for the past few years, and ask them a straightforward question: "Before you started out, did you have a clear idea of the realities of the world you were getting into?" The straight answer will always be: "No way. It was much tougher than I could ever have imagined."

My advice in this book can never cover each specific problem or difficult situation you will face, or each snap decision you will have to make. You'll have to rely on your own cold-blooded, commonsense, hard-nosed vision of the real business world, with all its warts and blemishes (and the occasional beauty spot), so that you can call your own shots quickly and correctly.

Better the devil you know . . .

Awareness of the Outside World

It's not just the "rose garden syndrome" and the distorted vision of reality that this creates. It's also that your vision has to be external. Your small business, even if it's operated from an old desk, a beat-up computer and a single telephone line in a corner of your bedroom, *exists and survives in the outside world.*

Not just in your bedroom.

The outside world has a nasty habit of creeping up and sucker-punching small businesses when they least expect it. Much of what happens to your small business, both good news and bad news, will relate to the outside world. Sometimes just around the corner, sometimes on the other side of the globe.

Too many beginners in small business feel that all they need to know is the narrow specifics of the particular business they are entering. "Hey, I'm great at Italian cooking. Let's open a little pasta joint."

That's asking for trouble. Some of the serious problems that can happen arise for external reasons that often have little or nothing to do with the specific nature of the business itself. You can serve the world's greatest pasta, you can have customers waiting in line at your restaurant door–and you can still go bankrupt very, very easily and for any number of excellent reasons that have nothing whatever to do with how delicious your pesto sauce tastes.

Grasping the Details, Staying Informed

As you move through this book, we will progressively cover everything you have to know about each and all of the survival priorities, without getting overly hung up on too much detail. We'll cover all the essential areas but avoid overloading you. It's the main messages that matter; details will be much easier to grasp once you've got the survival priorities in focus.

In Bob Dylan's words, "You don't need to be a weatherman to know which way the wind blows." *But you do need to know which way the business wind is blowing and how hard.*

When we're finished, you'll feel comfortable with what you thought were difficult, complex business subjects and you'll no longer be intimidated by them. From then on, I strongly recommend that you make a personal habit of keeping up-to-date by regularly–even if superficially–reading the business pages of your local daily paper or the better business magazines. It won't exactly be fun reading, but it'll take only a few minutes of your day, and it'll always give you an "edge." That way, what you've picked up in this book will stay fresh and up-to-date.

That edge just might, one fine day, spell the difference between your success or failure. By staying well informed, you'll always have an advantage, since you'll have a realistic perspective from which to be thinking through solutions to problems that arise. You'll make your decisions faster and better, because you'll have more self-confidence that you can see "the big picture."

Remember, in this book we're talking about today's "big picture." But the world is changing constantly, at a faster and faster pace. Things will look different, maybe very different, just a few years from now. We don't have a crystal ball to tell you what's headed your way. So keeping up-to-date and well informed is a daily business habit, like brushing your teeth, which will always be good for your business health.

Obviously, there will always be further details I don't and won't and can't cover. That is your responsibility. As you become familiar and comfort-able with all the areas I discuss (and remember, not all of them will necessarily apply to your specific situation, although they will all help build your overall business knowledge and self-confidence), you must develop the self-discipline to progressively teach yourself the additional detailed knowledge that you will continually need in your specific business activity, as you grow and develop.

Many successful entrepreneurs are often self-taught and they keep learning until the end of the game. They never fall into the trap of thinking they know it all.

Don't feel overwhelmed: the techniques, skills and business knowledge you will need to stay on top of your small business are simply not that complicated. There's often a lot of detail to master, but we're not talking nuclear science or managing General Motors; it's all pretty basic stuff. You just have to make sure you understand what's going on and work at getting a solid grasp of those details that apply to your own business situation.

Enough with the preliminaries.

Let's start work on the business of Small Business.

1

WELCOME TO SMALL BUSINESS:

Sure, It's Tough ... Yes, It's Risky ...
But It's Still Your Best Choice

You're Not Alone

Statistics show that about 750,000 new businesses are started every year in the United States. Almost all of these are small businesses. But the actual number is much higher; that 750,000 figure is based on the actual legal process of incorporation of new business entities. It does not include one of the major trends of the '90s, the one- or two-person small business usually operated out of a home, garage, or one-room office. These businesspeople operate as "self-employed." To save costs and hassle, they file taxes as individuals. If they have a business name, it is usually a "d/b/a" (doing business as) name, not an actual corporation.

These different trends make for confusing statistics but we can safely say, without risk of overestimating, that new small businesses are being formed in the United States at a rate of at least 1 million per year. That is far higher than in previous decades. And how many small businesses, new and old, are there in all? Here again, different statistical sources give different numbers, but it's a fair guess that the total is close to 30 million small businesses in the country.

So when you consider starting up your own small business, take comfort from the fact that you're in good company; you're riding the wave of the future. There are good, solid economic and

> Today, almost 10% of American workers are self-employed—reflecting a trend toward independence and entrepreneurship bolstered by increased labor market turbulence over the past decade. Some have struck out on their own simply to stay afloat after being laid off, others to gain flexibility and autonomy, and still others to pursue the American dream of upward mobility.
>
> —Gene Koretz, *Business Week*

social reasons why all this is happening and there's nothing crazy about wanting to do so. It makes eminent good sense.

But the good sense has also to be applied to running your small business, not just starting it. Starting it and joining the national small business club is the easiest part. Running it day-to-day and paying the annual dues is a damn sight harder.

So What's a "Small Business"?

We can roughly group small businesses into three categories, working from the largest to the smallest:

"BIG" SMALL BUSINESSES

These businesses have somewhere between twenty and one hundred employees and have usually been operating for a number of years. Sometimes bad luck or mismanagement will bring one down but in general they are home safe. They've grown from nothing, made all their big mistakes and survived . . . they've learned their lessons well. Their management is usually professional, they're efficiently organized and they're on top of their business, whatever it may be.

Such "big" small businesses are often run by owner-managers, who still maintain the dynamism, simplicity and informality of a small company—and prefer it that way. There's a simple rule of thumb that says that once companies get past the 100-employee level, they start thinking and operating like Big Businesses.

There are large businesses that still manage to keep their "small" personality intact, through the personal preference and style of the owners. But there is a clear point in most companies' growth (if they continue to grow) when they start to lose the flexibility, informality and dynamism of a small business and start adopting the more rigid organizational style and administrative structure that are found in large corporations.

Some owner-managers of these "big" small businesses deliberately choose to stay the same size, innovating and improving year by year to stay on top of their competition, but resisting the temptation to keep striving for further growth in sheer size. These companies, through progressive improvements over the years in efficiency and productivity, can often increase sales and profits year by year, yet still stay roughly the same size and still maintain the personality, characteristics and style of a small business.

In general, these "big" small businesses are modern and sophisticated in their management methods . . . they have to be, at that level.

"MID-SIZED" SMALL BUSINESSES

The majority of small businesses fall into this size bracket, with about five to twenty employees. Here you're looking at the millions of retail stores, restaurants, storefront services, gas stations, repair shops, machine shops, studios, printers, bookkeepers, business services and the like. Many of these are franchise operations, operated and managed by their owners.

Here, levels of management sophistication and efficiency vary widely and wildly, from modern franchise operations with all their accounting, controls and systems supplied (and monitored) by the franchiser, to old-style businesses, comfortably secure in their niches and run pretty much as they always have been.

Among this large diversity of types, shapes and sizes, you can't say that any one is better than the other. Different strokes for different folks. But you will find a remarkable consistency among those that have survived and are making a decent profit. They all keep their eye on the basics we are talking about in this book . . . even if their ways of doing so range from the latest computer technology to handwritten entries on file cards and notebooks.

"SMALL" SMALL BUSINESSES

Many of these small, one- to five-people businesses are home based. You will also find a large number working out of one-room offices, small storefronts and assorted holes-in-the-wall. Some of them will grow, get better organized, start making more money and eventually move up in the ranks. Others will stay the same small size long-term, focused only on providing their owner-managers with independence and a decent livelihood.

Nothing wrong with that. Constantly growing bigger is not necessarily what some entrepreneurs want to do, once they have achieved their primary financial goals and a secure position. They'd rather not face the extra hassle. That's one of the rewards of small business: you decide what you want from your business in personal terms. The business doesn't decide for you . . . unless you let it.

One painful fact is that the mortality rate is highest among these, the "babies." But that fact should not discourage you. It's pretty natural when you stop to think about it. Just like babies anywhere, they're learning how to walk and talk, they're building up immunities to disease, they're learning to take care of themselves. Some "baby" businesses just don't make it through this period of vulnerability. You can learn lessons by looking at the ones that unfortunately didn't make it and asking yourself what they did wrong.

Business Mortality: The Bad News

The bad news is that on average a majority of small businesses don't make it. They fail or fold in their first year or two.

This news should bother you, and that's all to the good. Running a little scared is the best way to run a business and the surest way to stay alive. Knowing how easily others have failed will stiffen your spine when the time comes to make hard decisions.

There's a widely quoted statistic that's been around since they invented business schools and started teaching Statistics 101. It says that over 70 percent of new business ventures fail or close down in their first two years.

Nobody knows what the exact percentage is today and it really doesn't matter. The key point is, it's damn high; it's certainly well over 50 percent. The message is clear and deadly: most new businesses—meaning small businesses—are not prepared, in some form or other, for what they are about to face. When the first hiccup comes (and it always does), they don't have the financial resources or staying power to make the necessary adjustments, correct their mistakes and keep battling on. They get wiped out by the first salvo in the battle.

So what does that tell you? That the ones who folded were unprepared and ill informed. They went into the poker game without an adequate bankroll, without studying the rules, without knowing how to calculate the odds and without checking out the other players in the game. It may sound heartless, but they had it coming. Feel sorry for the others, who made all the right moves but then got blown away by the unpredictable storms and tempests that sometimes happen in the business world, in spite of their best efforts.

SUDDEN DEATH
It's a Sad Truth about Small Firms: They Go Out of Business All the Time . . .

By their very nature, small companies are far more vulnerable to abrupt failures than large businesses. For one thing, they tend to have less access to credit and capital when their cash flow dries up. They also lack product diversity—the one item they're counting on to be hot may become passé or never take off at all. As a result, a setback that perhaps would only knock a dollar off a big, diversified company's stock, might be enough to put a small company out of business.

—Rodney Ho, *The Wall Street Journal*

Business Survival: The Good News

And the good news? The good news is that the survival rate has been improving in recent years.

Recent research is showing that the 70 percent death rate–that longstanding, oft-quoted piece of statistical wisdom–is dropping. There are more survivors.

The explanation for this drop in the death rate of new businesses is that ours has become a much better informed world. Much as people may grumble and complain about the deteriorating quality of television, the press, radio talk shows and education in general, the fact is that recent years have seen a stunning, remarkable surge in the amount of information being thrown at the average citizen. And a good part of this steady stream of information relates to business, finance and economics.

Years ago, business news was for Businessmen, with a capital *B*. Dad, in his comfortable, secure job, did not need to know anything other than the technicalities of the business in which he worked. Mom had to know how to bake tuna casserole and change diapers.

The Information Revolution and the other assorted social, cultural and economic revolutions currently being fought out have mixed things up nicely. Now there isn't a single reasonably intelligent, reasonably balanced, reasonably normal man or woman in the United States today who is not: (1) concerned about their personal finances; (2) worried about their jobs; (3) aware of firings, downsizing, bankruptcies and other business phenomena; and (4) informed of general business and economic news. It's a different world.

So the folks who are now starting out on the same small business path as their predecessors (who generated those chilling statistics) are just naturally better prepared and more realistic about what they are getting into.

The latest statistics are telling you that if you make a real effort to inform yourself about business realities and if you work hard at preparing yourself for your small business venture, that alone should switch the survival odds in your own small business venture–from 70/30 against you, maybe to 30/70 in your favor.

AFTER YEARS OF NEGLECT, A GOLDEN AGE DAWNS FOR SMALL BUSINESS

This could be the best time in decades to run a small business. Why?

More money will be flowing into the small business sector from a growing number of sources. Venture capitalists are more flush with cash than ever. . . . Banks . . . should be opening their coffers too. . . . Some are exploring ways to expand in the small-business market.

The star of small business is also rising in Washington. . . . Some form of tort reform, tax reform, and overall simplification of regulations looks certain. Even if the changes aren't large at first, it's clear that the currents are moving in the direction of free enterprise.   –Peter Nulty, *Fortune*

Why Choose Pain and Sacrifice?

If and when a small business fails or folds, the pain and financial losses are extreme. Most of the burden falls on the businessperson responsible for the failed venture and his/her family and close friends. It's not a fun experience, to put it mildly.

Yet even if you do prepare well, work hard and survive in your small business venture, it's still going to be a tough, hard grind, for who knows how many years. Who needs that? Why not just hold on to that comfortable guaranteed-for-life job at International Widgets Corp. and calmly live out your allotted lifespan, blissfully safe and secure for the duration?

Because, pal, starting your own small business may well be the only attractive alternative you will have, the way the business world's headed these days.

Jobs like yours are going the way of the dinosaur. International Widgets will probably be taken over next quarter by Global SOBs Inc., who will unceremoniously can your redundant (as they view it) ass, with two weeks' severance pay and a Mickey Mouse watch in grateful, heartfelt appreciation of your twenty-five years of faithful, dedicated service. Welcome to Al Dunlap world.

Or you may have already lost that well-paid job, through no fault of your own. Or your well-paid job may suddenly have become a lousy, badly paid job. Or you may have been forced into early retirement. Or you may be young, smart and talented, and your job prospects are limited to Greaseburger Heaven, at $5.75 an hour, part-time, twenty hours per week.

Or maybe you have some cash stashed away: hard-earned savings, retirement funds, an inheritance, a graduation present, insurance money from the late lamented spouse, whatever. It's money but what good is that going to do you? Start spending it and soon it'll be gone. Put it into stocks, bonds or CDs, and it's probably not going to generate enough

ENTREPRENEURIAL SPIRIT ENTERS HIGH SCHOOL
Teens See Business Ownership as Shelter from Corporate Layoffs

Many of America's teenagers believe they've found a way to avoid becoming corporate layoff victims of the next century: Start a small business.

Nearly 70% of high school students want to launch their own small business, according to [a survey]. By contrast, only half of adults surveyed expressed an interest in small-business ownership.

Young people seem to be listening to their families' dinner table discussions about economic uncertainty and major corporations' layoffs.... "The kids said they don't trust government and they don't trust big business."

—Stephanie N. Mehta, *The Wall Street Journal*

If we're old enough to kill each other, then we're old enough to start our own business.

—Patrice Tsague, 21, president of [a company] designed to foster entrepreneurship in young African-Americans, quoted in *Fortune* annual income to keep you alive, carefree and happy. Instead, you may want to give serious consideration to investing it in your own small business. It's a good investment option, so long as you give up on the idea of "carefree and happy" for the next few years. Because you're going to have to work hard to protect that investment.

So, whatever your personal circumstances, you may well discover that in this modern, turbulent and unpredictable world, starting your own small business may be the best alternative you have for making a decent, well-paying living long-term, and controlling your own career and financial fate.

If the price of having chosen this direction is the need to make considerable personal and family sacrifices, for a number of years, you may consider it a fair trade-off. Unless you still believe in rose gardens, free lunches and fairy godmothers.

Hitting the Jackpot

Of course, there's always that other seductive, enticing reason for starting your own small business.

The dream of glory, success and Big Bucks. Of the good life, the fun life, the carefree life. When your business becomes a wonderful, stunning success, everything comes together and everything works out perfectly.

When you hit the jackpot.

It actually can happen. The odds are pretty long but it has happened to a number of successful entrepreneurs. Often it's plain dumb luck. Sometimes it's outrageous smarts. Usually it's just endless hard work. But it can and does happen to the lucky few.

However, hitting the jackpot must *never* be your main objective. It's not something you'll ever be able to guarantee. If it happens, so it happens. But it can be a fatal distraction if it becomes your main motivation in starting your own business.

Some small businesses fail precisely because their owners allow their wild dreams of hitting the jackpot to distract them from short-term priorities, from the grungy, sweaty work that often needs to be done, and from the day-to-day problems that need to be resolved. They take their eye off the survival ball, they start dreaming of next year's successful jackpot instead of tomorrow morning's tasks, and . . . pow! They're blown away by costs, customers, competitors or whatever else snuck up behind them while they were dreaming and sandbagged them while their guard was down. The dream never had a chance.

So, for your own protection–and sanity–think of your business, first and foremost, only as a better way of making a decent living and taking control of your life. Not as a ticket to fame, riches and the good life.

If you get lucky and your small business becomes a huge money machine, wonderful. I'll be happy for you. Send a postcard from Tahiti.

Just don't ever count on business jackpots.

They're in the hands of the gods. Not yours.

The Rewards Are for Real

Now that I've finished administering the nasty medicine, let's relax a little and talk about the good side. Yes, indeed, there is a good side.

Although small business has its hardships, it also has its rewards. You'll appreciate the rewards that much more, because they come hard won. Here's a short list:

Remuneration: Once you've got your business up and running, you should be able to pay yourself at least as much salary as you would receive in a regular job, and probably more. In some cases, much more.

> Some women who have dropped out [of corporate careers] are avoiding the issue [of returning] by starting their own businesses. Given the recent spate of corporate downsizings, a growing number of women opt for self-employment. . . . Once they discover the rewards, most do not want to return to corporate life.
>
> –Deborah Jacobs, *The New York Times*

> Women are starting businesses at three times the rate of men. Whether they've hit the glass ceiling, fallen victim to downsizing or want to find a way to juggle work and family, women are looking for ways to succeed through self-employment.
>
> –Susana Barciela, *The Miami Herald*

> Contrary to the image of women-owned businesses as small and struggling, a study . . . shows they are not only flourishing, but are more likely to succeed than the average American company.
>
> –Rachel L. Jones, *The Miami Herald*

Perks: You're the boss. So long as you don't tread too heavily on the IRS's toes, you can creatively grant yourself a bunch of little advantages that you'd never see as an employee.

Expenses: Here again, while keeping a careful eye on Big Brother IRS, there are many expenses that your business can absorb–and legitimately deduct–that would otherwise be your personal expenses.

Job Security: As long as you stay in business, no one can fire you. Your only concern becomes the security (survival) of your business. The freedom from "boss people" with life-or-death power over your job security is a major plus, especially in this downsizing business world.

Games and Politics: You're free of the frustrations, irritations and time wastage from the internal games and company politics that are a key part of protecting your job in many large corporations. If games and politics start happening in your own small business, you're the boss and you're to blame. You have the power to stop it.

Personal Efficiency: Unlike the corporate world, where good performance often goes unrecognized and unrewarded, in small business the results of working better are all yours to enjoy. Every effort you make to improve your personal working efficiency is totally to your and your business's benefit. There's a huge personal payoff in learning to work better. You actually enjoy figuring out how to improve your efficiency.

Personal Time: You work hard, you put in long hours, you work nights and weekends when necessary. But you also learn the real value of every hour, to yourself and your family, and you learn to manage your personal time better. So you don't have guilt pangs when you treat yourself to a late morning, a midweek afternoon off, a long weekend, or, God forbid, an actual vacation.

These rewards all come with one major precondition: your sense of responsibility to your business and yourself must be total. There's no fooling yourself in this world. You get to start collecting the goodies only if and when your business can afford them . . . and you're the only judge of that. You've got to work at keeping yourself honest. If you start spending money the business doesn't have or wasting precious time when urgent problems need attention, your small business will quickly end up joining the 70 percent crowd, the ones who don't make it.

So here's one final recommendation: fine-tune your conscience and your self-criticism before you start your small business. You'll need them.

And the biggest reward? Remember that horribly overworked phrase *job satisfaction,* so loved by personnel managers, corporate psychologists and management gurus? A phrase that has become steadily more hypocritical and meaningless in this Brave New World of restructuring, reengineering, layoffs and downsizing.

Job satisfaction is still very much alive and well in the small business world.

> The 1990s are turning out to be one of the greatest bonanzas for entrepreneurs in recent history. Entrepreneurial gambles have been the fastest road to riches since the days of Marco Polo, and today remain a major creator of jobs in the American economy.
>
> –B. Bowers and U. Gupta,
> *The Wall Street Journal*

It takes on a whole new meaning when you're running your own show and the show's running well.

It's the best reward of all.

It's the greatest feeling.

It's what makes the hard work, the strains and the worries all worthwhile.

So welcome to Small Business.

DEEP WATER: AT SEASIDE MOTEL, NEW OWNERS LABOR TO STAY AFLOAT

Last December, Paul Pfaff, a silver-haired 42-year-old, quit a $75,000-a-year job, sold his family's home, and risked everything to purchase the Edgewater Lodge [in Long Key, Florida Bay] for nearly $1.4 million, mostly borrowed. For $400,000 less, he could have bought a spanking new McDonald's franchise, but he was looking for a venture with atmosphere.

He got it. Though the 17-room establishment needs a face lift and a swimming pool, it boasts 600 feet of shoreline on Florida Bay, including five fishing docks. . . .

Within four years, Mr. Pfaff may be able to sell the place for a $400,000 profit—if he doesn't go broke or collapse from exhaustion before then. . . .

"I really got tired of the corporate garbage and sitting at a desk unable to do anything more with my career. This is what I've wanted to do for a very long time—work in a place where I can create things, make them better and make money at it, on my own time."

No matter that the Edgewater consumes nearly all of his waking hours. "I used to sit at a desk all day doing nothing and I was dying," he says.

—Lyda Longa, *The Wall Street Journal*

Now how's that for job satisfaction?

2

THE PERFECT SMALL BUSINESS OPPORTUNITY:

*The Beauty of the Enterprise
Is in the Eye of the Entrepreneur*

Where Are the Perfect Opportunities?

If I had a precise map showing where to dig for entrepreneurial gold, and if finding the right business opportunity was all it took to be successful, I'd already be disgracefully rich. And I certainly wouldn't be giving you and the rest of my readers my secret map, would I now?

I'm not rich, I don't know of any secret formula, and no one else does either. Never believe any guru book, entrepreneurial magazine or motivational seminar that promises you the secrets to finding entrepreneurial opportunities. It's either BS or a hustle–neither will be good for your financial health.

The truth is that there's no handy answer and no sure way of finding the ideal small business opportunity.

If you've already bought one of those laundry list business books, touting "The Thousand and One Best Business Opportunities in America" or whatever, you've wasted your money. What are you going to do? Throw darts at it to decide which of the thousand you're going to gamble your money and your future on?

New small businesses don't succeed unless, in one way or another, they incorporate some element of the hopes, desires, dreams, abilities, personality, emotions, guts, experiences, skills, knowledge–whatever–of their owner-operators. If they've got what it takes, they'll find some business opportunity that fits at least reasonably well with that peculiar and unique mix of characteristics that they possess, and they'll make it work. You're not looking for the *perfect* fit . . . only a *reasonable* fit.

That's the key. It's a highly personal process. Like picking out a new pair of shoes . . . or choosing a spouse. There's got to be a minimum level of comfort before you buy the shoes and walk out of the store . . . or out of the church. And both the shoes and the spouse need breaking in, before they fit well.

It's the individual owners who make any business opportunity an actual success, never the other way around. It's not: just find the perfect opportunity and it's guaranteed to work.

That notorious 70 percent failure rate includes many small businesses that were correctly focused on fantastic opportunities but just didn't make it, only because there was no good "fit" between the nature of the business and the nature of the entrepreneur.

Great Businesses, Lousy Businesses

Few small businesses fail just because they went into a dead-end activity. There are very few inherently rotten business areas. Look around you and you will see people making good money in all kinds of weird, unattractive business activities. It works for them, even if it might not work for you. Different strokes, different folks. Never forget that Wayne Huizenga, the Blockbuster business genius, made his first millions in the garbage business. Didn't make for great cocktail party conversation ("Find anything interesting in today's trash haul, Wayne?") but it did make for great success.

Consider the many new restaurants that close their doors after only a few months of operation. There is nothing inherently good or bad about the restaurant business, in itself. It's who you are and how you operate the business that determines the ultimate outcome. You'll hear all sorts of success stories to confirm how good it can be. You'll hear all kinds of disaster stories to show how lousy it can be. It's neither one nor the other.

The failures happen for hundreds of good and specific reasons, all usually related to the owner-operators, their decisions and their abilities: lousy location, too much local competition, inadequate financing, poor cost control, employee theft, crummy food, overpriced menu, you name it.

WHO ARE THE REAL ENTREPRENEURS?

Entrepreneur is not a meaningless word. . . . I'm talking about the conversion of ideas into viable businesses by means of ingenuity, hard work, resilience, imagination, luck, and all the other ingredients that go into a successful start-up. . . .

In my book, entrepreneurs are people who, starting with nothing more than an idea for a new venture, have the ability to take it to the point at which the business can sustain itself on its own internally generated cash flow. . . .

The entrepreneurs' job is to put everything together, wearing 10 different hats, juggling 20 different balls, relying on their own knowledge and instincts and creativity to get them to positive cash flow.

—Norm Brodsky, *"Street Smarts," Inc.*

Yet too often, when the funeral's over, you'll hear instead, "Oh, the restaurant business is one lousy business."

No, that's not the reason. It's that the owners didn't get it right, for whatever reason, good or bad. It may not even have been their fault. Nevertheless they just didn't get it right in that particular restaurant, and you can't place blanket blame on the restaurant trade, from their single unhappy experience. The right owner-operator can make a reasonable success out of even a lousy business. But a great business can't make a success out of a lousy owner-operator.

So forget the very idea of "choosing the perfect areas of opportunity," as if they're just sitting out there, waiting to be plucked off the tree.

Instead, start with a cold, hard look at yourself.

Know Thy Business Self

Bill Gates started Microsoft because he was a computer nerd in high school. Same goes for Steve Jobs, who built Apple. Henry Ford was a mechanic. Sam Walton of Wal-Mart was a small-town merchant.

These are all exceptional cases but they illustrate the point. Starting a small business starts with self-awareness. Not in any touchy-feely, philosophical sense. Just a hard-nosed, commonsense awareness of who you are and what you want; what you're good at, what not; what turns you on, what doesn't; which sacrifices you're prepared to make, which not.

You absolutely do *not* need to be a certified genius or have some incredible talent in some special area. We can't all be Stephen Spielberg. Small business is a remarkably equal-opportunity jungle environment. Nerds and plodders make it just as frequently as prima donnas and hotshots. Possibly more so, because they're less cocky and run more scared.

But the ones who make it all have traits in common: *self-awareness and self-criticism.* They believe in their own potential, but they also know their abilities and limitations. This self-critical ability to "know yourself" is key, both in deciding where to start and in actually

> ### RELISHING THE FLAVOR OF A RESTAURANT STAKE
>
> For many successful executives, the restaurant business has proven irresistible. . . . Outside investors contribute [funds], the chef and management put in their own funds and more efforts are made to set fiscal controls. That's all for the best . . . because more than half of all restaurants fail within the first year. . . .
>
> Businesspeople need to realize, that just because you know your own business well, there's no guarantee you can understand the risks of a restaurant investment.
>
> —Jill A. Fraser, *The New York Times*
>
> I learned more from the one restaurant that didn't work than from all the ones that were successes.
>
> —Restaurateur Wolfgang Puck, quoted in *Inc.*

running your own business. If you don't have it–and some people just don't–don't even *think* of starting a small business. You'll fail. We've already said enough about the jungle environment surrounding small businesses for it to be fairly obvious that only realists can survive.

Realists know themselves. Dreamers don't.

Everyone thinking of going into their own business has at least some vague idea of what type of business that might be. Work from there. Develop that idea, develop ideas in related areas, even in long-shot areas. But always start with an honest self-assessment of your own strengths and weaknesses, as the foundation for the idea. Somewhere there must be that gut-feel telling you: "Yes. This is the kind of thing I can do."

In apparent contradiction, you will sometimes read of entrepreneurs who start successful small businesses in areas about which they know nothing and that have no apparent connection with their personal characteristics. Here's why: in such cases, they were already experienced business managers. They went into a business where the one key ingredient for success was going to be good, solid management, not any particular skill or special ability. So in fact they did know their capabilities and how to apply them, even if they were not experts in any specific area, technically speaking.

(A warning, however. Don't confuse broad management experience in the corporate world with the ability to micromanage a small business singlehanded. It's not the same thing, as some downsized former executives have learned to their regret.)

So specific, what-business-should-I-choose advice is impossible to give. Only you can search out and define the business opportunity best suited to yourself. The best broad advice I can give you is this: *Make your selection from a survival perspective, not a success perspective.*

SHEEPSKINS UNNECESSARY

What's critical to becoming a successful entrepreneur? Certainly not a college degree. [A survey] of 151 highly successful entrepreneurs–all ranking among the richest 1% of Americans–found that only 46% completed their college educations. An additional 29% never went to college, while 27% started and didn't finish.

Even those who completed college don't give their degrees much credit. . . . more important to success: starting a venture early.

–The Wall Street Journal

What does that mean? It means choosing an area where you feel you have the best odds of still being in business, with your nose above water, after a year or two. Even if it does not seem as glamorous, as fun and as potentially moneymaking as other alternatives. Why? For the reasons we've already discussed. The start-up odds are not in your favor and your personal priority must be to survive. You are much more likely to survive if you select a basic, down-to-earth, doable project, rather than one which is geared to some vision of wild short-term success.

Almost all businesses that survive their first couple of years evolve and improve and change, especially in this fast-moving modern world. So you will have your crack at success later on, when you have a stable and solid small business base from which to grow.

Think Wayne Huizenga. He didn't start with Blockbuster; he started with trash. He first survived with his garbage business; that later became his business platform for future success.

Are There Enough Business Opportunities?

Are there sufficient business opportunities out there?

Enough of them for you to find one that fits your needs and personal characteristics?

Yes, indeed there are. Far more so than at any time in modern business history. All the wrenching changes that are creating such turmoil in society and in the modern business world have their entrepreneurial advantages. They are creating hundreds of thousands of new opportunities for small businesses, on an unprecedented scale.

• **Downsizing:** After the wild corporate self-indulgences of the conglomerating craze in the '70s and '80s, large corporations have switched directions. They are now discarding a mishmash of subsidiary businesses that they once avidly collected during their quest for the ultimate "Big," to concentrate instead on their "core competencies," as the gurus love to label it (all they actually mean is "basic business"). This latest switch in Big Business priorities means all kinds of smaller businesses are being freed up from their previous corporate owners. This is creating opportunities for entrepreneurs, although usually the bigger ones with the deep pockets.

• **Outsourcing:** This buzzword is used to describe the process of eliminating all kinds of internal services and

> **SMALL PRODUCT-DEVELOPMENT FIRMS SHOW SOLID GROWTH**
> **Entrepreneurs Fill a Void as Big Concerns Trim Their Internal R&D Staffs**
>
> With many large companies scaling back internal research and development, small [firms] are seizing a chance to pick up the slack. . . .
>
> Corporate downsizing has decimated many research and development staffs. But as the economy has strengthened, many companies have chosen to pump more R&D money to outsiders, rather than keep it in-house. At the same time, rapidly improving computer technology has enabled small entrepreneurial firms to design products more quickly and more cheaply than ever before.
>
> —Rodney Ho, *The Wall Street Journal*

firing every imaginable nonessential employee, from the janitor to the receptionist . . . to then swivel around and contract the services of small outside companies to do the same jobs, often using the former employees. Some of it makes sense, much of it doesn't, and most of it is poorly executed. But that is all excellent news for small service businesses, which are mushrooming everywhere to offer all sorts of goods and services to bigger corporations.

• **Reengineering/Restructuring:** Hot buzzwords, trendy labels to describe the wholesale elimination of layers of employees, aiming to get the same work done with less people, earning lower salaries. This is causing considerable pain and suffering, but it is also generating many nice little business opportunities for small companies, as the big corporations shoot themselves in both feet and then have to scramble to find outside small companies to do what their good employees once did. It's a bit different from "outsourcing," which is at least a more rational process in its intent. This is opportunity generated by chaotic cost cutting and misguided management. But it's opportunity, nevertheless.

• **New Products and Services:** Technology is changing at an explosive rate. This is generating myriad new products and new services, often faster than there are suppliers and people to make them, sell them, distribute them, transport them, service them and so on. This creates "piggyback" opportunities for small businesses to work for the larger companies that are generating these changes, yet often cannot handle all the work internally, or don't want to.

• **Trends in Modern Lifestyles:** Everyone is working harder and longer, getting more stressed out, with less and

---

HOW TO SUCCEED IN THE ODD HOURS
Market Grows Among Time-Deprived

The fiercer pace of work in the 1990's, especially the longer hours for many . . . is Matthew Ryffel's bread and butter. Mr. Ryffel, 30, an engineer who started his own one-man company, is an on-call computer repairman, available 24 hours a day to serve time-stressed work-at-home telecommuters, after-hours executives and anyone else who has transcended the boundaries of 9-to-5. He has fixed authors' hard-drives in the middle of the night, and reprieved lawyers caught on Saturday with their word processors down.

"Nobody works stranger hours than me. . . . I sleep with a beeper under my pillow."

His company is one of a new crop of businesses founded to serve a growing market: the time-deprived. Although round-the-clock service and entertainment are nothing new, newer companies specialize in providing the utterly mundane at times and places of convenience.

From corporate office parks where workers can get their shoes repaired or their car's oil changed or buy a new suit or a set of pots and pans without leaving work, to vendors at railroad stations who sell hot gourmet meals, to doctors who will see patients before sunrise and chiropractors who make office calls, the margins of ordinary commerce are stretching into some extraordinary territory. . . .

"Two people come home and they're tired, and that's it," [an economist] said. "That's what's creating all the opportunities for these new little niche firms."

–Kirk Johnson, *The New York Times*

less time for personal and home responsibilities, especially in families where both husband and wife work. The upside is that these trends are creating many opportunities for businesses such as take-out restaurants, dry cleaners, child care services and every other imaginable home or personal service.

• **Evolution in Society:** Society is changing dramatically, in many ways. People live longer and there are thus more old people; immigrants change the demographics and habits in many cities; many more women work and so on. These changes are constantly creating opportunities for new products and new services, which can often best be provided by small businesses.

• **New, Cheap Technologies for Business:** The availability, low cost and ease of use of PCs, business software, printers, faxes, copiers, modems, scanners, cellular phones, answering machines and all sorts of other modern business devices have generated a stunning impact in creating opportunities for starting new ventures. Businesses that only ten years ago might have required twenty or thirty employees, plus large investments, to become operational, can now get up and running with maybe only two or three people (including the owner) and maybe one tenth or less of the investment. This is making possible myriad small business activities that would have been unthinkable or economically impossible, only a few short years ago.

• **Home Business Opportunities:** A major offshoot of this technological revolution, combined with the social and lifestyle changes sweeping the country, is the ease of operating minibusinesses out of your own home. Short years ago the idea would have seemed nonsensical.

THE ECONOMICS OF AGING

Americans are getting older . . . the numbers heading for Golden Pond are staggering. Today, about 1 in 8 Americans is 65 years or older, compared with 1 in 25 at the turn of the century. By 2030, 1 in 5 Americans will be elderly.

And senior citizens are around for a lot longer. Life expectancy at birth was 47 years in 1900; in 1993, it reached 76 years . . . the fastest-growing segment of the population is the so-called oldest old—those 85 years or more.

Elderly Americans will live longer . . . and be better educated . . . as well as healthier . . . and better off financially . . . get more from their parents . . . own more stocks and bonds . . . and not be a burden to the community.

The senior citizen market may be an economic bonanza.

—*Business Week*

HEALTH CARE SHIFTS FROM HOSPITAL TO HOME AND HEARTH

Home is where the heart is. More and more, it's also where the health care is. . . . Hospitals are discharging patients as soon as their condition is stable, to finish their treatment and recover at home. . . . Home care is the fastest-growing segment of U.S. health care.

Home care embraces everyone from new mothers and their babies to the elderly with chronic health problems. Needs can be as simple as changing a gauze bandage or as sophisticated as giving oxygen, intravenous drugs and nutrition.

—Marilyn Chase, *The Wall Street Journal*

Now, in economic terms, it is perfectly feasible to generate a tidy annual profit–often enough to substitute for a salaried job–out of a mini home business, because of the very low operating costs of using your home as a business base. Such businesses could never have existed before, because they would have required a business location, paying commercial rents and carrying other high operating costs, which meant they could never have produced a profit.

• **Traditional Small Business Opportunities:** Don't forget the obvious: the many traditional areas where small businesses have always done well. Small retail stores, professional services, services to homes and businesses, traditional restaurants, fast-food outlets, and so on. These traditional activities continue to be as attractive for aspiring entrepreneurs as ever, although more caution is needed (we'll discuss competition and franchising in later chapters). They may not be as glamorous as other areas, but often they bring with them the considerable advantage of lower risk and greater security.

Buying Existing Businesses

You may be interested in buying someone else's existing small business. There may be advantages, you may be getting a good deal, you may get started faster, but please . . . be awfully, awfully careful. You may also be buying someone else's past mistakes, lousy decisions, horrible location, poor management and generalized mess.

Look at it this way. It's hard enough as it is to decide on a new business activity, do all the homework needed to be sure of your decision and then do all the work needed to get the business started.

Why add all the additional work of trying to train yourself as a business detective and financial auditor, to check whether you're about to be taken for a sucker? Or are you going to believe everything that the current owner tells you, or that the business broker who's peddling the deal (for a commission) says? There are more horror stories in these kinds of deals than you can begin to imagine. And if you have been fooled or conned, there's no way you'll ever see your money again.

The only attractive, safe deals of this nature are where you have known the business and the sellers well enough and long enough to be sure of what you're getting. That is seldom the case.

If you are determined to buy someone else's business: (1) Be deadly suspicious of everything you're told; (2) Do detective work and legwork, looking for concealed bad news; (3) Ask for documented proof of everything important; (4) Hold back a large chunk of the money until you have operated for some months; (5) Only buy the assets, never buy the business (and all the potential liabilities that may come along with it).

Buying existing businesses tends to be a game for corporations and investors who have adequate financial, legal and professional resources to make exhaustive checks on anything and everything and to protect themselves against being suckered. Very few new entrepreneurs have either the resources or the experience to play this game.

Making Your Choice

The opportunities are out there. Many of them, popping up all over. With sensible self-awareness, you should be able to identify the right kind of small business opportunity for your needs.

The decision to start a small business is highly personal. What might be a great opportunity for one person could be a disaster for another, only because of differences in their personal characteristics, not because one is any better than the other.

So, instead of specific advice, here are my general notes of caution:

1. Start with the self-analysis. Make it cold, make it objective . . . make it hurt. It's the foundation for everything you're going to do in your own business. The better you know yourself, the better choices and decisions you will make.

2. Stick as close to home as possible, figuratively and literally. By taking advantage of familiar territory and existing strengths, you will simply be reducing the number of danger areas where you could make disastrous mistakes, in your vulnerable first years. Your risks will diminish and your survival chances will improve.

3. Trust your gut as much as your brain. Your brain can start inventing clever justifications for doing unwise things, while your gut may be pointing in an opposite direction. If it somehow doesn't feel right, the decision is probably "no," and if it feels comfortable, the decision is probably "yes."

4. Just as I can't help you decide on a business area, often neither can your family or friends. You can and should talk to them about *whether* to run

the risk of starting a small business, since they'll suffer along with you. But they usually can't help you decide *what,* any more than I can. Yes, they know you better, but they often can't evaluate your true potential in untried areas. Their well-meaning fears for your safety can very easily cloud their good judgment, one way or the other.

5. If you don't already have a clear idea of what you intend to do in small business (many already do), don't rush yourself. Wait a while, take your time to observe and to think. Observe everything that's happening around you, in your home, outside, at work, driving, shopping, traveling, eating out, wherever, whatever . . . always looking at what's going on from a business perspective. The more you "think business," the more you'll start seeing business opportunities that weren't apparent before. Read the business news in the local newspapers daily, even if it bores you. Not business theories but *business news . . .* who started up, who folded, who sold out, who bought who, who introduced new products or services, who screwed up, etc. It will help open your eyes.

6. Never allow yourself to get rushed into a deal or a decision of this importance and magnitude. *Never, ever.* The reason you are going into your own small business is not to buy an entrepreneurial lottery ticket and guess what business will be the McDonald's of the year 2020. You want a solid, decent area of opportunity that will work reasonably for you, in the near future. There are many. If you missed one by waiting too long, there'll be another along in a couple of weeks. Don't sweat it. You can blow your one chance at starting up your own business by taking a hurried decision, because you didn't want to lose that "great opportunity." *There are no great opportunities, only good ones.* Slow is sensible–at least in looking, evaluating, thinking and deciding. Remember, once you've decided, you'll be running like crazy for years. So don't start running until you absolutely have to.

STATE TARGETS BOGUS DEALS FOR STARTING A BUSINESS

State and federal regulators launched a nationwide blitz on companies peddling bogus be-your-own-boss businesses, ventures that swallow entrepreneurial dreams.

In a massive crackdown, called Operation Missed Fortune, business opportunities and work-at-home schemes were targeted. . . .

While get-rich-quick enterprises vary from vending machine distributorships to assembling toys at home, the pitch is always the same: invest, then just rake in the dough. The reality: lots of work, questionable profits.

—Audra Burch, *The Miami Herald*

7. If it sounds too good to be true, it probably is.

Decision Time

If you have already made your choice and are already operating your own small business, the best advice I can give you is: try to stick with it, try to make it work. Whatever disillusionment and problems you may be encountering–and everybody does–they will seldom be as great as they would be if you switched and started over in some other new business area.

If you are still making up your mind about the kind of small business you want, first finish reading this book.

Then read it again, a second time.

What we'll be discussing in the coming chapters could have a profound effect on how you judge what may, right now, be looking to you like the great opportunity of a lifetime.

It may not look quite that way after you've finished the book.

3

FRANCHISING, THE EASY OPTION:

Looks Easy, Feels Safe . . .
But the Lunch Ain't Free

Franchising: The Dream Solution?

Dream away. Sign on. Pay up. Start operating.

Then wake up to the realities of franchising in the late '90s.

Ouch! You may well have bought yourself a small business lemon.

It's a once-upon-a-time story. Once upon a time franchising was glorious. Franchising is a beautiful operating concept and a highly effective business and economic model. It started flourishing in the United States after World War II, then expanded rapidly around the world. It has been a huge success. In general, it has worked very well for both franchisers and franchisees for many years. It is a wonderful cooperative method for combining the resources and know-how of the franchise company with the capital, individual management and personal dynamism of an entrepeneurial franchisee.

It worked beautifully and harmoniously *only* while there were great new popular businesses suitable for rapid expansion (for example, fast-food restaurants) and lots of room and opportunity for expansion all over the country and around the world. While that was happening, franchiser and franchisee saw eye-to-eye; they were on the same team, capturing the same opportunities.

That was then. This is now.

There are far fewer fresh, new and attractive franchise concepts being introduced each year; a new McDonald's isn't being invented every day. And many of the existing concepts (the good ones) have expanded to their market limits, so that any new franchisee faces highly restricted growth opportunities and savage competition, often from other franchisees in the same system.

So franchisers face a very difficult sale. If they were to be completely truthful about what they are offering and entirely realistic about the likely future profit potential of each franchise they are selling, most potential franchisee-investors would race for the exits.

So what do franchisers do? They hustle, they hype, they hard-sell. They flash genuine success stories from the past, to convince you that the future will be a repeat performance, even though much of the evidence points in the opposite direction. They highlight all the attractive features in their system, but bury descriptions of dangers and downsides in the fine print of their brochures. They tighten up on every clause in their standard franchise agreements, because they know new franchisees are going to squeal and squiggle when they find out what they have got themselves into.

The trap has to be airtight, once the piggy's inside.

None of this means that it's impossible to find a good franchise opportunity for yourself. They do exist and they can be found. Hard but not impossible. What it means is that you must apply exactly the same hard-nosed realism and skeptical attitudes that you would to anything else that relates to your small business plans. Much more so, in fact, since there's such a strong temptation to trust the polished sales pitches of big-name franchisers. Whatever the defects in their systems, these guys are all superb marketers of franchise agreements; often all their profit comes from the business of selling franchises, rather than the actual operations of their franchise system.

Think of them as used car salespeople and you'll be better able to defend yourself. If you want to see their heavy-duty hype in action, go visit one of those national franchise trade fairs that are held around the country. These fairs are much closer to old-style carnivals than to serious professional events, but they are a good education in showing you what you are up against.

Never allow the seductive ease to carry you away. That is the overpowering temptation of a franchise deal. As you start doing your small business homework in preparation for getting started, you begin to realize how much hard work and how many time-consuming, nitty-gritty details are going to be needed, just to get your new venture up and running.

Suddenly–poof!–your fairy god-mother materializes from the pages of one of those glossy franchising magazines, grinning away like a maniac, waving this

After a long career as a broadcasting executive, Gene Swanzy decided to take early retirement five years ago to run his own business.

Impressed by Mail Boxes Etc. . . . [he and his wife] bought two of the postal and shipping services franchises in Arlington, Va.

Today, Mr. Swanzy is sorry he ever heard of franchising. So far, he and his wife have invested $300,000 in the two stores, and still are $250,000 in debt without taking out a dime in salary.

"It's been a horrendous experience," said Mr. Swanzy, now 63. "I blew my retirement money, and now I'm trapped."

–Earl C. Gottschalk Jr., *The New York Times*

franchise proposal at you where *everything*, absolutely *everything*, is done for you and delivered on a plate, neat and tidy and ready to roll. Just make your down payment, sign on the dotted line, jump in and drive off in your shiny, spanking new, rose-colored franchisemobile.

So you still believe in fairy godmothers, huh? What you can believe is that this particular fairy godmother is getting a fat commission out of everything you pay the franchiser.

There are no free lunches, folks, especially not in franchise land. Operating a small business is always tough and always demands hard work. There are no exceptions to this rule, especially not in franchise deals. As we discussed in the previous chapter: if it looks too good to be true, it probably is.

The franchise free lunch has its cost. One way or the other you, the naive, trusting franchisee, will pay for it over the long term.

Franchising is a cold-blooded, hard-sell business these days. Franchise operators will try to sell you the We're All One Big Happy Family Here story, but the reality is far closer to The Masters and the Slaves.

Franchising: An Overview

A recent report estimated that about half of all new businesses opened every year in the U.S. are franchise operations. So there's a fifty-fifty chance you may be thinking of buying a franchise.

There are franchise systems offered for everything you can possibly imagine and some you can't: fast-food outlets, casual-dining restaurants, consumer services, retail stores, business services, home-based systems, telephone-based systems, and so on. Walk around any shopping mall, flick through the yellow pages; many of the businesses you see will be franchises. They come in all shapes and sizes. You'll find them advertised in the business pages of local papers, business magazines, industry magazines.

Finding franchise opportunities is not the problem. There are many to choose from.

> ### TRADE-SHOW ORGANIZERS AGREE TO SETTLE FTC LAWSUIT OVER FRANCHISERS' CLAIMS
>
> The legal action arose from an unprecedented nationwide investigation of trade shows, which have become an increasingly important franchise-marketing tool. . . .
>
> Some trade shows have become "unchecked free-for-alls," marred by cavalier violations of federal regulations that bar undocumented earnings claims and income projections for potential franchisees. . . .
>
> At one trade show, a franchiser illustrated his promise of certain riches by displaying a plexiglass box filled with dollar bills. In another instance, a banner over the exhibitor's booth claimed that the franchiser was "certified by the FTC"–even though the agency has no certification authority. . . .
>
> "The people who are marketing business opportunities are saying whatever they think people will believe or want to hear," says [a Michigan assistant attorney general].
>
> –Michael Selz, *The Wall Street Journal*

The problem is selecting one that is a good business deal for both you and the franchiser . . . not just the franchiser.

The basic franchise arrangement, for the small businessperson, works roughly along the following lines: You sign an agreement for a long term, usually ten to twenty years. You buy the right to use their system in a given location or area. They determine almost all the details of the business. They promise to provide certain help and services to you. You follow their rules. You pay a one-time licensing fee, followed by a regular percentage of your sales, as royalties, plus other charges, such as advertising contributions. You make all the investment necessary to set up the business. The agreement document is extensive and spells out hundreds of obligations, most of them yours.

When a franchise system works well for both parties–and it sometimes does–it can be excellent. The theory of franchising is very sound, and there is nothing fundamentally wrong with the basic concept. You are combining, on one side, a professional package of sophisticated features only a large corporation can afford to develop, fully tested and ready to execute, and on the other side the small entrepreneur's close attention to detail, dedication, long hours and hard work.

In theory, a perfect marriage of mutual convenience.

So much for the beautiful theory.

In real life, this theory all too often blows apart, for the simplest of reasons: one party, the franchiser, holds all the cards and the other party, the franchisee, holds only one solid card (the money to invest) and desperately wants to believe that everything he/she is told about the investment will come true. Once the money's been invested, the franchisee is left holding no cards at all.

Franchisers are selling promises of future earnings, from an investment that you–not they–are going to make in their franchise system. The temptation for an unethical–or merely incompetent–franchiser to cheat or cut corners can be overpowering.

ACTIVIST FIGHTS FOR THE RIGHTS OF FRANCHISEES

Susan Kezios is rapidly emerging as the most prominent activist for the nation's more than 400,000 franchisees. . . . Ms. Kezios has managed to meld franchisees from different franchising systems into a united political force.

Franchisees, who pay fees and royalties in exchange for using franchisers' business formats, have become much more militant in recent years about what they see as mistreatment by franchisers.

Ms. Kezios is seeking federal and state laws to give franchisees more power in franchise arrangements. Among her goals: creating legally protected exclusive territories for franchisees.

Many of her adversaries wish Ms. Kezios would resume her career as a disc jockey.

She "is doing a real disservice to the franchise business," says [a senior V.P.] of Blimpie International, a sandwich-shop franchiser. "She is becoming a thorn in the side of franchisers."

"I'll tell you who's making trouble for franchising," she says. "It's the franchisers who continually write onerous, one-sided contracts with franchisees."

–Jeffrey A. Tannenbaum, *The Wall Street Journal*

Franchisers: The Bad Side

To be fair, there are good franchise organizations and good franchise opportunities, even though they become rarer as the years go by. If you apply the same commonsense, cold-blooded attitudes that you would in investigating any business opportunity, franchise or not, you may get lucky and find what you're looking for: a good, fair deal. Maintain your objectivity, don't fall in love with the deal and it may work out fine. There's little advice to give you on the good guys; they're not the problem.

It's the bad side of franchising that presents the biggest dangers to small business newcomers, and that's what I need to review with you. When a franchise system turns pernicious and unfair (as it too often does), the reasons are usually one of the following:

• **Plain Dishonesty:** There are more outright scams and horror stories in the franchise field than you can possibly imagine. It's just too damn easy for an unscrupulous franchiser to fool a gullible potential franchisee. The system is an invitation to cheat. It takes many months for a franchisee who is being duped to finally wake up to what's going on. By then, it's usually too late to repair the damage or to recover the lost investment. Franchise con artists know how to stay ahead of the law.

• **Lousy Businesses:** The franchiser offers all the external packaging of a business–signs, logos, menus, decoration, layout, design, whatever–that is, the external, visible, flashy, glitzy, fun part of the business. But the real problems always lie in the guts of a business and they are usually impossible to detect at first glance. The franchiser representative is a salesperson, whose objective is to close a deal. Even an honest one will emphasize those glitzy features, instead of the boring, possibly negative business details. The potential franchisee wants the dream to come true and usually does not have enough expertise, especially in the particular type of business being negotiated, to ask all the key, hard questions and insist on frank, detailed answers. So the hype wins out. Only months later does the sobered-up franchisee find all manner of defects and problems in the operation of the business. By then, he/she is too far in to pull back out and often has to stick with a lousy business for many years. Very similar to buying a used car from a persuasive salesperson . . . the problems only appear later, when you've been driving the car for a while. By then, you might as well keep driving.

• **Franchiser Incompetence:** Managing any business demands competence. The operators of a franchise organization need to be *better qualified* than your average businessperson, since they are managing not one but two businesses, simultaneously. They not only have to manage their basic franchise operational concept (say, operating fast-food outlets), profitably and efficiently, but they must also manage what is in effect *an entirely different service activity*, serving the needs of a group of fairly amateurish franchisees (say, providing supplies, accounting and control systems, administering advertising programs, etc.). Instead, franchisers are often *worse qualified* than the average businessperson: they're often managerially incompetent. This is why so many franchise systems end up literally falling apart. The people running the overall system are quite simply not up to the managerial demands of a complex dual activity. Of course, it's still the franchisee who loses his/her investment. Even if there may be grounds to sue, there is usually nothing left in the franchiser's business to pay for restitution.

• **Franchiser Collapse:** There are many cases on record of new concept franchise organizations that get off to a rapid start-up, sign up a number of franchisees who make substantial investments and then collapse. The reasons can be the simple incompetence mentioned above or inadequate capitalization or plain fraud. Whatever the reasons, the dramatic consequence is that *even if the franchisees are doing well*, they will usually be taken down by the collapse of the franchiser. Whereas an independent small business may not be affected by the collapse of one of its major suppliers, franchisees are so operationally dependent on their mother franchise organization that they get dragged down too. Here again, usually they lose their entire investment, with no chance of recovery from the franchiser.

> W. Michael Garner, a well-known New York franchising lawyer [described] a common problem: franchiser failures that burn franchisees. When a franchiser runs into problems, "it is all too easy to abandon the venture and leave the franchisee with nothing," the attorney told the House Small Business panel.
>
> —Jeffrey A. Tannenbaum, *The Wall Street Journal*

• **Conflicts of Interest:** Far too often, the franchise organization puts its self-interest ahead of the needs of the franchisees. Some examples: forcing franchisees to buy supplies only through the system; overpricing supplies; forcing the purchase or lease of unnecessary equipment; diverting franchisee advertising contributions; allowing too many franchisees in a given market area, purely to increase royalties and fees. There are laws to prevent such abuses, but it's far too easy for an unscrupulous franchiser to circumvent them.

Big Business Franchisees

One reason that there are so many conflicting stories, good and bad, about franchise systems is that, just as in the regular business world, the franchise world also divides into the two separate worlds of Big Business and Small Business.

There are many successful franchise systems, where both the franchiser and its franchisees are big, professional companies, each with their own experienced, well-qualified staffs, who both know their business inside out. In the restaurant trade, for example, you will find large franchisee organizations (sometimes called area development franchises) with many outlets and exclusive territories covering entire states and generating hundreds of millions of dollars in sales.

Here, there is a reasonable "balance of power" between franchiser and franchisee. Maybe the franchising company has an edge because of its relatively larger size, but it would never be so unwise as to try to take unfair advantage of its large franchisees. First, because each franchisee is too big and too important to the success of overall system; neither party can afford a major, disruptive quarrel. Second, because both parties know what they are negotiating, detail by detail, when they work out their franchising agreements and they are pretty evenly matched; one cannot take advantage of the other's ignorance. Third, if the franchiser did anything blatantly unfair or even illegal, the franchisee would catch them at it very quickly, and then take quick and aggressive legal action to defend themselves and to sue for indemnity.

So the scams and the horror stories almost never occur in this civilized, genteel and professional enclave in the franchising jungle. That's why you'll find both franchisers and franchisees who will indignantly protest that the ugly stuff I'm talking about is untrue and exaggerated. So far as their experiences are concerned, they're probably right. Naturally they don't relish being lumped together with the lowlifes and rip-off artists to be found in fair abundance, when one turns over a few rocks in Small Franchise World. It lowers the tone of the neighborhood.

So these folks spread the message that franchising is a clean, professional and upright industry. They may feel that way about their own neighborhood, but unfortunately they're not talking about your side of the tracks.

> ### NPC INTERNATIONAL ACQUIRES 126 RESTAURANTS
> NPC International Inc. acquired 126 restaurants from Pizza Hut Inc. for $56 million. . . . NPC is the world's largest Pizza Hut franchisee, with 544 restaurants and delivery kitchens in 14 states. The company also operates and franchises 182 Tony Roma's restaurants and the theme restaurant Famous For Ribs.
>
> —*The New York Times*

They're not referring to the franchise world you will encounter as a small entrepreneur. If you decide to enter the small business world through the franchise door, you're going to have to be very, very cautious indeed. Just remember that, if you buy into a small business franchise, you've got a good chance of finding yourself dealing with a franchising outfit that is possibly dishonest or incompetent or out to take unfair advantage of you, in some form or other.

You're small. You're a target.

The Territorial Saturation Trap

Later, in the chapter on competitors and competition, we will take a look at the "territorial saturation" problem, where too many similar businesses are working too close together, all serving the same type of customer. Everyone loses in such saturated situations.

Except the franchisers who signed up the franchisees who are now bleeding to death.

Territorial saturation is the single biggest danger you face as a prospective franchisee. However, it's something you can prevent at the time you negotiate your agreement. Or at least walk away from the deal, if you don't get the guarantees you need.

So listen up carefully, please. This one's a life-or-death issue.

This is the biggest and most prevalent problem. Here, the happiest of happy franchisee families can come royally unglued. Here, even the best franchise organizations with honest, professional managers can still end up seriously hurting their franchisees.

No matter what guarantees the franchiser gives you, no matter what they say or promise, no matter what convincing arguments they present, no matter what clauses they put in the agreement, *they will never, ever give as much of a damn about direct competitors in your market area as you will.*

That's simply a fact of franchise life. Your little franchisee ass is much more directly in the line of fire. Theirs isn't. Competitive damage, if it happens, will hurt you ten times more than your

RETAIL FRANCHISES APPEAR RISKIER THAN OTHER START-UPS
Survival rates for franchise start-ups appear low in retailing.

Overcrowding in retail-franchise niches such as fast-food is generating lower profitability and higher failure rates for franchises, compared with nonfranchise start-ups in the same field. Many disgruntled franchisees complain of brutal competition in retail sectors—often within their own chains.

—Jeffrey A. Tannenbaum,
The Wall Street Journal

franchiser. At most, they'll lose some royalty fees on your reduced sales; you may lose your entire investment and livelihood.

So the cards are not equally stacked. They're somewhat rigged. Against you.

That means two things:

1. They'll try to restrict your geographic area of exclusivity as much as possible–if possible, even avoid granting you a protected area. You can be sure that if yours proves to be a successful and profitable business location, and if your customers love you, it won't be too long before you'll be looking at a competitor with the same franchise name over the door, just outside your exclusive area. Surprise, surprise. You'll lose say 10 or 20 percent of your sales when the other franchisee opens. The franchise operator will lose nothing . . . instead they'll gain, having received another lump-sum franchise fee, plus collecting monthly royalties on the combined sales of you and your neighbor.

2. They'll want your operation up and running for their "system" to be covering as much geographic territory as possible, against other competing "systems." Without being aware of it, you may well be heading straight into a "saturation trap." When you open or shortly thereafter, two or three competitors in the same type of business as yours–all franchisees, believe it or not–may open as well. All of you will bleed, some to death, because there just won't be enough business to keep you all alive. Your franchiser representative will say how sorry they are that so many competitors saw this great opportunity in that territory at exactly the same time but, hey, that's business. Just be patient. You got your exclusivity, didn't you? So do you really believe that a truly competent franchiser could not have smelled the "saturation" risk and warned you off in time? But if they'd done that, their franchise system would not be present in your particular neighborhood, would it now?

Not all franchise organizations behave this badly. Really good, ethical, professional franchise systems certainly do exist around the country. Such

> Ronald Myers, manager of a Downey, Calif., Subway Sandwiches & Salads franchise, says the outlet is "still profitable, but barely." Besides facing competition from nearby Kentucky Fried Chicken, McDonald's and Jack-In-The-Box outlets, among others, the store competes for sales with three newer Subway outlets within a two-mile radius.
>
> Average weekly sales were $8,000 before these units opened, but now are only $6,500.
>
> –Jeffrey A. Tannenbaum,
> *The Wall Street Journal*

franchisers can offer small businesses first-rate opportunities for safe start-ups. Both franchisee and franchiser can have common interests in many matters.

But when it comes to discussing your territorial exclusivity and the risk of excessive competition, you two are on different sides of the bargaining table and always will be. Don't ever forget it. There's an inherent conflict between your different interests, and always will be.

Get It Right or Walk Away

So how do you find yourself a decent, reliable franchise deal–where, if you do everything you promise to do as a franchisee, and if you work your butt off, you're not going to get screwed over at the end of it all by factors totally outside of your control?

Unfortunately there's no easy answer, but here are a few recommendations to improve your chances.

Prepare very carefully for the negotiations with your potential franchiser. Don't get hung up on the small details; that's not what's going to kill you. Think cynical, be cynical: list all the potentially damaging things that could happen to your franchised small business, by checking around and talking around with franchisees in the same type of business. Even franchisees from the same system, if you can find them. Caveat: make sure these are not the ones recommended in the franchiser's literature; they may well be shills.

You will not find this process too difficult; it's all fairly obvious stuff and franchisees who've suffered some of these problems are seldom reluctant to talk about them. They like to get it off their chests. They'll be happy to warn you of the things that can go wrong.

Based on your investigations, write up a long list of potential "bad news happenings." Be as specific as you can and as nasty as you want; it's your small business future that's on the line and this is not a popularity contest. When you're ready, sit down with the franchiser's representative and say: "Look, no offense intended, but here's a list of the potential dangers that I'm really worried about and want to be protected against. I'm not saying you'll do these ugly things, but I need to be sure you won't. If you can guarantee in some reasonable way that your company won't allow these things to happen and you will put it in writing, we'll be able to work on the rest of the details. If not, we're going to be wasting our time, because I'm just not prepared to run the personal risk that any of these nasty events might happen. Clear 'nuff?"

If you get the right reaction, proceed. You're probably dealing with professional and honest businesspeople, who know *exactly* what you're worried about, who think you're smart and courageous to have been so forthright, and with whom you may be able to build a solid long-term business relationship.

But if they get offended, walk. They have no right to feel offended.

But if they say "we'll talk about that later," walk. They won't.

But if they won't put it in writing, walk. They can't be trusted.

And walk fast. Because there is *nothing* in business life *worse* than being stuck with a bad long-term franchise agreement with a lousy franchiser.

You can't get rid of the business. They won't buy it from you. No one else will buy it. You can't change it. You don't want to invest in improving it. You have too much money tied up in it to allow it to collapse. You don't want to risk putting any more money into it. You'll never get decent income out of it. You will always keep paying for the mistakes and incompetence of the franchiser.

It's pure business hell and a form of business slavery. It's the pits of business life.

Whereas if you go your own way and create a little business on your own, however many mistakes you make you will always have the freedom and the flexibility to correct those mistakes at some time in the future. It's one thing to work away at fixing your own mistakes and avoid repeating them; it's quite another to keep paying for the franchiser's mistakes and incompetence.

No franchiser is doing you a big favor by offering you a franchise deal. Never fall for that old "it's the last great car at this price on the lot" pitch. There are always other good franchise systems and new franchise opportunities to investigate. Take your time.

Only close a franchise deal when you're absolutely comfortable with all aspects of the deal.

Or Go It Alone

The advantages of being part of a first-class, top-notch franchise system are all pretty obvious. It's a prepackaged, ready-to-go deal, with lots of help and support in areas where you have little experience or know-how.

But what if you can't find the ideal arrangement?

If you can't find it or anything comparable, in my opinion you're better off on your own, instead of settling for some second-rate alternative and maybe condemning yourself to the Eternal Franchise from Hell.

Sure, going it alone will take you longer and be a lot more work. In compensation, you'll be saving the fees and the royalties you would have paid for a franchise. That can be a considerable amount of extra capital that you can then pump into your own operation.

Setting up your own small business without the help of a franchise system is much easier nowadays than in the past. You can do far more investigation, preparation and planning on your own than you might imagine possible. This is a free country; as long as you do nothing illegal, you can take advantage of all the information that is accessible to the public. With a little chutzpah and a great amount of legwork and desk work, you can often discover all kinds of very useful start-up information, just by doing basic business detective work: observing, photographing, measuring, talking, walking, phoning, questioning and simply digging around. Feel free to imitate every single good idea you see, as long as it's not protected by trademark or copyright or is clearly proprietary.

This kind of preliminary legwork may take you, say, a month or two or three, which you would not be wasting if you were going straight into a prepackaged franchise situation. On the other hand, you're gaining substantial savings in fees and royalties, and avoiding the other major dangers we've just been discussing.

I know franchisees who have privately admitted, with great regret, that they came to realize too late that they could have put together a similar small business on their own, instead of signing a franchise agreement. None of the business's details turned out to be as mysterious or as complicated as they had imagined; all it would have required would have been the time, work and patience of making their investigations and doing their own detailed planning and preparation.

Your independent options may be just as good or even better than a franchise opportunity. So keep an open mind, look at all the options and don't get hustled by the hype of franchise operators. It's only business. You're allowed to say no.

About "New Concept" Franchises

This high-velocity business world has greatly increased the rapid rate of birth, growth and death of new fads in business. Almost all of these "new concept" businesses are franchise systems. Here's how the cycle operates. Some bright guy comes up with a clever new concept. Within months, it's hyped all over the country. Imitators spring up. You see it everywhere. Franchisees want to "get in on the ground floor" on this great trend of the future. They plunk down their money. By then, solid, established competitors have had a chance to zero in, find the flaws and go for the jugular. Or the concept has some fatal flaw of its own that only surfaces after the business has grown. At the end of the cycle, everything collapses.

The franchisees are left hanging, twisting slowly in the wind.

Most people only get one shot at setting up a small business. Don't blow it all on a roll of the dice, which is what many of these new concepts are.

Okay, so maybe one in a thousand may turn out to be a huge success . . . twenty years from now, maybe?

And what about the other nine hundred and ninety-nine?

Want to be one of them?

Resist the temptation of a killer new concept franchise. If you are going to go into a franchise deal, at least make sure it has been around long enough to establish a solid track record, one you can verify and investigate for yourself. As you've seen in this chapter, franchise deals already present enough potential problems of their own. Why add to them the total unpredictability of new forms of business that have very little chance of proving a success?

> **PERILS FOR NEWCOMERS**
> **Chances for Success Look Slim for New Franchise Systems.**
>
> Among 138 companies that began selling franchises in 1983, 104 were defunct a decade later, says Scott A. Shane, assistant professor of management at Georgia Tech.
>
> At a time of increasing controversy over the success rate for new franchisees, the study suggests that potential franchisees must be particularly wary about embracing untried franchise concepts. The risks faced by new franchisers are even higher today than in the early 1980s, when the franchising market was less saturated.
>
> A new franchiser's successful operation of a prototype unit doesn't guarantee that a franchise system will take hold, Dr. Shane cautions. Indeed, he argues that building a franchise system requires completely different skills from those needed to run an underlying business. . . .
>
> —Jeffrey A. Tannenbaum, *The Wall Street Journal*

Multilevel Marketing Ain't Small Business

Multilevel marketing powerhouses always hype their deals to prospective novitiates as *starting your own business, setting up a home business, becoming an entrepreneur, being your own boss* and so on.

Don't believe it. It's not really small business, it's not really an entrepreneurial activity and it isn't really franchising. What most of it really is, is really disgraceful. So you will find the multilevel marketing circus covered in one of the short memos in the *Odds 'n' Ends* appendix to this book.

Franchiser-Franchisee War Stories

So you wonder if maybe I've exaggerated in this chapter?
Read the clippings that follow; judge for yourself.

CARVEL STRATEGY FROSTS MANY FRANCHISEES

Carvel creations, once sold exclusively in Carvel Ice Cream Bakery Stores, are now available in supermarkets.... Carvel says it needs supermarket sales to survive. Though it is a big name in the East Coast ice-cream world, the chain has shrunk to fewer than 500 stores.... Franchisees, who run nearly all the stores, are sharply split over the new strategy. Some are so angry they are fighting back in court.

"My last name may be Hughes, but my first name isn't Howard," says John G. Hughes, a franchisee. "I don't have a bottomless pocket to subsidize Carvel's bad ideas." Sales at his Carvel store, which totaled about $340,000 last year, might fall below $300,000 this year, he says. He blames the 24 supermarkets within five miles that now sell Carvel products....

The president of a franchisee group that opposes the supermarket strategy, says some franchise stores have seen sales declines of 20% or more, since supermarket sales began.

—Jeffrey A. Tannenbaum, *The Wall Street Journal*

IS GENERAL NUTRITION (GNC) HEADED FOR CIVIL WAR?
Claiming the Company Favors Its Own Stores, Franchisees Are Trying to Band Together

GNC has been widely promoted as one of the country's best–and fastest growing–franchise operations. But growing pains are straining ties with franchisees.... While rapid expansion has been highly profitable for GNC, some franchisees complain that it is coming at their expense. They claim poor distribution has left stores unstocked, even as they face increased competition from new franchisees and price-slashing company-owned stores....

With supplies tight, franchisees complain that GNC ships popular products to company-owned stores more often, while their shelves remain bare. "All my outside suppliers can ship to me in three days, max," says [a franchisee]. "But I wait five weeks for GNC."

One franchisee in Boston now battles three company-held Nature Food Centres within two blocks of the shop. "I'm in competition with my franchisor," says the franchisee.

—Stephen Baker and Keith L. Alexander, *Business Week*

THE FADED COLORS OF BENETTON
Picture Flat Sales, Family Conflict, and Angry Store Owners

Problems stem from Benetton's franchise-style operation.... [It] relies on a system in which local entrepreneurs put up capital for new stores. The method allowed Benetton to grow explosively, but it's showing increasing cracks and strains. In the late 1980s, American store owners charged in dozens of legal disputes that Benetton encouraged too many stores to be built, too close together, and failed to supply them adequately.... From around 500 stores in the late 1980s, only 150 remain.

—John Rossant, *Business Week*

TREACHER'S ANGER
Angry Franchisees Spew Vinegar about a Fish-and-Chips Chain

Twelve current and former franchisees of Arthur Treacher's Inc. have alleged to the FTC that the Jacksonville, Fla., fast-food franchiser misled them about costs and other issues. The 12 people who wrote the FTC say they have collectively lost about $3 million as franchisees and master franchisees. Their letter alleges that Treacher's failed to disclose significant facts to prospective franchisees.

"I would like to see Arthur Treacher's put out of business," says [one franchisee]. "I'm very angry because Treacher's doesn't give needed support," adds [another].

—Jeffrey A. Tannenbaum, *The Wall Street Journal*

SALSA'S AND SISTERS SETTLE WITH UNCLE SAM–BUT NO REFUNDS LOOM

The FTC moved against what it described as one of the biggest franchising frauds in years. In federal court in Phoenix, the FTC filed charges against four franchise promoters and eight of their companies for allegedly delivering little or nothing of what they promised to more than 400 franchisees. The case mostly involved Salsa's Gourmet Mexican, Pizza Chef and Blazer's All-American Barbecue food outlets, as well as Winner's Circle and Risque apparel stores. . . .

Under an FTC settlement . . . [the promoters] are barred from offering any franchise or business opportunity in the future. But FTC officials say they will be able to recover little, if any, of an estimated $6 million in fees and royalties paid by franchisees.

"I'm not getting a dime back," says [a franchisee]. He claims he lost more than $40,000 on a Winner's Circle outlet. . . . "All this settlement will do is release me from my contract."

–Jeffrey A. Tannenbaum, *The Wall Street Journal*

INVESTORS TO GET $600,000 BACK
FTC: Companies Misled Business Seekers

Federal regulators have negotiated a settlement in a business opportunity fraud case involving 18 South Florida firms. At least $600,000 may be refunded to investors.

The firms marketed distributorships featuring everything from weight-loss products to lingerie. But consumers, investing an average of $9,000 each, complained the products did not earn the amount of money promised. . . . The FTC sued the firms . . . after at least 300 investors complained. The FTC charged the firms used shills, or phony references, and misrepresented the earnings potential of the business. . . .

The firms, advertising in newspapers, marketed display racks featuring products such as cosmetics and gourmet coffee, popcorn and cookies.

–Audra D. S. Burch, *The Miami Herald*

ENTREPRENEUR TURNED SLEUTH HELPS FTC ASSAIL CONCERN

Thomas Woodward, a mortgage broker, recently went to extraordinary lengths to check out a business opportunity. . . . The FTC praises his tenacity in investigating Dr.'s Choice, a Sunrise, Fla., purveyor of store display-rack distributorships for diet products and related items. . . . Mr. Woodward's detective work provided "critical" evidence in building a case against the company.

In its complaint, the FTC alleged that [the owners] made false earnings claims to investors and gave company shills as references . . . and didn't provide profitable locations for displays as promised.

FTC lawyers estimate that about 500 individuals have invested at least $2.5 million in Dr.'s Choice. None of the investors seems to have recouped any of the initial investment.

–Barbara Marsh, *The Wall Street Journal*

SPEEDEE UNITS DIDN'T GET SPEEDY HELP–AND WERE MISLED . . .

California's Dept. of Corporations filed a sweeping lawsuit against Speedee Oil Change Systems Inc. According to the suit, California franchisees received "little or no" promised training or other support from subfranchisers. . . . The suit alleges that the majority of the California buyers never were able to open their units. . . .

Most franchisees never achieved a profit, much less the promised annual profit level of $100,000 in three years.

–Jeffrey A. Tannenbaum, *The Wall Street Journal*

FROM AN ARTICLE IN *FORTUNE*: "Trouble in Franchise Nation"

Demand for New Outlets Is Booming. But Markets Are Crowded, Lawsuits Are Flying, and the Risks of Getting Burned Have Never Been Higher.

The current state of franchise nation can be summed up in two words—deeply troubled. For all their past successes, precious few systems are minting money for franchisees today. Most markets are crowded, and expenses are rising. Even worse, new evidence suggests that the whole franchising model . . . is so riddled with problems and ill will that opening a franchise can often be riskier and less desirable than simply starting up your own business. . . .

"Most people think of franchising as some kind of bonanza," says [a director of an SBA Center]. "The reality today is if you get a solid operation, work damn hard, and you're making $40,000 a year after four years, that's good."

A McDonald's Story:

McDonald's franchisee Allen Whitehead opened his McDonald's in a low-income section of Hartford in 1983. . . . His operation was a quick-serve hit. Annual sales rose steadily, peaking at $2.3 million—well above the national average—and he was making what he calls "a very healthy income." But in 1987, McDonald's put in a restaurant 2.6 miles away from his store. Over the next several years it added four more close by. Since then his sales have dropped to $1.5 million.

Whitehead acknowledges that some McDonald's franchisees do prosper. "I think about a third of them are doing really well—like I was," he says. "A third are hanging in there. And another third are barely making it. I can't see the situation improving if the company keeps pushing in more stores." Whitehead's advice: "Remember, the franchiser is in the business of maximizing his revenues, even if that means saturating your market with competing stores."

A Failure Story:

One other danger that prospective franchisees should be aware of: higher-than-advertised failure rates. Franchisers like to brag that their business is safer than starting up a business on your own. . . . Economist Timothy Bates has found that almost 35% of franchises had shuttered their doors by 1991, vs. 28% for other small businesses. . . .

Why would today's franchises be more prone to flop? "I think the golden era of franchising might be over," says Bates. "Buying a McDonald's 20 years ago was a great business. Buying a Subway today is nowhere near as attractive."

No need to tell that to Greg Kane. The 35-year-old Navy flyer with a master's in management science bought a Subway franchise in Hanover, Mass. "Subway said its franchises had only a 2% failure rate," says Kane. "That was the big hook." . . . He borrowed $60,000 from his in-laws, who took out a second mortgage on their house. Kane lost his store last year after a new food court across the street chewed up his business. . . .

Was Kane able or incompetent? "When I was making money, I got high marks from Subway," he says. "When the food court opened and I started losing money, Subway marked me down for being messy." Now Kane is suing Subway, as are scores of other franchisees. He claims that the company "misled me with their statistics—the failure rate is much higher than 2%."

Some pointers:

• **Lessons one, two, and three:** It's the contract, stupid. Few would-be franchisees are aware just how inequitable the agreements are that franchisers typically foist upon them. "Most treat franchisees like indentured servants," says [a lawyer]. "They have fewer rights than employees." . . . "Franchisees have to dig, and they have to fight," says Susan Kezios [the franchisee activist]. "When a franchiser tells you he can't negotiate his contract, that's complete b.s."

"Franchise contracts are inordinately one-sided. I'd never sign one again unless I could make major revisions," says [a franchisee]. "The contract had a lot of scary-sounding details, but my lawyer and the company said it was just boilerplate. It turns out those details mattered a great deal."

• **Be prepared for hefty up-front costs. . . .**

• **Be especially careful to investigate any new or unfamiliar franchise system.** Few of the hassles you could encounter are as potentially costly as taking a flier on a fly-by-nighter who lures you with the five most dangerous words in franchising: "This is the next McDonald's."

• **Be prepared to walk away. . . .** Above all, future citizens of franchise nation, learn to say no. If something, anything, doesn't feel right to you, walk away. Remember, you're the boss. Isn't that why you wanted to become a franchisee in the first place?

—Andrew E. Serwer, *Fortune*

4

THE WELCOMING COMMITTEE:

Watch Your Back . . .
Hide Your Wallet

The Cannibal Syndrome

It's not a social club. It's not an emotional support group. It's not Entrepreneurs Anonymous. It's not us versus them.

It's them versus you. You, all on your lonesome.

All your contacts as you start up and develop your small business will be with people who want something from you and your business: a piece of your spending money, while you still have it to spend.

Why this selfish attitude?

Because it's business, is all. That's the very essence of business contacts. To sell things, to buy things, to obtain useful information . . . to profit from the contact with you, in some way or other. It's in the nature of the beast.

Be a nice girl or guy, and give in to the many constant pressures to spend more than your business can afford, and you will become a prime candidate for the 70 percent club.

There will not be a single exception to this rule, other than members of your family and close friends. They're the only ones who love you for who you are (maybe?), rather than what you can do for them.

Expect only self-interest from other businesses and professional services you'll be dealing with when you start up and you won't be disappointed. The rare Good Samaritan that you encounter may reestablish your faith in the basic decency of human nature, but it certainly won't change the realities of the business jungle or the normal patterns of behavior of its hungry inhabitants. They'll eat whatever they can get. If that happens to include you, as meal rather than fellow guest, so be it. Nothing personal, you understand.

Cannibalism is acceptable business behavior.

It's difficult to explain the Cannibal Syndrome to beginner entrepreneurs and get them to accept that it is a very real problem, which can have a dramatic effect on how efficiently they spend their limited capital when they are starting up and have little or no revenues flowing back in. Newcomers are often idealistic; they'd like to believe better of their fellow businesspeople.

So I'm often accused of cold-hearted cynicism and gratuitous meanness when I bring up the subject. It goes against everyone's better nature to accept that so many new small businesses get ripped off (or would you prefer "taken advantage of?")–gently, nicely, quietly and politely–by so many older, established businesses and so-called "professionals." And that such behavior is so prevalent that it is one of the underlying causes of many small business failures in their early years.

They buy stuff they don't need. They pay too much for things that should cost less. They sign onerous contracts and agreements that they can't get out of. They pay for expensive professional services that are irrelevant or unnecessary or postponable. When all the bills come in and accumulate, the small business flounders and drowns . . . for no good or clearly apparent reason. The start-up entrepreneur doesn't even get to strut his or her stuff . . . the business dies of financial asphyxiation before the show can even get on the road.

Hey, It's Only Business

One reason that all this is hard for newcomers to believe is that the stickup artists don't wear ski masks or wield semiautomatics.

They're just regular ol' businessfolks, just like you and me, just trying to make an honest living. If you were to question their morals or ethics on the subject, their indignant answer would be: "Hey, it's only business . . . so what's your big problem, pal? You're the one making the decisions in your small business, aren't you? Why blame me if you made poor decisions?"

They're right, unfortunately.

It *is* only business. They *are* only selling and hustling and hyping, which is

MASS MARKET

Look inside any entrepreneur's mailbox these days and you will discover a dizzying array of offers from major long-distance phone companies, Big Six accounting firms and giant computer makers. In trade magazines and local business journals, too, you will see countless advertisements for office-supply superstores and huge bank-holding companies.

Corporate America clearly has discovered that there is big money to be made selling to the nation's more than 20 million small businesses.

—Stephanie Mehta, *The Wall Street Journal*

perfectly acceptable business conduct. *Your problem is that you're at the sucker end of their business activities, because you're new and wet behind the ears.* If enough newcomers smartened up and hardened up, fast and early, and became much more cautious about how they commit their small business's precious bucks, it's those other businesses and professionals that would feel the pinch.

Check out Charles Darwin's theories on evolution and survival of the fittest; he's the original business guru. It *is* a business jungle. One's survival *is* often the other's demise. Dog *does* eat dog. And you, pal, start off as a puppy among the bigger, hungrier dogs. Getting smart, fast, will improve your odds of survival.

Businesses and "professional practices" whose revenues come mainly from new business clients do not like to hear this kind of talk. Makes them irritable. The longer you and other newcomers continue as trusting innocents, the better for them, naturally enough. Also, their feelings (yes, they have them) can get hurt and they can start whining that they are the victims of "bashing." Lawyers are particularly sensitive souls on this issue, probably because their fees are the most onerous for a new small business. The higher the fees, the greater the sensitivity. They'd all prefer a tactful, respectful silence, instead of all this mean-spirited talk. It could be bad for business . . . theirs.

This isn't a whistle-blowing campaign, but I have to remind critics that the title of my book is *Beating the Odds in Small Business* and that its commitment is to improving the odds of your survival in your own new small business. Which leaves me with no alternative but to convince you of the key message in this chapter, which is:

They need to take advantage of you while you're still green and gullible; it'll be too late for them, once you've smartened up.

Clear 'nuff?

So smarten up, watch your back and clutch your wallet, from Day One.

New Businesses as Targets

No one likes to be taken for a sucker. As a modern consumer, you have your defense mechanisms well honed. You don't fall for con jobs, sales pitches and advertising hype. You don't buy what you don't need or can't afford. You've been exposed to marketing pressures since you were a child and you're fully trained in blocking out the tempting messages. You don't get taken easily.

Yet you are far more likely to be suckered as a small businessperson than you would be as a consumer. Because it's a new and different game, where your opponents are experienced and well trained, and you are not.

Here's what happens, all too often:

1. Most small businesses that are going to fail will fail in their first years. Everyone knows this except the entrepreneurial newcomer, who believes he/she will be the natural exception to any such pessimistic predictions. So the pressures come early, while you're still in business.

2. Almost everything the new business's owners pay for in that first year–merchandise, equipment, contractors, lawyers, consultants, construction, real estate, leases, agents, whatever–is usually something they've seldom or never done or bought or negotiated before.

3. They have the most money to spend when they're starting up . . . and inexperienced. After some time has passed, they're beginning to run on empty and get much tighter with the cash . . . and smarter, of course.

4. They're buying from other businesses and professionals. People much like themselves. They're inexperienced and unsure of themselves, and they tend to trust the recommendations of such "fellow" businesspeople more than they would listen to the advice of, say, a store salesclerk.

5. Professionals who sell services (lawyers, consultants, brokers, agents, contractors, etc.) to new businesses don't *realistically* expect to have a "continuing long-term client relationship," even though they talk up the idea–*"We'll be here for you always, pal."* The way they see it, after the first year the client will probably have folded. If not folded, will certainly have wised up and be in a tight cash position. So they take advantage while they can, while the client's still innocent and trusting . . . and able to pay the bills.

6. The same goes for most "onetime" suppliers of machinery, equipment, furnishings, etc. Realistically, they don't expect their new small business customers will be around for the long haul, much less be giving them more business in the future . . . so they try to get it while they can.

7. The honorable exceptions to this predatory behavior can be found among regular wholesalers, distributors and service companies, who serve their many small business customers on a routine basis (daily, weekly or monthly). They have little to gain from a short-term quick hit. They have more to gain from building a healthy long-term relationship, and want to be still supplying their client after he/she has survived the initial phase and wised up. These trade guys deserve gold medals when compared to the so-called professionals.

8. Another exception is suppliers who also sell to the general public (Office Depot, Staples, Kinko's, Home Depot, etc.). These retailers *know* they can't screw the general public and get away with it for long. So they don't screw their business customers either. More gold medals.

So Who's Broadcasting the Bad News?

But, you may ask, if new small businesses are regularly taken advantage of to such an extent, why don't you hear about it and read about it more often?

Because, folks, the message wouldn't benefit anyone but the prospective suckers. No one else wants to hear it. Or were you expecting some kind of public service radio and media program, called maybe *Save Our Suckers*? If so, don't hold your breath . . . it ain't going to happen.

The correct message is that most people you'll be dealing with when you start up will be trying to take unfair advantage, in one way or another, of your temporary vulnerability as a business newcomer. Not the most joyous message to be sending out to all those optimistic people planning to start up their own small businesses.

Established businesses with something to gain from serving new small businesses prefer to broadcast the opposite message. Upbeat hype about the glories and joys of owning your own business . . . about rose gardens and how they can help you grow them . . . at a price.

Consider for a moment some of the consequences if the more downbeat but realistic message were openly and regularly discussed in the media:

• Some people would get scared and would shelve their plans to open their own small business. That's sales, fees and commissions just got blown out the window, which would otherwise have ended up in someone's pocket.

- Those who didn't get scared off would be rougher and tougher on their lawyers, consultants and other service providers and in many cases would dispense with them altogether. That's more fees just blown away.

- They would also become more aggressive in bargaining for better prices on machinery, furnishings and similar purchases, and in looking for better deals. That's somebody's gross margins just got hammered.

- New businesses would not buy so many nonessential gadgets, trinkets and assorted doodads, once they realize they can and should do without them, while they are going through the difficult start-up period. That's more lost sales for someone.

- Upset advertisers might start pulling their ads from those papers, magazines and TV channels that aired the downbeat message. That's someone's advertising dollars just went up in smoke.

- Politicians and government officials might complain that such scaremongering is having a depressing effect on economic activity, job creation, tax revenues and so forth.

So this kind of realistic talk is not exactly popular stuff.

And you want to know something?

If your new business becomes successful and it begins selling to business customers, there will come a time when you will also chime in: "Let's not exaggerate, now. Let's not spread such depressing news, such unfair criticisms. Let's not . . . " and so on. You'll be looking at those sprouting little companies, ready to open their freshly stuffed wallets, anxious to buy your products or services, and you'll also be thinking, "Yummy, yummy. Dinner is served."

It's in the nature of the beast.

Welcome to the Cannibal Syndrome.

These are things you need to know. These are things people don't like to talk about. *These are things that happen all the time.*

The Hype and the Hustle

So you've taken off your well-worn consumer's hat and put on your brand-new business owner-operator's hat. Immediately you find you're the target for a whole new type of marketing, smoothly, seductively selling the overwhelming need for stuff and for services for your new small business. You have little or no experience in judging what's good, what's bad; what's essential, what's unnecessary; what your business can afford, what it can't; what's sound advice, what's hype; what's responsible selling, what's hustle.

As a wet-behind-the-ears entrepreneur, you are now faced with convincing, sophisticated hype, for all sorts of services and products that you've never had to evaluate before. You know you have to make decisions but you're unsure of yourself, naturally enough.

That makes you a vulnerable, choice marketing target.

Just as America's marketers are the world's experts at selling their consumer goods, they are equally proficient at marketing goods and services to business buyers. Businesses, as a buying segment, are as important in dollar terms as the consumer market. So get prepared for polished, expert hype of

Selected Advertising Gems:

From AT&T:
Starting a new business is simply a matter of knowing where to turn. The uncertainties of starting a business could corner you. You need information, but don't know where to find it. Quickly and easily . . . now there's help. Introducing AT&T Resources for New Business. . . . One call . . . can help you navigate through the difficulties of starting a business.

—Ad in The Wall Street Journal

From Sprint:
Real business challenges demand Real Solutions. The new program that's helping businesses boost their bottom lines. . . . Call us for a free top-to-bottom analysis of where your business stands, with information. . . . Talk to a professional business consultant. . . . They'll work with you on strategies to manage finances more efficiently.

—Ad in The Wall Street Journal

From Bell Atlantic and Blue Cross:
Looking for data systems and solutions that'll insure the health of your business? Call me. . . .

—Ad in The New York Times

From Chemical Bank:
Unleash the entrepreneurial spirit. It can turn your company around. Alert to every opportunity. Quick to pounce. Proud to carry off the prize while the competition fumes. . . . We'll help you seize opportunities that can vanish in a flash. . . .

—Ad in Business Week

From American Express:
You have what it takes to make your small business into whatever you want it to be. We can help you in ways you never thought of. From accounting services to lines of credit to corporate cards. American Express is here for you.

—Ad in Time

If you believe that these advertising messages are sincere and heartfelt, there's an attractive, previously owned bridge in Brooklyn I'd love to sell you, to ensure that your small business bridges the gap to glorious success.

which you, the neophyte business owner, are now the designated target. An honor, no doubt, if only it weren't so damn costly and so potentially destructive to the financial health of your business. It comes from different directions:

• **Business Media:** Upbeat articles, news items, capsules . . . in the business section of your local paper, in business magazines, in the business segments of TV and radio programs. All describing the wonderful things successful businesses are now doing. With their newer, faster, more powerful computers. With their high-tech communications systems. With their latest training seminars and motivational courses. With their computerized order-taking, filling and dispatching systems. And so on. It's fascinating, glamorous business news, but the stories are always about the exceptions. Regular news about regular businesses, just plodding along doing the best they can with whatever limited resources they can scrape together, just isn't newsworthy. The Business Star Wars stuff makes better reading.

• **Business Advertising:** In those same papers, magazines, TV and radio programs, you'll find these persuasive ads. The businessperson's equivalent of ads for perfume, liquor and luxury condos. Blindingly fast laptop computers. Business software that'll run your company for you. Telephone systems for warp-speed communication. Web sites to strut your stuff in cyberspace. Office furniture that'll double your employees' productivity. Insurance programs that'll protect you against every calamity. Financial services to turn your cash flow into torrents. Consulting services to guarantee perpetual profitability. And so on. All very seductive. But your small business has as much need for this stuff, or the financial ability to pay for it, as you do for that luxury condo.

• **Direct Mail Deluges:** Once you're on assorted mailing lists (it'll happen), you'll start receiving never-ending direct mail, offering business stuff that no self-respecting entrepreneur can afford to be without. Business organizations you must join. Books and magazines you can't be without. Lectures you can't miss. Seminars that will transform you. Specialized software, office services, temp organizations. And so on. Some of this literature is worth glancing at, but most of these offerings are luxuries that will waste your time or money or both.

• **Consultants, Lawyers and Assorted Advisers:** These guys have their own marketing techniques. Nothing crassly commercial. Through letters, reports, meetings, telephone conversations, proposals, diagnostic reviews, over lunches, these guys sell their stuff as well as Nabisco or General Motors. Their technique subtly works the fear element, the insecurity element, the lack of experience element. You'll be held personally liable for anything and everything. You'll lose your company, home, spouse, kids and pet parakeets. Awful, spine-chilling things will happen to you, if you do not contract their indispensable services. The marketing pitch is: use our services or the earth will open under your small company's tottering infant feet and it will drop into a bottomless pit, where you will roast in perpetual hell for your irresponsibility in not working with us. We know what's best for you. You don't.

• **Looking Entrepreneurial:** The image angle . . . Rolex, Jaguar, BMW, Armani, expensive restaurants, whatever. The pitch is: if you want to be a successful entrepreneur, you've got to look and act like one. The truth? Nowadays it won't make the slightest difference to the success or failure of your small business if you work in jeans and a T-shirt, drive a pickup truck and travel economy class. Nobody cares. Too many well-dressed dudes, driving the right cars and wearing the right watches, have caused too many business disasters and financial scams in recent years for anyone to be fooled by appearances anymore. Bankers, investors and suppliers are only interested in your ability to survive and pay your bills.

Self-Defense

Once you accept the reality of the Cannibal Syndrome, you'll learn to defend yourself. You'll become one royal pain in the butt. You'll ask hard questions and demand straight answers. You'll doubt the experts and insist they explain themselves. You'll challenge fees, invoices and charges. You'll cancel orders, you'll return goods. You'll threaten lawsuits. You'll scream bloody murder. All in all, you'll become one hard-nosed SOB when people try to take advantage of you and your business. Even if you're a pussycat at home. And when they turn on you and bitterly complain about your distrustful attitudes and tightwad ways, you'll have the ready answer:

"Hey, pal, it's only business."

Watch for the Crooks, Scoundrels and Swindlers

The smarter members of the criminal community just love cooking up schemes for fleecing businesses. Especially small businesses. For much the same reasons mentioned in this chapter: the victims' lack of experience, their gullibility and the pressure of work.

You and your small business could be the next target.

Awareness that such things happen is your best defense. Read on . . .

STINGING SMALL BUSINESS
There's a New Breed of Swindler Out There—and Entrepreneurs Are the Prey

Small-business formation is booming, propelled by a generation of entrepreneurial innovators and the huge layoffs in Corporate America. But this eager class of risk-takers is discovering that the risks can be greater than they ever imagined. To all the normal bedevilments of small business—tight financing, unsure markets, strong rivals—add another: a new breed of unscrupulous moneymen who prey on entrepreneurs.

Con artists have been around for ages, of course. But the fatal combination of entrepreneurial fervor, need, and financial naïveté makes small-business owners easy marks for a new variety of scamsters. Filled with enthusiasm for their own ideas, they can be startlingly inexperienced in finance . . . what makes emerging companies easy marks is their often desperate thirst for capital.

Entrepreneurs are left to swim in shark-infested waters: the world of stock promoters and brokerage firms that specialize in small-cap companies.

—Michael Schroeder, *Business Week*

A CRACKDOWN ON PHONE MARKETING
Tougher Rules Are Aimed at Fraud Against Gullible Consumers

The Government proposed sweeping new rules to fight criminals who coax money over the telephone from Americans who are too ready to believe, too harried to care or too greedy to check.

Law enforcement authorities say abuses in what is known as telemarketing represent the nation's fastest-growing form of consumer fraud.

Deceptive telemarketing firms use fake invoices and other schemes to coax at least $40 billion a year from companies and consumers, particularly small businesses and elderly retired couples.

—Anthony Ramirez, *The New York Times*

BUST-OUT SWINDLES APPEAR TO BE BUSTING OUT ALL OVER
More Firms Are Fleeced by "Buyers" Who Order Goods but Don't Pay

In bust-out fraud, swindlers order merchandise, never pay for it, and make their money reselling the goods. . . . Small businesses are often the targets of bust-out artists, say law-enforcement officials. These concerns commonly lack the resources and time to do thorough credit checks of new customers. Increasing competition in many fields has also pushed large numbers of businesses to relax their credit standards. When firms "get a little desperate to move product off the shelf, the con men come out; it's like watering a plant," says a deputy sheriff. . . .

Bust-out artists sometimes make small initial orders at very large firms to give them credibility with small businesses. If many smaller companies "see a Procter & Gamble as a reference, they will just give credit to the con artist without further checks on his creditworthiness," says [an investigator].

A loss that a large firm can shrug off can mean the difference between life and death for a small company. One small plastic-bag manufacturer in California was forced out of business after losing $300,000 to a bust-out that operated from the Chicago area.

—John R. Emshwiller, *The Wall Street Journal*

5

IT'S THE COMPETITION, STUPID:

Eat Your Lunch . . .
Or Have It Eaten for You

Charles Darwin Feels Your Pain

Remember that famous line from a presidential campaign: "It's the economy, stupid!"?

Well, in your case: "It's the competition, stupid!"

Forgive the *stupid*. It's to get your attention. No offense.

Knowing your business is a survival necessity, which requires no explanation in this book; it's obvious. But your competitors know their business too, certainly as well as you do. It's *knowing your competition* that gives you *strategic know-how*, to add to your business know-how, and a *strategic edge*, to better defend yourself in the struggle for survival. All too often small businesspeople find excuses for not doing their competitive homework. And they pay for it with their business lives.

So let's make this one really clear: however small your business may be, in-depth understanding of your competition, from its narrowest sense to its widest definition, is a top survival priority. Before you start, after you've started and forever after. Competition is always there and never goes away.

There is a tendency for newcomers to argue: "Yeah, sure, sure. *Of course* I'm going to have competitors and competition. I'm not stupid; that much I do know. Tell me something I don't know. Competition's to be expected. That's what business is all about. Can't do anything about it. So let's get on with starting up the business and getting down to work."

They don't prepare themselves, by checking out the opposition.

Big mistake. These are the newcomers who most often get sandbagged by some competitive threat that they did not anticipate. Situations where a little foresight, observation and preparation might have made all the difference in terms of self-defense and self-preservation.

Look at your problem of business competition this way. Business success results from many things, but one key ingredient is to generate adequate survival income from sales, fees, commissions, royalties or whatever it is you do to turn a buck in your particular business. When that happy event takes place, whether you were aware of it or not, *you just took food away from a hungry competitor.*

Likewise, business failure can have many causes, but one universal reason is that your company's income drops below what it needs to stay alive. Should that sad event take place, *it will be because competitors saw your lunch sitting out on the table and ate it.* Potential customers still spent their money; they just didn't spend it with you.

The more you can learn about potential competitors and overall competition in your field before you start up, and the more you can keep learning once you're rolling, the better prepared you'll be to eat their lunch before they eat yours.

Just because your business is very small, don't fool yourself into thinking that it won't be visible and thus won't attract competitive attention. You don't need to attract attention directly, in order to feel the effects of competition. However small you may be–even if it's only a one-person home venture–you're in business to receive payment for something you do or something you supply. Whoever is paying that money may decide to spend it some other way or with some other supplier.

That, folks, is called competition. And it hurts.

Or they may decide not to spend it at all.

That nonspending decision is also a form of competition. It also hurts.

Think of "competition" not just as other businesses identical to yours, performing exactly the same business activities as you. That's far too narrow a definition. Think of it as a malevolent, threatening cloud, hovering over your potential or existing clients, constantly bombarding them with good reasons why they should apply their money in other ways, elsewhere. The more you get to know what's in that cloud, the better you

If Darwin were alive today, he'd be a professor at the Harvard business school studying small enterprise. Talk about a laboratory of evolution and survival.... Half of all new companies don't last more than five years. Of the survivors, most live with profit margins that are razor thin and margins of error that are thinner still. Alertness and speed reflexes are essential.

A giant like Wal-Mart can arrive in the neighborhood like a mountain-size vacuum-cleaner and suck a Main Street dry of customers in a few months.

Face it–entrepreneurship is a fast track to humility.

–Peter Nulty, *Fortune*

can counteract its negative influence. The less you know about it, the more vulnerable you will be to unpleasant surprises.

It's not just learning to "compete" in the obvious sense. It's learning everything your competition can teach you about your market and your customers. Studying the competition is one of the best ways of ensuring your own survival.

Charles Darwin showed the way: in a competitive environment, the fittest survive, and they do it by constant adaptation to the threats around them.

Competition: A Fact of Life

Recently, a newspaper article ran an upbeat little story about a bubbly new restaurant owner, talking about how great it was to have all these neat, friendly competitors around him, because "the more there are of us, the more customers we will all attract." He wasn't thinking too clearly . . . or maybe he didn't express himself well.

Yes, he has a short-term "geographic allegiance" with the neighboring restaurants, in drawing customers away from other competing eating areas in town. No, it isn't happy camper time, as he'll quickly discover when his local area becomes oversaturated, as too often happens in the restaurant trade. Those formerly friendly competitors will then start worrying only about themselves. They will revert to their role of unfriendly competitors, cutting prices, stealing employees, offering discount coupons, whatever. Whatever works, whatever brings in the customers.

You can temporarily work with your competitors when it's to everyone's short-term advantage. But they will always continue to be competitors, and will always revert to their naturally competitive roles, when the right time comes. As you will, too.

It's a Darwinian jungle where, to a greater or lesser degree, everyone has to fight everyone else . . . sometimes to the death . . . for their share of the limited food supply–the food being customers and their dollars.

For small business newcomers, it's even tougher. They are fragile and vulnerable to the slightest competitive blow. Older, bigger, better-established

THE COMPETITION
Another problem is ignoring competitors. It's amazing how many business plans I have seen and how many entrepreneurs I've talked to in the very early stages, who are basically saying, "We don't have any competition. There's nobody like us out there. We're unique. Nobody is selling this stuff."

Then they're out of business in three months or six months, and they sing a very different song, because they have suddenly discovered that these other people came out of nowhere and they've got all kinds of competition. . . . The reason they didn't think about it is perhaps they didn't want to.

—Interview with Wendell E. Dunn,
in *The Wall Street Journal*

businesses can usually take a few hard competitive knocks, fall down and still pick themselves up.

New small ones are often out for the count.

True, the modern world, with its rapidly accelerating pace of change, is steadily creating more and better opportunities for small businesses and is also making it much easier to start up small businesses. That's the good news.

The bad news is that the same applies to everyone else.

So competitive pressures are also constantly increasing. Both from other businesspeople also starting their own new businesses, and from existing businesses, small and large.

Well Scared = Well Prepared

So why point out the obvious? Of course you're going to have competition in whatever line of business you enter. Of course nobody expects a free ride or a monopoly.

However, simply *knowing* that you're going to face competition doesn't do anything for you, other than scare you. But being both *scared* and *prepared* forces you to take effective countermeasures. Small businesses are more vulnerable to being sandbagged by an unexpected competitive challenge and more likely not to see it coming. It's the old "learning curve" problem . . . only after a few nasty skirmishes in the jungle will you refine your skills at defending yourself from predators. And learn to counterattack.

When you start a new business, your attention is usually heavily focused inward, on everything needed to get set up and moving ahead. If the threatening competition is out of your field of vision, you may simply not see it in time to prepare yourself. Back to that jungle analogy: you must lift your head frequently, to look for dangers and sniff the wind for nasty smells.

Something unpleasant may be coming your way.

My warnings have only one purpose: to convince you to regularly spend time checking out (1) specific competitors and (2) competition in general, and thinking through your defensive moves. Before you start, while you're starting, and forever after. You can never assume you already know it all. You

> **FEAR IS NOTHING TO BE AFRAID OF**
>
> The workplace is never free of fear—and it shouldn't be. Indeed, fear can be a powerful management tool. . . .
>
> As Intel CEO Andy Grove points out in his book, "Only the Paranoid Survive," fear is crucial to creating and maintaining the passion necessary to win in the marketplace. . . . Fear of complacency and stagnation is almost always good, as is fear of losing your customers, profitability and market share. . . . Nothing motivates like the fear of losing the big account.
>
> —George Bailey, *The Wall Street Journal*

never know it all. And if you do know it all today, tomorrow it will have changed; competition moves very fast these days.

Check, cross-check, double-check, triple-check. Study the enemy closely. The better you know your competition, in as much detail as possible, the better overall chance you will have of surviving, and the better your business will perform. You will be able to take advantage of your competitors' good ideas (yes, it's okay to copy their ideas . . . after all, they'll copy yours), avoid repeating their goofs and thus stay ahead of the game.

Competing for Customers' Limited Bucks

You're always competing for the client's buck. For a chunk of the spending money of clients who, in this tight modern world, have become much more selective about how they spend their precious cash. They may simply prefer to spend it on something entirely different, instead of your particular product or service. There doesn't have to be a competitor creeping around, offering something similar at a lower price. The competition can be invisible.

Consumers nowadays are acutely conscious of the value of a buck. They are very knowledgeable about the dollar cost of most things they buy. They see prices every day–in direct mail catalogs, in TV ads, in newspaper ads, in store windows, on supermarket shelves–and they remember them well. They usually know what stuff costs and may simply prefer to spend their money on something other than what you are offering, good as it may be. In which case, you have a serious problem.

Business customers likewise. Profit margins have been steadily squeezed in recent years. Business customers are under constant pressure to control every dollar they spend. They may prefer to spend on alternative purchases or not to spend at all.

Your small business may be selling a better mousetrap, but before starting up you should check as best you can not only who else (that's the visible competition) is selling mousetraps and at what price, but whether your potential customers really want to spend money on mousetraps at all, however great they may be and whatever they may cost (that's the invisible competition).

And maybe they don't have mice.

STUDYING THE COMPETITION PAYS OFF WELL FOR SMALL BUSINESS
Market intelligence isn't just for big companies: Many small shops routinely visit their rivals, question suppliers, socialize with competitors and scout trade papers for tips. . . . A chef who owns two Atlanta restaurants gives managers a food allowance to dine out and bring back ideas. [The owner] of a used-clothing-store chain in San Francisco, asks workers to "keep their ears open and mouths shut" at parties.
–"Business Bulletin,"
The Wall Street Journal

Or maybe they have mice and don't care.

New entrepreneurs too often allow their enthusiasm for their project to blind them to reality. Knowing your competition is knowing reality. Sometimes it will tell you things you would rather not hear. Better that you hear it while there is still time to change and adjust, rather than when it's too late.

Constant Change, Constant Competition

Business life was once calmer and more secure. Not that many years ago, anyone with a nice little business that was doing well could often look forward to years of peaceful coexistence with competitors. Nobody rocked the boat too much, everyone made a decent living.

Ah, the good ol' days.

Now, even if you and your close competitors wanted to try that–without breaking the law, in case you're thinking of fixing prices–it wouldn't work. Change is constant. It happens at an ever-increasing pace. New products, new technologies, new services, new ideas . . . they keep appearing almost daily, from businesses that you would never have thought of as competitors only the day before. But the new stuff, in one way or other, may threaten to take the place of your stuff. You may soon be out of business, unless you saw it coming and had your defenses organized.

LIFE AMONG THE GIANTS TAKES PLANNING, PASSION

Running a small business—even a successful one—can be full of peril. . . .

Whether you're in a law firm, an accounting firm, a print shop or a parts distributor, you're bound to be competing with a company that's either regional or national in scope. And at times—many times—it can seem like an unfair fight.

We live in a world of economic Darwinism—survival of the fittest. And the fittest often are the biggest.

Big companies can buy in bulk and therefore, offer lower prices. Bigger companies can achieve economies of scale impossible to imagine for the small-business person. Big can offer benefits and wages unreachable for smaller companies. And big can advertise and promote and market and target and crush.

But there are ways for the small to succeed.

—David Satterfield, *The Miami Herald*

The pace of change in the computer industry is an example. First mainframes. Minicomputers started replacing mainframes. Then personal computers took center stage. Then successive generations of faster, better and cheaper PCs replaced each previous generation. Then portables. Then laptops. Each generation surviving for only one or two years. Printing was first done on clunky dot matrix machines. Then compact, faster dot matrixes. Then expensive laser printers. Then cheaper, better laser printers. Then ink-jet printers. Faster and faster, with the pace of change always steadily accelerating.

People have become used to change and no longer resist it. On the contrary, they love it. A few generations ago, people clung to tradition and it was harder to break ingrained habits. That gave some protection and stability to many businesses. That no longer exists. The best survival strategy for any business, in this high-velocity world, is to learn to live with change and accept it as a fact of business life.

Go with the flow. You can't fight it.

It's not just products and services that are changing so rapidly. It's lifestyles, work habits and personal preferences as well, with stunning rapidity. The ground is constantly shifting, creating both dangers and opportunities.

Learn to love it. Learn to profit from it. Learn not to let it bring you down.

Information Flows, Competition Grows

An integral part of this phenomenon of rapid change is the speed with which information now flows. The rapid flow of information makes changes happen even quicker.

Twenty years ago you might have developed a better gadget, widget or whatever, but it could take years for the product to become widely known and accepted. It took time to spread the word.

The "communications revolution" has changed all that. Companies that develop new gadgets and widgets can spread the word much faster, to a much wider audience. So new products that might once have taken a couple of years to introduce and start selling, can now cover the same distance in only a couple of months.

From a competitive viewpoint, this means that your reaction time to defend yourself against competitive threats has shrunk greatly. Competition can sneak up and jump you, faster than ever.

Saturation: Too Much of a Good Thing

The saturation thing is a modern-day business minefield, directly generated by the rapidity of change phenomenon, but only in recent years has it become so widely prevalent and so dangerous. It can and does cause unbelievable grief to small businesses. Yet so many newcomers just will not do the obvious: lift their eyes, look around them, sniff the wind, and read the obvious danger signals. They're too in love with their new businesses; the signals can't apply to them.

Here are a few scenarios to chew on.

You drive down a suburban highway near your home, for the first time in a year or so. Within a few miles of each other, you find a wonderful selection of new eateries: Chili's, Friday's, Applebee's, Outback Steakhouse, Chi-Chi's, McDonald's, Burger King, Wendy's, Boston Market, and more. They all opened in the past twelve months. They are all fine places, offering good food at reasonable prices. Yet all of them are losing money. Why? Simply because there are just too many of them, too close together, serving a single neighborhood with only so many residents, able to eat only so many meals per week. Only after another year or so will the weaker ones fold, leaving the survivors to finally start making profits. Unless new restaurants open up.

Is this where you want to open your delightful little pasta joint?

Another scenario. You used to have your calling cards made at Ye Olde Print Shoppe on Main Street at $99 per box, and they took a week to deliver. Pip's Printers opens in a nearby shopping center, with modern computer-based equipment. The same cards cost $49 per box, ready in two days. Then Ye Olde Print Shoppe switches to a Sir Speedy franchise, with even more modern machinery; the cards drop to $39.95, ready in twenty-four hours. Then a super-equipped Kinko's opens nearby; now it's down to $29.99 in twelve hours. And the local paper says that an Office Depot will open in sixty days with a superdiscount printing department.

And you're still thinking of buying a print shop franchise?

Or another scenario. Sammy's Artistic Signs would handpaint a store sign and have it ready for you in a couple of weeks. A Fast Sign franchise opens nearby, offering computer-generated signs, ready in forty-eight hours, at half Sammy's prices. Then a Best Signs pops up, with even cheaper prices and faster delivery. Sammy's converts to a pizza outlet and drops out of the sign game. But then you hear that that same new Office Depot is also going to install the latest generation sign-making equipment, offering signs at deep discount prices.

And you're still negotiating with that sign franchise outfit?

What's going on here? Has everyone gone crazy?

Are all these supposedly sane, intelligent restaurateurs, retailers and service companies actually some business variety of suicidal lemmings, blindly following each other over the edge of the cliff?

No. It's a modern-day business phenomenon, which can be called "high-

SHOOTOUT ON RESTAURANT ROW
Overbuilding Is Taking Its Toll on Casual Dining Chains

There's a three-mile stretch of road in Addison, Texas, just north of Dallas, that's a virtual shrine to the American chain restaurant. Both sides of the busy thoroughfare are lined with joints offering everything from fast-food burgers to seafood. In all, there are 115 places to eat–about one every 45 yards–and they're often packed. But don't be fooled by the traffic: Belt Line Road may be the nation's most visible sign of what's wrong in the restaurant industry. . . .

"There's going to be a huge shakeout," predicts the CEO of Applebee's.

–Business Week

velocity competitive saturation." Sometimes things just move too fast for everyone. Normally, any sensible businessperson carefully checks out the competitive situation before plunking down two or three hundred thousand dollars on a new location. Nobody's that dumb, to start up in an obviously supersaturated market area. Trouble is, it may not be obvious.

Commercial real estate developments can move so fast nowadays–and nobody wants to miss out on a good opportunity–that these saturated competitive situations can develop almost overnight, because nobody guessed that their future competitors were also moving fast, on a parallel course. By the time all the new businesses are committed, open and operating, there's no way out. Then, only red ink flowing in the streets will decide who survives.

Excess speed has its dangers and can prove fatal, if you and your competitors are all speeding to the same road crossing at the same time, and there are no traffic lights to determine who goes first.

New small businesses can save themselves grief by doing a little cold, calm "what if" thinking, double-checking their facts and suppositions before making final commitments that could land them in such saturated competitive situations. In all the scenarios just described, a little amateur detective work, just strolling around and chatting, could have saved some of the participants.

So it couldn't happen to you? Such saturation situations are the leading cause of failure of franchise operations. And franchises represent 50 percent of the business activities chosen by new small business operators.

So yes, it sure could happen to you.

The lesson is: think long, carefully, slowly and cold-bloodedly about potential competition and where it might spring from, and your chances of getting hammered will be far lower. Get wildly enthused and go barreling in blind without a thought to potential competition, and you may well regret your lack of caution.

It's that old cliché: look before you leap.

Category Busters and Big Boxes

Recent years have seen the explosive growth of another competitive monster: the "category buster," usually operating out of a "big box." Although its competitive dangers are most obvious in the retail area, don't think it can't happen in other types of business. Where the

> **RETAILING**
> Merchants opened so many stores in the Eighties that even hordes of shop-til-you-drop consumers can't keep them all in business. Huge discounters like Wal-Mart and Target have put smaller and weaker competitors under enormous pressure. . . .
> *—Fortune*

economics of giant size and massive concentration favor a category buster, it can happen in almost any line of business.

Take those friendly folks at Wal-Mart, who have probably bankrupted more small-town retailers throughout the U.S. in recent years than all who went bust in the Great Depression. Other category busters you will recognize: Toys R Us, Staples, Office Depot, Office Max, Home Depot, Builder's Square, FootLocker, CompUSA, Sports Authority, Blockbuster Video, and so on. Even organizations like McDonald's must be considered as category busters; if you're thinking of opening a hamburger stand, think twice.

The key to successful category buster organizations is their mammoth size, their concentration on a clear category that the public can easily identify, their ability to purchase huge quantities of merchandise at exceptionally low costs and then sell at equally low prices, counting on extremely high sales volumes in giant locations (big boxes) to make the overall business economically profitable. And, of course, the creation of a virtual monopoly situation in local market areas, as smaller competitors are forced to drop that category of merchandise. Or are simply wiped out.

Is it wrong? The customers love it, how can it be wrong?

It takes hundreds of millions of dollars to finance a category buster business, but Wall Street is usually more than happy to subscribe the necessary capital. Smart investors know the long-term economic advantages of such businesses, and the benefits of a regional near monopoly once most small competitors have been duly squashed. And the beauty of this near monopoly is that it's all perfectly legal. No need to worry about antitrust legislation, restraint of trade or whatever.

You've probably seen the movie *Jurassic Park*, so I shouldn't have to point out the inadvisability of fooling with dinosaurs. Anyone planning a new small business in this day and age should first check the risks of some category buster monster coming stompin' along all over the local countryside. And get well out of the way if the risk exists. Or do you want to be told all the gruesome details of the demise of thousands of small computer stores that disappeared overnight when Computer City, CompUSA, Office Depot and other chains moved into the PC market? And other horror stories, to make the point?

The Copycat Thing

The smallest businesses (typically home businesses) should probably worry more about copycat small competitors than being stomped by the monsters. At least you can see the dinosaurs looming on the horizon, clomping your way. Copycats are sneakier. They're most often found among your friends, acquaintances, neighbors and ex-employees.

Here's an all-too-typical scenario: with a small investment, you start your own small business, probably out of your home or in a minuscule office or small store. You work hard. After a tough start it all comes together. Clients are happy. Everything clicks. You start making decent money. You're happy, the family's proud of you, your friends congratulate you . . . and everybody talks up your success.

Suddenly, your old buddy Jack (or Jill) opens an almost identical small business in the same area, targeting the same customers . . . but maybe just a little bit cheaper. Coincidence? No way. If you confront the erstwhile friend, you'll either hear, "Oh, come on, the market's big enough for both of us. Don't be so selfish!" or a more honest, "Hey, buddy, it's only business." Suing them won't work. Your only defense will be attack; smother the SOB with price competition or whatever else you can dream up, while you are strong and they are new, weak, vulnerable and unsure of themselves . . . just don't make it a criminal offense. Get nasty; that's what former friends are for.

The competitive damage by a copycat can be very painful, because most very small businesses operate in very narrow market niches, where it takes only two or three close competitors, on exactly the same turf, to ruin the business for everyone. A minisaturation problem.

The best advice, to avoid the risk? Do what all smart business owners do. Keep a low profile, and your mouth shut. Talk as little as possible about your successes and as much as possible about your problems. When asked, tell everyone how miserable business is. Complain constantly. When you really feel the need to celebrate, make sure it's only with trusted friends and family.

Of course, if your business is growing and expanding, naturally a time will come when you're strong enough and big enough that you'll automatically provoke competition. But you should be able to live with it by then. Copycats won't bother you. They'll be smaller and weaker than you. With your jungle instincts nicely developed, you'll be able to make their business lives miserable. With a clean conscience. You did your time.

Neither Kind Nor Gentle

So I've said what needs to be said about competition. Not to scare you needlessly but to alert you to the realities of competitive dangers, too often overlooked by new entrepreneurs until it's too late.

The rest will be up to you.

In fact, most neophyte small business operators, after the first shocks and scares, begin to relish the competitive battle and get a considerable charge out of outsmarting and outmaneuvering the competition. They acquire a taste for the battle. It can be fun.

The realities of business competition in the entrepreneurial world mean you have to get used to wearing two different mental hats, and develop what amounts to a split personality and a double standard of conduct.

Yes, you can and should be personally friendly with competitors and treat them considerately and cordially, as individuals. Civilized, courteous behavior should be how you conduct yourself in business, always. There's never any profit in acting like a jerk. The competition you face in business is usually not personal, and you should try not to take it personally. It's only business.

But the realities and dangers of competition will always be there. You must be alert, wary and prepared to fight back ferociously, to defend your territory and protect your business interests. It means being hard-nosed, coldblooded and (let's admit it) pretty damn self-centered. It's you versus them.

Not everyone is comfortable having to think and act this way. All I can say is that if you feel genuinely uncomfortable with this double standard, you should think twice before proceeding with your small business plans. You may not have a natural "instinct for the jugular" and might consider something else.

Ballet, anyone? Poetry reading?

Yes, it would be so nice if it were a kinder, gentler business world.

But it ain't, and I don't see it changing to kind and gentle any time soon. To the contrary. Much to the contrary.

6

WHOSE RISK, WHOSE REWARD?

*Finding the Money . . .
Scrambling for More*

Capital Dreams

So you need money for your new small business?

So you'd like an example of how other folks do it?

Check out this quote from *The Wall Street Journal* on Steven Spielberg's company Dreamworks, and of the start-up cash he and his pals raised with a couple of phone calls before breakfast. . .

as a little object lesson in the kind of business fairy tale that will *not* happen in your small business life.

Some story. Fat-cat investors elbowing each other and beating down doors for the honor of handing over wads of money for piddling shareholdings. Major banks groveling to make giant long-term loans, at low interest rates with no security, as if they were lending to General Motors. Dreamworks' take totaled something like two billion dollars–and counting–and these guys didn't even have an office with their name on the door. They were still working out of their homes in their pajamas, f'crissakes.

Think of your own cash needs and eat your heart out.

> **DREAMWORKS SKG SWEETENS THE TERMS OF $1 BILLION CREDIT LINE**
>
> Dreamworks is backed by some of Hollywood's biggest talent and nearly $1 billion in equity, a hefty cushion for bankers to lend against, but it has no track-record.
>
> [A New York bank] underwrote a $1 billion (syndicated loan) at aggressive terms and conditions, but found that many big U.S. banks believed it was simply too sweet a deal. . . . "It's venture capital money disguised as a loan," said one lender. . . .
>
> Dreamworks [then] agreed to pay slightly higher fees and make other changes to encourage banks to participate. . . . It shortened the tenure from 10 years to eight, which is still unusually long for bank loans. The fees and interest rates will remain at rates typically charged to investment-grade companies.
>
> [Two banks] have now committed $250 million each. . . . Other banks were expected to join the syndicate.
>
> —Steven Lipin and Thomas R. King,
> *The Wall Street Journal*

But there's logic here, business logic . . . and a lesson to be learned.

You see, Spielberg, Geffen and Katzenberg have something you don't have, which makes them "bankable": total credibility and impeccable track records in exactly the same entertainment field their new "small business" is entering. And genius, of course, which maybe you have but only you know that so far; certainly not your banker, anyway.

The point here is: everyone *knows* these guys are gonna make it.

What's the risk in Dreamworks? None.

No one, yourself included, can tell if you'll make it in your new small business, even through the first year. Statistics say you won't.

What's the risk with your deal? Total.

That has everything to do with raising money.

The Fear of Risk

All this goes to the root of the problem that faces every small business when it tries to raise capital: *risk and the fear of risk*. You're afraid to risk your own life savings in getting started; your family and friends are afraid to risk theirs by helping you; investors are afraid to risk part of their capital in backing you; banks are afraid you won't be able to repay their loans.

So get comfortable with the notion that *there is risk and always will be risk*. In anything involving funding for your small business, everyone, yourself included, is going to be running scared of you and your adventure and of the downside risk. Don't get mad, don't get upset, don't get offended when you face skepticism, doubt, noncooperation and possibly ridicule. It's normal. It's to be expected. You have to overcome it. It won't go away.

If you have the self-confidence, the ability and the staying power–and assuming, of course, that yours is not some crackpot scheme–you'll find ways to get together the money needed for your entrepreneurial venture.

By working the other side of the "risk" coin.

Namely, reward.

The Lure of Reward

"Reward" comes in different forms, not necessarily just cold hard cash.

If you are to overcome your fear of the risks and come up with the necessary

> **WINNERS**
>
> Former schoolteacher Jan Davidson, founder of Davidson & Associates, was confident enough her educational software company would triumph that when she needed extra startup cash, she took $6,000 from a college fund she and husband Bob had started for their three kids.
>
> Not that it was an easy call. "Taking that money was a pretty hard decision, because we were very serious about our children's education," says Davidson. She needn't have worried. Twelve years later, the kids have stock in the company now worth $99.6 million.   *–Fortune*

capital out of personal or family savings, you and any family members involved must have some reasonable common agreement on the "reward" expected from the venture. Maybe it's not only the prospect of earning more than you did as an employee, but also of enjoying the freedom, independence and security of being in control of your own business fate, in these downsizing times. Maybe for close members of your family who are risking their money, the opportunity of helping you realize that dream is reward enough. They'll be happy to see the money back whenever–if ever–you can repay it, but their true reward is in helping you achieve your dreams.

Depends on how well you get along with the family, of course.

If it's your close friends, part of their reward is in helping you succeed, but they would also like a fair share in your good fortune, if you are successful. If not, no hard feelings, so everybody lost.

If it's acquaintances and private investors, their reward becomes strictly monetary. But if they have enough confidence in you, they may be willing to wait a long time before seeing any return. Maybe part of their reward will be in boasting later: "See how smart I was? I made this all possible. I saw the potential in this new business. I was willing to wait until the business got on its feet." If they get the praise and you get the opportunity, it's a fair trade.

If it's banks, their reward is the interest you pay and the degree of certainty of getting their capital back at the end. If you can find ways of increasing their degree of certainty, they'll be more willing to risk making the loan.

So, as a starting point to any calculations or plans of how you come up with the money, keep reminding yourself that everyone involved in your funding will want to have some idea, some notion, of what their reward will be. Only the prospect of reward will counterbalance the inevitability of risk.

Who knows, for those folks investing in Dreamworks, maybe the real reward is getting to knock back a cold beer with Spielberg every so often. It's whatever it takes. It's still a reward.

STARTING OUT–A LITTLE HELP FROM THEIR FRIENDS
Rule #1: Don't make your buddy your banker.
Rule #2: If you ignore Rule #1, at least minimize the risk.

When actor Don Johnson wanted seed money for DJ Racing, a venture to build and race speedboats, he didn't bother with a bank. Instead, he turned to his friend Martin Ergas, a Miami real-estate investor.

The star obtained an interest-free $300,000 loan on a handshake. But a year later, Mr. Ergas filed suit, claiming Mr. Johnson had reneged on his oral agreement to repay the loan within a year. In court documents, Mr. Johnson alleged he had five years to pay back the loan. The disagreement was settled out of court.

It may sound like a bad script, but as Mr. Johnson has discovered, making your buddy your banker engenders real risk. Legal fees and bad-debt headaches aren't the half of it. Fallout from soured loan agreements can destroy close relationships, especially if such arrangements are treated with the informality often accorded best friends and favorite cousins.

–Alex Markels, *The Wall Street Journal*

The process of first raising the start-up money and then maybe having to find more soon after, can be frustrating, agonizing, depressing, humiliating and horrendously time-consuming. Without doubt it's the worst part of starting a new business; it can drive you nuts. Putting yourself in the mind of the other parties and seeing how they might be thinking "How much risk am I running?" and "What's my reward going to be?" will help you think out your approach and keep your cool in your discussions. You'll need all the cool you can get.

Remember, potential investors and you yourself actually have a lot in common, as you both battle with your consciences and your demons, sweating out the possible answers to "What are the real risks to me and my family?" and "What are the future rewards for us?"

Enough philosophy. Let's talk about the money.

How Much to Get Rolling?

No matter how much pure guesswork has to go into it, some estimate of your total cash needs, however rough, is far better than no estimate at all.

It's amazing how often entrepreneurial hopefuls, who already have some starting money in the bank, decide impatiently, "What the hell, I'm just gonna go for it," with little planning, no sound estimates of capital needs and no interest in the risk-reward equation. This is the jump-in-the-deep-end-then-learn-to-swim style of entrepreneurial start-up. Otherwise known as the Las Vegas School of Small Business Financing.

Their guts and supreme self-confidence are impressive and I can't say they're always wrong; there are some amazing small business success stories that have started that way. However, as you can guess, the survivors are few and far between. Most of them don't learn to swim fast enough to avoid drowning in the deep end. Entertaining business stories but lousy examples to follow.

I strongly recommend that you avoid this school of business start-up and this philosophy of business life (and death). The laws of economics continue to apply, and they are not in favor of this approach. Even if your small business gets off to a quick start, if it cannot pay its start-up bills, that'll be the beginning

HOW MUCH?

Classic Problem: . . . By not accurately estimating cash flow and capital requirements, many small companies routinely short-change themselves.

Figuring the correct amount of capital for starting a business can be a tough balancing act. If companies ask for too little capital, they may lack the funds to grow; sometimes, they lack the funds simply to survive. On the other hand, if they ask for too much, investors balk.

Similarly, if they borrow too soon, they lack revenues to finance the interest payments. But if they wait too long, they may find themselves in so much trouble that nobody wants to lend to them.

The lesson in one entrepreneur's travails: Calculate the unexpected into your financial planning.

—Udayan Gupta, *The Wall Street Journal*

and the end of your brief burst of entrepreneurial heroics.

The opera will be over; the fat lady will have sung.

Why allow that to happen? Why not be more cautious and methodical, do your preliminary homework and start off by arming yourself with at least a rough estimate of your capital needs? Such basic steps as:

- **Worksheet:** Open a blank spreadsheet on your PC (more about that, later in the book). Title it "Rough Estimate of Start-up Capital Needs," and use it to keep continuing track of your estimates as you pull them together.

- **Fixed Assets:** Draw up the most detailed list possible (at this stage) of all the fixed assets (furniture, equipment, remodeling, etc.) your business will probably need. Get cost estimates from suppliers or even "eyeball" the numbers, but at least put some dollar value on each item, however unsure you are. A dollar value, any dollar value, is far better than a question mark.

- **Start-up Expenses:** Draw up a list of all your probable start-up business expenses (that is, initial costs before your operations start and your revenues begin flowing back in). Put a rough estimate on each item.

- **Working Capital:** Think through the different components of working capital your business will need in its first months, and estimate the total working capital (piggy bank) your business will need to finance its day-to-day operations for at least the first six months. (More on working capital and cash flow, later.)

- **Personal Needs:** You need a roof over your head and food on the table while you're setting up the business. If you expect to spend, say, six months without salary before business income starts kicking in, you'll still need to pay your home rent or mortgage, grocery bills, gas and so on. Estimate your personal monthly cash needs and be realistic about how many months you may have nothing coming in.

- **Cushion for Errors:** Add everything up. Then add an additional 20 or 30 percent to the total, as a fallback cushion for the mistakes you will have made and for the unexpected extras that will inevitably crop up.

Now at least you've got a starting point: your *Estimated Start-up Capital Needs*. Whether that's $10,000 for a home-based microbusiness or $1 million for a full-service restaurant, the work in preparing this estimate will be very different but the principles are pretty much the same.

The key is to do this homework sensibly and rationally, substituting commonsense estimates for pure wishful thinking.

And How Much More, Later On?

You may be one of those fortunate ones who hit their initial money calculations right on the nail, get rolling fast with a profitable business and positive cash flow and never look back. It happens.

If so, congratulations and bon voyage.

But you'll be in the minority. More often than not, initial estimates prove too low. Don't feel too bad if it happens to you; you'll be in good company with many others facing the same problem. It's not unusual and doesn't mean to say you're doomed to failure.

Most new ventures discover, either right away or some months later, that they are going to need to inject more money than they had first estimated. It can happen for different reasons:

- Your initial estimates don't pan out. Your total outlays in investments and start-up costs exceed what you had budgeted. If enough money does not start flowing in quickly from the new operation to cover the shortfall (and it probably won't), you will need additional funds to pay for the difference. Pronto.

- Your new business has a different working capital profile from what you had originally expected. Maybe you're having to extend more customer credit than you had planned. Maybe suppliers aren't giving you the credit terms you had expected. Maybe you're having to carry larger merchandise inventories. Whatever the reason, your business is going to need a larger working capital "cushion" than you had first estimated. And you're going to need this fairly fast, so as not to cripple the growth of your new business just as it's beginning to take off.

- You are losing money in the first months and the loss is steadily draining cash from your small working capital reserves; you are stealing from your own piggy bank. You need those working capital funds to finance your day-to-day operations, so you are going to have to replace the stolen funds somehow, until the business turns the corner and starts filling the piggy bank from profits.

- Sales are booming, the business is nicely profitable, but it has a negative cash flow profile . . . the more it sells, the more working capital it needs, to finance the higher level of business activity. A nice problem to have–but not if you can't raise the cash to keep growing.

Don't get depressed or embarrassed if these things happen. There is no such thing as certainty of future events in business. They don't sell crystal balls for entrepreneurs, and risk is part of the game.

As the T-shirt proclaims, shit happens. So you must battle on.

Capital shortfalls have happened to many bigger and better businesses than yours that have succeeded in the end. You'll not be the first to get caught in this kind of cash crunch. You certainly won't be the last. The important things are to understand *exactly* what is happening and why, to resist the temptation to panic, and to move really fast in covering your business's ass, one way or another.

You're much more likely to find a solution if you keep your cool. Panic solves nothing.

Using Your Own Money

Most small businesses get started with their own capital–the personal savings of the owner and/or family. Usually there's no alternative. There's almost no practical way of raising outside money for an untried, untested, brand-new small business, where the owner-operator has no track record. If that's your case, you'll be wasting time trying to raise your start-up capital from venture capitalists or through bank loans; the frustrations and wheel spinning will probably kill your enthusiasm for your project and you may never get off the ground.

That means digging into personal savings, borrowing from other close members of the family, selling stuff, moving to a smaller home, whatever it takes. It's painful. It really hurts. To go through with it, you have to believe strongly in yourself and what you're plannning to do.

This can be very hard on other members of the family. Inevitably, not everyone in the family shares the same degree of enthusiasm, confidence and personal commitment to the venture. The arguing, the recriminations and the accusations can start flying, usually at precisely the moment that the owner-operator is working hardest, totally stressed out, under tremendous pressure, nervous as hell and needing all the moral support he/she can get. It can lead to bitter family relations, constant quarrels, domestic violence, divorce, bloody murder.

No kidding.

If it's all your own personal money and you have no spouse, no dependent children, no aging parents, no one to love you and care for you, you may well be one lonely, miserable SOB, but you're perfectly suited to the life of a struggling entrepreneur and are far more likely to succeed than the average responsibility-laden family man or woman.

Who needs all that stuff anyway? Get a cat, if you're lonely.

Kidding, just kidding. Maybe.

Avoiding Family Strife

So if family funds are going to have to be the source of your small business's start-up capital, at least try to reach a clear understanding from the start with every family member involved, as to the two separate needs for money: (1) the estimated capital needed to get started; (2) the fallback emergency cushion, agreed to in advance, which will *only* be "called" if more money is needed, for the reasons just mentioned.

You, as owner-operator, must do everything in your power to use only that first amount, and fall back on the emergency cushion only when your back is to the wall . . . and never ask for more than that.

Unless of course you *have to* ask for more . . . but at that point domestic life will start getting decidedly stressful, if it hasn't already. Unless your family members are rich or saints. Preferably both.

To pull through those hard times and reduce family strife, the bunch of you should try to keep everything in perspective and keep reminding yourselves of the expected future rewards, of why you're making all this effort in the first place. It's too easy to lose sight of the end goal and to give in to the temptation of throwing in the towel prematurely.

When the going gets tough, remind yourself: once the start-up pressures are over and you have a stable operation, you'll be running a small business that is 100 percent yours and your family's (probably), generating good income (hopefully) and the future of the business will be yours to decide. You can stay comfortably as you are, you can grow slowly and cautiously or you can shoot for the stars.

There are obvious advantages to you, the owner-operator, when the start-up investment (or loans) are from your own savings or from members of your family (or even from close friends). As long as there is no quarreling going on, there is no pressure (1) to pay back the money within a narrow time frame, or (2) to pay it back with high interest, or (3) to make a quick profit by selling part or all of the business, the moment things go well.

You can work hard and diligently at making the business grow if you're not under these kinds of short-term external pressures, which can be highly disruptive and can destroy your concentration and motivation. You won't have this luxury, if you have cut a deal with outsiders or managed to arrange bank loans.

Never, ever forget to do the paperwork on the deal. All too often these personal, family arrangements are made informally, in a hurry, and are not properly documented, since everybody knows each other. Later, maybe much later, this can generate disruptive, even destructive disputes and disagreements. Years of work can get blown away when such family quarrels get started.

HOW TO BEHAVE LIKE A BANK
Get Terms from Friends in Writing; Charge Interest

When friends and family turn to you for a helping hand—one with money, that is—how can you say no? Frequently you can't, or don't want to. It may be a noble way to live. But financially, it's not too wise. Many loans to friends and family often go unpaid.

"Never loan money you cannot afford to give away," says [a specialist].

Get it in writing

Next time friends or kin treat you like a bank, behave like one. That means drafting and signing a promissory note, setting an interest rate and agreeing on repayment terms. Cold and unfriendly? On the contrary. "In order to maintain the friendship, it should be done in writing," he says. Even among relatives, a written document is the way to lend money. . . .

Being upfront about your expectations about getting repaid goes a long way to ensure that you will get paid, experts say. Otherwise, the borrower may misinterpret your expectations or fail to give it priority, thinking that it isn't important to you to get paid. If the person who lends the money just says, "Pay me when you can" what does that really mean?

Allow the borrower to propose his or her repayment terms. "If the borrower doesn't keep the terms, you can say: You're the one who told me you could do it, and I expect you to keep your word," says [the specialist]. . . . There's another reason to document loans made to friends and family. Should the bad debt qualify as an income-tax deduction, you need proof that you made the loan. . . .

What the IRS requires

You have to prove that the money you gave Uncle Joe was really a loan and not a gift, since gifts aren't deductible. A promissory note with specific repayment terms will prove the lending intention. Even if Uncle Joe pays you back, you still want a promissory note. You want to be able to show the IRS that those deposits in your account aren't income, just loan repayment.

—Alina Matas, *The Miami Herald*

Even with the best of intentions, people's memories of what was agreed can be dramatically different, years later. When the business has grown and become profitable, some people forget the hard times and the personal sacrifices; greed takes over. Also, one or another of the parties may get hit with unexpected tax consequences, simply because the documentation was not adequate for the purposes of the IRS.

For all these reasons, put your deal with your family's funds in writing. A short uncomplicated document will usually suffice. For most small businesses, your friendly accountant can provide you with a model document and help you polish the final version. If possible, avoid using lawyers, for all sorts of good reasons. More about them later; nothing too complimentary, as you may guess.

Banks . . . the Catch-22 People

It's also hard to say anything complimentary about banks and bankers, from the entrepreneur's and small businessperson's point of view, in the start-up years. There's nothing to compliment them for. They may be helpful to you later on, when your business has grown bigger and is securely profitable . . . but when you're starting up? Fuggeddabouddit. At least for *business* loans.

How so, if the big banks are running major advertising campaigns, touting their wonderful loan programs for small businesses? Because those loan programs are either for well-established businesses with at least two or three years of solid financial statements to show (which will not be your case) . . . or they're simply offering personal loans (with all the responsibilities these entail), gussied up to look like business loans. The end purpose of all their marketing fuss is simply to get their hands on your business's banking account (with all the fees and charges and interest-free balances it gives them), without running any risk in making you a *genuine* business loan.

A Dun & Bradstreet survey . . . emphasized that "although bank loans are important sources of credit for small companies, the owners are very adept and creative at finding the financing they need to stay in business," says [a spokesman].

The survey found differences between older businesses and new ones. Firms in business for more than five years are more likely to use commercial bank loans (38%) than newer businesses (21%).

—*The Wall Street Journal*

Banks make money by lending money and collecting interest. They'd always like to do this with zero risk. That is, by lending to people or businesses that are so secure that whatever happens they will repay their loans. The problem is, of course, that the clients who are that secure often don't need the loans . . . whereas the businesses that need the loans are often in precarious condition. Shit, as bankers well know, happens–and, as they also well know, it happens most often to small businesses.

This makes bank loans to new small businesses pretty much a nonstarter and a waste of everyone's time, especially yours. You'll never meet their requirements, especially the one that probably says you have to demonstrate two or three years of good results in your business. Hmmm . . . now how do you do that, if you've only just started up?

Bankers wrote the book on catch-22, even before the book itself got written.

That's the nature of the banking game. So fine, there should be no cause for complaints. Except for the singularly irritating fact that the marketing bozos at the major banks and their ad agencies just *adore* the mystique and aura surrounding small business. You've seen it on television. . . . *We foster the entrepreneurial spirit that made America great. . . . We nurture the future corporate giants of the U.S.A. . . . Come talk with us about your small business's most intimate needs and we'll be behind ya, buddy* . . . and so on. They'd like some of the glamour and excitement to rub off on their miserable, conservative selves. They also would like to get their hands on your checking account.

But loans? Real live business loans? Actually do something constructive for struggling small businesses, like maybe lending them real money? And run real risks that the money may not be repaid? No way.

LENDING WOES STUNT GROWTH OF SMALL FIRMS

The Fed tightens credit . . . but a lot of small businesses are asking: When was credit ever loose? These companies have benefited from the economic expansion . . . for many, revenue and profit are up, and they need capital to finance their growth. But they aren't getting it from banks. "There's supposedly billions of dollars in capital out there, but not much is going the way of small businesses that have sales of less than $2 million and need a $500,000 loan," says [an investment banker].

It certainly isn't going to Hydrokinetic Designs in Coral Gables, Fla. [which] had two bank-loan applications rejected, even though the maker of twin-nozzle shower heads expects sales . . . of $1 million, says David Black, founder and president. The banks refused to lend against Hydrokinetic's $450,000 of inventory and receivables . . . instead they wanted the debt secured by such fixed assets as plant or equipment—collateral Mr. Black says his company lacks because it farms out production to a contract manufacturer. "It's still very challenging getting a loan as a small, growing business," Mr. Black says, noting his failure to raise financing is limiting his company's growth.

Small firms lacking fixed assets aren't the only ones struggling to secure bank financing. . . . Young companies with little operating history are still getting snubbed. . . . So are older companies that have suffered setbacks. "Banks are looking to expand credit, but they are mostly expanding existing credit lines, not opening new ones," says [a financier].

—Michael Selz and Udayan Gupta, *The Wall Street Journal*

Reality says that you will only get your crack at bank loans for your small business after you have been operating successfully for a number of years, have substantial business assets and balance sheets and P&L statements that show it. And, of course, have been giving them your banking business for all that time.

There are other bank angles to consider:

- If you have a good personal credit record with a bank, plus liquid assets (such as certificates of deposit) that they can hold as security, they might make a direct loan to your business, so long as you also give your personal guarantee. In truth, it's really nothing more than a personal loan, but at least you are starting to build up a credit record in the business's name, rather than your own. That could help you later on.

- Your personal credit record has become more acceptable as a criterion for granting business loans, at least with a few of the more enlightened banks. Their reasoning is that, if you have spent all those years building up your credit record, you are probably not going to "walk" on your business's loans, even if it gets into trouble. You'll probably still have to provide personal guarantees, of course.

- The Small Business Administration (SBA) has different loan and credit programs for assisting small businesses, some of them quite attractive. These programs are always processed through a commercial bank and will still require most of the usual credit information and personal guarantees. However, since the banks are "insured" by the federal government for most of their potential losses, they can be less stringent and more flexible. SBA programs may be worth your time to check out.

- Other special loan programs for minorities and specific business activities can sometimes be found. Investigate with your local banks and SBA center. You may get lucky. But be prepared to waste a lot of time; the more of a "giveaway" deal it is, the more bureaucracy you will face.

But a bank loan is a bank loan is a bank loan. So, whether bank loans or SBA programs, be prepared for difficulties and disappointments. They will want to check that your business operations make sense. You will have to show that you have invested your own money and that it is on the line, at risk in the business. Your personal credit must be good. You will have to have some collateral. And they will get you to sign off on everything, so that your ass is also firmly on the line in guaranteeing their loans.

> They want it all.
> It's in their nature.
> They're bankers, aren't they?

Squeezing Working Capital

"Squeezing" working capital can be a practical method for generating a little extra cash in the middle of a financial crisis, or at least for avoiding having to raise additional working capital.

Often small business owner-operators have a resigned attitude toward the different components making up the working capital of their small business: "It is what it is and I can't do anything to change it." They're afraid to start unpleasant hassles with suppliers or customers when they try to make changes that will help their business.

> **LOWDOC JUMP-STARTS BUSINESSES**
> **Streamlined Process Moves Money Faster**
>
> Jerry Lerner never bothered with financing from the U.S. Small Business Administration. It would have cost too much in accounting, legal fees and time to get a loan package together. So he used his own resources for Compro Enterprises, an 8-year old commercial property maintenance company.
>
> Then he heard about the SBA's LowDoc program.
>
> "From start to finish it took maybe three weeks, and all I had to use was our accountant," says Lerner, who got a $95,000 loan for equipment and operating capital through Flamingo Bank. . . .
>
> LowDoc cuts red tape for loans under $100,000 and reduces much of the paperwork to a one-page form plus the applicant's personal financial statement–a marked decrease from the two-inch stack of documents business owners had to file with their loan applications.
>
> For loans over $50,000, the SBA also requires the borrower's corporate tax returns for the past three years. The SBA guarantees up to 90 percent of bank loans to small businesses. The average loan in the new program is $57,000.
>
> —Dale DuPont, *The Miami Herald*

They forget that, mathematically, a small number of gentle squeezes, here and there, can often add up to a sizable overall reduction in total working capital, which may be all they need to cover for their shortage of funds. So what if they have to tread on a few toes to make it happen? Such measures as:

- Reducing customer credit terms
- Getting tougher in billing and collection methods
- Obtaining advances against orders, or partial prepayments
- Improving credit terms from suppliers
- Delaying payment to undemanding or disorganized creditors
- Speeding up bank deposits of checks and cash receipts

Sure, it can be a tedious and unpleasant task, making all these small squeezes, customer by customer or supplier by supplier. Did anyone promise you that the life of a small businessperson was going to be easy? You do what you gotta do. If that means a few days of applying pressure, writing letters and working the phone, in order to slide these changes by customers and suppliers without generating ill feelings, then that's what you gotta do.

CAN'T MEET PAYROLL? BUSINESSES USE PLASTIC TO GET CASH INFUSIONS

Business owners are turning the surge in cut-rate credit cards into a big source of company financing.

Consider Thespine Kavoulakis. As owner of a Pittsburgh chemical-testing concern, she had three business-loan applications rejected. But as a consumer, she has lenders stuffing her mailbox with enticements to borrow. "They keep mailing me offers and I keep taking them," she says. [She] has used cash advances from four credit cards with a combined credit line of more than $20,000 to buy supplies and equipment and even pay her three employees. Her current total balance of $15,000 accounts for three-quarters of [her company's] debt. . . .

Fierce competition among credit-card issuers spurs the trend, enabling some industrious entrepreneurs to patch together as much as $100,000 in business financing through Visa and MasterCard.

Some 26% of the owners of small and midsize businesses are using credit cards to fund their companies. . . . Credit-card debt has become the third most popular source of financing . . . [after] bank loans and business earnings.

A lot of small-business owners don't mind higher rates as long as they can borrow. "I don't look at the credit cards as debt. I look at them as buying time," says Ms. Kavoulakis.

—Michael Selz, *The Wall Street Journal*

Think how much better you will feel, when you see that the overall result of these efforts freed up, say, $10,000 or $20,000 or more from your business's working capital needs.

Personal Credit

In small business, these days many owners are using their personal credit cards to get started or to stay afloat.

If you have been keeping your nose clean with your credit cards, car loans and home mortgage, you can often use your credit cards to make purchases for your business or to draw cash on the lines of credit. Depending on how many cards you have and their limits, you can be looking at amounts of $10,000 to $20,000 or even higher.

It could save the day and the business. Do you need more justification than that?

But remember: (1) This should only be as a short-term financial solution. The interest rates are too high to make financial sense, if you keep at it all the time. (2) Keep the transactions clearly separate in your bookkeeping and talk to your accountant to make sure that you are handling the credit card transactions correctly. You are mixing up personal and business matters and you must keep them well separated and documented, both for your own controls and to avoid unpleasant tax problems.

Venture Capital and Angels

Venture capitalists: the label can apply as much to your rich uncle who makes the occasional private investment in a promising business situation as to professionally organized investment companies who specialize in bankrolling start-up businesses. The private individuals who make these investments are often called "angels" in the investment trade . . . because that's what they often seem to be, to the floundering entrepreneur.

These guys are the capitalist heroes of the entrepreneurial world and rightly so. They are willing to risk their money, often large bundles of it, by investing in promising young businesses with innovative products, services or ideas, and helping them overcome the many hurdles and obstacles until they become successful and profitable.

However, as always, there's no free lunch. Venture capitalists are not charity organizations. They're in it to make a buck–a very large buck–as a reward for the very large risks they run. They'll be your partners, fans and supporters . . . but don't ever think of them as friends or family.

It's still business, only business:

- They're not interested in very small, common or garden-variety businesses, the kind you may be thinking of primarily as a means to make yourself a living. Thus many small businesses will have no appeal to them, since they will have little growth potential or "exit" potential.

- Almost always (unless you're Steven Spielberg), the business must already be operating and showing its tricks, even if it's not yet profitable.

- You will have to have your money at risk and your ass on the line (even if you *are* Steven Spielberg), along with them. If it sinks, you all go down together. They view this as a powerful incentive for you to work your butt off, trying to keep it afloat.

- They're looking for start-up businesses that have something special or unique about them, where a large injection of money ("seed capital") will enable the business to grow much faster than would otherwise be possible.

- They want the business to have "profit potential" in the future and they want to see some pretty solid arguments and reliable calculations, to convince them that this will happen if they risk their money. The profit does not have to be there right now, but it better look feasible, once all that money has been pumped in.

- They're pros. They will want solid numbers and reliable information. You may have the greatest business in the world, but if you don't have decent internal information and good controls, you won't be able to communicate with venture capitalists in the language they understand–facts and figures.

- They will want a big "piece of the action," a fat share in what you see as *your* business. Once you're married to them, it will become yours *and* theirs. It's at that point, with all that easy money sitting on the table, within your grasp, that you can make the mistake of exchanging it for too big a piece of your "action," and end up regretting it later. Some entrepreneurs have had bitter experiences, struggling to build a fantastic new business, only to discover in the end that they sold themselves too short and lost control of their own creation and business destiny.

- They will want an "exit strategy," and a profitable one, at that. This is also where things can blow up in your face. Venture capitalists will usually want to "cash out" in a reasonable period of time, say, three to five years. They'll do this by selling their shares to other investors (whose ideas for the future of the business may be radically different from your own), making a good profit for themselves but possibly nothing for you . . . you may still be left running the business. Or they may "take the company public," which is often the ideal "exit strategy." This can also be great for you, making you rich or at least no longer poor. But if you stay in, you may find yourself running a publicly traded company, which can drive an entrepreneur nuts.

Let's face it: if yours is that one in a thousand among unique small businesses where venture capitalists come eagerly knocking on your door, you'd probably be out of your mind not to take advantage of the opportunity. But you must keep reminding yourself, as you negotiate with them: *There's no free lunch, there's no free lunch, there's no free lunch.*

Then maybe you'll be a tougher negotiator and manage to cut yourself a well-balanced deal, which will pay off for you royally later on, when you have delivered the goods to the venture capitalists who backed you: a successful business.

Going Public

Or, to get the jargon right, "doing an IPO," that is, an initial public offering. That's when your venture has grown successfully enough that its shares can be offered on the stock market. A fascinating future course for a successful small business, but not a subject that fits into this book. That's a whole different ball game. By then, your small business will have grown far beyond the survival stage that concerns us in this book.

But this is America, so a brief mention must be made of this culmination of any entrepreneurial business owner's dream: to see their business up in lights, traded on the stock exchange. It can happen, it does happen.

So dream a little:

- You're going to need good, professional venture capitalists to get your business ready for the launch. You're looking at years, not months.

- You and they may make one pile of money when you launch the IPO and may still be able to keep control of the business. And maybe not.

- From there on, if you're still running the show (you may have lost control in the process), your business life will be measured by quarterly results, the price of the stock and the wise-ass opinions of a bunch of arrogant Wall Street analysts.

- You may not like any of this. But if you're rich and free to go your own way, say thank you to Wall Street and go start another small company with all the capital you now have.

That's life in the stock market fast lane. It can make you rich, but it may not all be roses. Anyway, you've still got a long way to go and a whole lot of time until then. Dream on.

No Funds = No Business

Entrepreneurs want to get on with the action, with the challenges of starting

---

VENTURE CAPITAL: NOT A LOVE STORY

Too Often, Entrepreneurs Who Join Financiers in Marriages of Convenience Are Headed for Heartbreak

Welcome to venture capital hell, a place of punctured egos and lost millions, where entrepreneurs and their financiers typically land when when things don't work out. . . .

Failure isn't inevitable, but the makings are usually present. Entrepreneurs and venture capitalists come together in a marriage of convenience, a potentially volatile mix of egos, wrestling over power and money. The company may be the founder's life's work, representing an enormous emotional commitment. For the venture capitalist, it's just another investment to get into and out of in five years, tops.

Can these marriages be saved? Sometimes not. Products fizzle, spending spirals over budget, founders prove lousy managers, investors become too intrusive. "There are more opportunities for the wheels to fall off, because there are too many unknowns," says [a venture capitalist].

—Richard Melcher, *Business Week*

Many high-tech pioneers see tapping traditional venture capital as a pact with the devil: Venture capitalists, they say, often have too little real-world experience, too short-term an outlook and too meddlesome an approach.

"I couldn't stand the thought of dealing with the standard venture capitalist, who I think of as a 37-year-old Stanford M.B.A., who's never hired anybody, never fired anybody, never built a company and never sold a product—but who somehow has all the answers," says [an entrepreneur].

—Paul Carroll, *The Wall Street Journal*

up and running their own show, with the exciting part. Finding the money and scrambling for more is always a frustrating, time-consuming, nervous-making exercise in spinning wheels.

Forward movement stops as they sweat out different alternative solutions, using their own money and/or funds from family, friends, private backers, professional investors, banks, personal credit cards or even loan sharks. Wherever they can find it.

You can't run away from it. Until it's settled, you're stuck in neutral.

So get involved, get it solved and then get on with business.

No money for start-up = no business.

You gotta do what you gotta do.

SHARON MCCOLLICK GOT MAD AND TORE DOWN A BANK'S BARRIERS

Sharon McCollick hit bottom when she and her husband were sitting on their bed, weeping. Banks do this to people.

Ms. McCollick makes work suits for women. Major clothing chains were clamoring for her designs. But she had missed three mortgage payments keeping her company alive, and her last shot at financing had just fallen through.

She was ruined at age 33.

Then, at a traffic light two days later, she discovered a secret weapon in her battle with bankers: her outrage. Today, she is sitting on $250,000 in working capital and heading toward her first million-dollar season. Credit wars, she learned, are no place for a conscientious objector.

[When young], she learned to recut old clothes, especially jackets. . . . Ultimately, she landed in a $100,000-a-year marketing job at Intel Corp., but continued making clothes—feminine work suits with a 1940s feeling. Colleagues asked where they could buy similar suits. The answer: nowhere.

Bingo. Business opportunity.

Ms. McCollick cashed in $60,000 in Intel stock . . . [wrote] a business plan and took the plunge. The woman lawyers and accountants she surveyed through professional organizations liked the designs so much they ordered $50,000 of product before she had opened her business.

But even in small business, there's such a thing as too small. J.C. Penney was enthralled with the designs but said she would have to install a costly on-line order system. Major NY clothing manufacturers sniffed at her meager orders.

She needed capital.

She went to her neighborhood bank and coaxed a lending officer to a breakfast meeting at Denny's. Lynn Ozer shuffled the papers and shook her head. No collateral. No track record. Don't even think about banks, she said.

Ms. McCollick finally found a manufacturer in New Jersey willing to handle her first season of production on credit; all she had to pay in interest was her entire profit margin. But she happily watched her '92 line fly off the racks at Filene's. . . .

She next resorted to factoring, which is the same as loan sharking, except that a) it's legal and b) it's secured by borrowers' receivables instead of the bones. The factoring company financed her '93 line at an interest rate of just 1%—per week. But she sold 2,500 suits. . . .

Resolving to make 1994 her breakout year, she landed a venture capital investment; the deal fell through. All cash within reach—her husband's income as a computer consultant, her mother's nest egg, money from friends—went into her overhead. She missed utility payments. She slipped $2,000 into arrears with the IRS—but she was still in business.

In the meanwhile, her neighborhood bank had been gobbled up by CoreStates Financial Corp., which was trying to set up small-business lending. Scouting for customers, a bank officer heard about a fashion designer named Sharon McCollick. "That name sounds familiar," the banker said. Three years after practically laughing Ms. McCollick out of Denny's, the banker, Ms. Ozer, agreed to finance Ms. McCollick's '95 line, thanks to a new program for women borrowers at the SBA.

But as the paperwork was being completed, the dirty little secret of Ms. McCollick's $2,000 in IRS arrears came to light. The federal government, she was told, didn't guarantee credit for anyone in arrears to the federal government.

The loan was off.

Two days later, in the depths of her depression, Ms. McCollick was staring at her local CoreStates branch through the windshield of her car. She turned in and stormed across the lobby. "This is my whole life," she bellowed at Ms. Ozer. "I can't take no for an answer. You've got to do something to turn this around."

The banker knew it would be highly irregular to pressure the SBA. But in 17 years of lending to small business, Ms. Ozer had never seen such a survivor. "OK, Sharon," the banker finally said.

She got the SBA to reconsider. Ms. McCollick scrounged the cash to pay the IRS. When the loan closed, 30 people swelled into the bank lobby to celebrate.

Sharon McCollick Enterprises Inc., just held its first Seventh Avenue show. And Ms. McCollick is already planning her memoirs. "I've got a title," she says, *"Clawing Your Way to the Top Without Nails."*

—Thomas Petzinger Jr., "The Front Lines," *The Wall Street Journal*

7

RUNNING THE SHOW:

Management and Organizational Theories?
Toss 'Em . . . Run It Your Way

You Need the Basics, Not the BS

From the avalanche of guru books, seminars and courses on the hottest theories and latest techniques for managing, organizing and structuring your business, many newcomers quite naturally assume that this trendy stuff has to have top priority for their time, attention, efforts and money when starting up.

It's a deluge of old theories, new theories, schools of this, philosophies of that, on organizing, structuring, delegating, centralizing, flattening, matrixing, team building, empowering, wowing, communicating, motivating, leading . . . never-ending "-ings."

For a small business owner, this stuff is at best irrelevant and at worst dangerous. It can seriously distract you from the immediate survival priorities of your fragile new business, at that critical moment when you are struggling to get on your business feet, when all your key needs are common or garden-variety basics: *basic management, basic operations, basic organization, basic administration, basic information and basic controls.* Not an "-ing" in sight.

But "basics" aren't sexy, aren't new, aren't trendy, and don't help sell gazillions of guru books or build reputations for cutting-edge innovation.

Your priority is learning to ride a bicycle without falling off. These jokers are instructing you on how to win the Tour de France.

> **ENTREPRENEURS KEEP IT SIMPLE AND STRIKE IT RICH**
>
> Top entrepreneurs these days tend to run relatively casual, decentralized organizations, seeking out more employee input and generally trying to make workers' lives easier.
>
> *—The Wall Street Journal*

These myriad theories and philosophies, even the stuff that has some merit, relate to the problems of organizing, managing and operating Big Businesses. These are weighty instruction manuals for piloting a Boeing 747, when what you need is a slim instruction booklet for flying a single-engine Cessna. You can make fatal mistakes in the takeoff phase of your small business plane if you're attempting to pilot it as if it were a 747.

In the start-up years, you and you alone are the key player in your show. So toss the theories and concentrate instead on the only thing that truly matters: your own performance and personal efficiency as owner-operator.

Your Personal Efficiency Is the Key

Organizational charts? Position descriptions? Mission statements? Philosophy of customer service? Strategic goals? Motivational seminars? Togetherness training?

In small business? Fuggeddabouddit.

CLEANING UP YOUR OWN MESS

Julie Morgenstern, a professional organizer, spends her days listening to the dark secrets of business-people.

"I can't think straight," they tell her. "I panic when someone calls and needs information," they confess. "I work incredibly long hours and accomplish nothing," they complain. . . .

"If you can't find anything, you can't get anything done," Ms. Morgenstern says. "Most business-people could add at least one more productive hour to their day, and feel a lot better about themselves, if they just got out from under their mess.

"You don't need most of what you think you do. As a rule, you can throw away 60 percent of the stuff on your desk and 80 percent of the stuff in your files.

"The last half-hour of every day," she said [to a client], "I want you to spend 15 minutes filing your papers and the next 15 planning the next day."

If your goal is to see your desk again, there are plenty of tools available. The best place to start is with one of the dozens of self-help manuals cramming bookstore shelves.

—J. Peder Zane,
The New York Times

At least until you're safely past the survival stage and your business is stable and successful. Then you can start following the teachings of the guru of the month, if that's what turns you on.

The single most important factor in the efficient operation of a small business is the owner-manager's personal work habits, self-discipline and basic competence . . . plus those of the one or two key managers who maybe work with the owner-manager, if the small business is one of the larger ones.

This nucleus of one, two, at most three people, takes the place of a corporate structure and of all the costly accoutrements of a large organization.

Large corporations and big organizations are structured in such a way that the top executives and managers follow a well-defined and documented set of internal rules and policies. It's the efficiency of the *overall organization* that makes for the success of the business, not the abilities of any one individual. It has to be that way because of their sheer size. Think of the U.S. Army, General Motors or IBM.

Small businesses have the advantage of guerrilla fighters or sports teams. Their smallness and intimacy makes it possible to operate as a tight unit, with instant communication between all the players. There is little bureaucracy to slow down decisions and their execution. Everyone knows pretty much what to do, with the leader pushing everyone and setting the example in work discipline and dedication.

"Organizational structures" cost money and slow things down. Small businesses can't afford such luxuries and don't need them, anyway. If they grow and enter the ranks of Big Business, then they may have to change and adopt more rigid rules.

So enjoy your smallness while you can.

However, I'm not saying it's easy.

The price for enjoying the flexibility, speed and efficiency of a successful small business is that *the owner-manager must set the example and must be the driving force.* In a large corporation, the chief executive may be almost invisible but, if the business is well organized, the company can work smoothly.

In a small business, you, the owner-manager, *are* the organization.

Invisibility is not an option.

So the efficiency of a small business is a direct reflection of the personal efficiency of the "boss person."

You are the organization. Your business will be as efficient and productive as you are, personally . . . or as sloppy and unproductive, if that's your problem. This applies to any small business. Even at larger sizes, the only difference will be that you may have a working partner or a key manager, but the same personal criteria apply to them as they do to you.

If you feel you need help in becoming more efficient and better organized, instead of buying management books or attending business seminars, buy one of the better "get-yourself-organized" self-help books. They will be of far more practical help than a best-selling business book. How to keep a filing system, how to organize your priorities, how to schedule your time, how to avoid drowning in paperwork, that sort of thing. It's business housekeeping, business personal hygiene. You should know enough to brush your teeth and wash behind the ears, if you're planning to run your own small business.

Here's an unglamorous reminder of basic personal duties for the owner-operator of a small business:

- **Controls.** There are essential control tasks that keep the business on track, such as bookkeeping routines, operational controls, updating your Management Information System and so on (more about these areas, later in the book). These vital controls just won't receive the management attention they require without the constant, personal involvement of the owner.

- **Office Routines.** Answering phone calls, opening and processing incoming mail, keeping pending files updated, having a well-organized filing system, getting the checks out, preparing the input for payroll calculation, etc., etc., etc. There are numerous tedious little tasks, daily, weekly and monthly, that many businesspeople are tempted to forget or put off. Neglect them for long and you're asking for major trouble down the road. Set aside an hour every day for "grunge work" and *just get it done.*

- **Written Communication.** Train yourself to be disciplined about writing up what needs to be written. Become proficient at basic letters, memos and faxes. Get in the habit, whenever possible, of "putting it in writing," after phone calls, meetings and discussions. Even if it's only a couple of lines. *Always* keep paper "hard copy" of important communications in your filing system, no matter what experts tell you about the marvels of the "paperless office." You can't rely on your PC's hard disk for that kind of business reference file; you'll never find what you need, when you need it, a year or two later.

- **Working at Home.** The ability to work out of your home is one of the great benefits of modern business life. PCs, faxes and the many other office gadgets offered by modern technology make it all feasible and quite easy. The savings in office costs and personal time are amazing. But the issue of personal efficiency and self-discipline makes it or breaks it. You have to have strong self-discipline, to force yourself to work as methodically and efficiently as you would if you were in a regular business office. If you are one of those people who like to sleep late, check out what's on the TV, hunt through the refrigerator, leave your business papers piled on the kitchen

One of the first questions for most entrepreneurs is whether to set up an outside office or to work from home. A management consultant says an outside office is "an appendage that can easily become an albatross."

He figures he accomplishes more working at his computer in his pajamas from 5 to 7 a.m. than most people do all day in an office.

—The New York Times

table . . . think twice. Either you whip yourself into shape and clean up your act, or you'd better forget about working at home.

Detail, Detail, Detail

Digging out and understanding the key details of your particular business activity is and must be your personal responsibility.

Each business has its own peculiar, individual set of critical operating and technical characteristics, whether it be restaurants, bookstores, auto repair, child care, grocery stores, copywriting, software design or whatever. Before you start up, the more you can absorb these details in advance, the better. If you're lucky, some of this knowledge may have come with you from a previous job. Once you've started, you will have to learn the rest of the details as you go along. Remember, the best source of technical details always comes from careful study of your competitors. It's amazing what a little dedicated detective work and footwork can teach you.

Nobody ever knows it all before they start up. But all successful owner-operators of small businesses end up acquiring a thorough, self-taught knowledge of the intricacies and details of their particular trade or activity.

You must be, have to be, a "detail person" to survive and succeed in small business. And you must try to know as much as possible, as quickly as possible. Your detailed knowledge of the technical characteristics of your particular business will always be one of your best weapons and most effective defenses.

If your ambition is to become the enlightened, illuminated, new-age Maximum Leader of your business, so focused on the Big Picture and the Major Issues that the scuzzy details can be left to the underlings, you've made a bad choice. Go try that one in Corporate America, pal, because in the small business world, it's a recipe for disaster.

Yes, of course you have to be your business's big thinker and strategist. That's obvious. But that can never be an excuse for not getting business dirt under your nails, digging into the detail work.

Leadership: the Glue of Small Businesses

Once upon a time, *leadership* meant something.

Now *leadership* has been turned into just one more management theorist's buzzword. You'll find courses in The Theory and Practice of Leadership; three-day seminars on "How to Become a World-Class Leader";

books on the 101 Leadership Habits of Leading Leaders . . . and away we go, for one more dizzy spin on the guru merry-go-round.

It's hard to say the word *leadership* with a straight face.

Yet leadership *is* of the most fundamental importance. Always has been, always will be. But seriously, if you need a whole trendy book to understand what the word means . . .

Leadership is the single most important human quality in the owner-manager of a small business, in giving direction, motivation and discipline to its employees (if you have any, that is). Especially because of the informal, loose and casual nature of a small organization. The personal leadership of the owner-manager is the glue that holds everything together, *instead of the strictures of an orthodox organizational structure.*

If you really don't understand what leadership means, you probably shouldn't risk going into a small business that requires employees. At least not until you've learned. It's *that* important.

If you do understand what leadership means, get it firmly into your head that, whether you have one employee or one hundred, *you are your business's leader.* You lead. You do not follow.

You set the example, you define the tone, you establish the style of the business. Don't ever be embarrassed or ashamed by the fact that any successful small business is always a reflection of a strong leader, its owner-operator. Successful small businesses have *character and personality: yours.*

Don't buy into any of the wimpy brands of touchy-feely management philosophies, which negate the role of a dominant, strong leader and preach that bosses and employees are all equal partners, loving associates, supportive equals, whatever. So what do you do when you catch employees with their hot little hands in your cash register drawer? Kiss them on both cheeks? Send them for counseling? Get real.

There's no evidence that touchy-feely philosophies produce benefits in Big Business and they sure as hell don't work in Small Business, where they work *against* the very notion of a strong and forceful leader who holds the business together.

About Personal Style:

The boss [at Bloomberg LP] is . . . hot-tempered, entrepreneurial, iconoclastic, snowboarding Michael Bloomberg. . . . The 53-year-old bachelor rules over a private company . . . with 2,000 employees. . . . Now that times are tougher . . . he's going to stick to those things that made him successful in the first place: quick reflexes, loose structures, and a culture where employees act like owners. . . .

While most companies Bloomberg's size form committees, hold meetings and write reports . . . Bloomberg himself makes most of the decisions, and fast. Says he: "I just do it. I go by my gut."

Instead of implementing tough management systems to keep people in line, Bloomberg works hard on a culture in which his people, a young, energetic crowd whose average age is 30, know almost instinctively how to do the right thing. He expects them to do it.

—Brian Dumaine, *Fortune*

A few observations on your role as your business's leader:

- Strong, forceful leadership is a plus, not a minus. All successful small businesses have strong leaders, even if not all of them are exactly the types you'd want to invite home to dinner.

- The best employees are always happiest working in a business with strong leadership and clear direction. It's more productive and less confusing all around.

- You are what you are, both warts and beauty spots, and running your own business is not going to change that. So make it clear from the start what your leadership style is, and those who don't like it won't hang around long. Less pain all around.

- Being a strong leader doesn't have to mean being an SOB. Good leaders are usually also fairly decent human beings.

Remember, you're going into business for yourself and you're the one running the risks. As long as you follow decent and civilized standards of management conduct, you're not obliged to adjust your behavior to suit anyone else's dictates.

That's one of your rewards and your rights.

It's *your* business.

Like Popeye, you have the right to proclaim, "I yam what I yam."

Quality Control: Your Job

Corporate America rediscovered the notion of quality control some years ago, after puzzling over why foreign

A GOOD EXECUTIVE IS A MATTER OF NATURE, NOT NURTURE

There's a lot of gum-flapping about the new breed of "team-building visionaries" occupying executive suites these days. To succeed in your management career, it seems, you must embrace "post-heroic leadership" or "distributed leadership" or "servant leadership" or "virtual leadership" or. . . .

Ah, but does that mean tossing out the old template and starting all over? Aren't some qualities of leadership immutable? And if changes are needed, wouldn't the true leader be flexible enough to make them? . . .

OK, so things have changed. But it still says here that one of the tests of the true leader is that he makes the needed adjustments.

Leadership "hasn't changed since the caveman, and anyone who says it has is crazy," insists [an executive search consultant]. "I want to know that the leader knows more than I do, that he's loyal, honest and courageous and that he's not going to abandon me when the saber-toothed tiger shows up. . . ."

What's the lesson here for tomorrow's leaders? Changing conditions may require new strategies and attitudes, but the qualities of a true leader—vision, credibility, courage, adaptability—don't change. In the end, you must remember this: A kiss is still a kiss, a sigh is still a sigh. The fundamental things apply, as time goes by.

Call it the Casablanca Theory of Management.

—Hal Lancaster, *The Wall Street Journal*

competitors were making so many inroads into domestic markets. Here again, what should be a basic management discipline in any good business has become a subject for management theorizing.

Books and theories on quality control invariably relate to the horrendous problems Big Business faces in trying to get its managers and workers to give a damn about the quality of their products or services. The problem never goes away, because it has everything to do with the work attitudes and personal motivation of each employee, which in turn is directly affected by the way they are treated and the personal fears they have about the security of their jobs. Shall we talk about downsizing, reengineering, restructuring, layoffs, executive salaries versus average wages, and so on? Corporate America reaps what it sows.

In small business, quality control never went away. Small businesses are always too vulnerable to competition and the owner-managers care too greatly about the risks of losing their few customers . . . and maybe their business. Quality control in small business comes naturally. It is a matter of life or death to owner-operators, and they watch it closely and personally; or at least the survivors do. In small business, quality control is not a set of procedures, routines, inspections, seminars and manuals.

It's a fundamental survival issue. It's basic behavior like:

- A restaurant owner personally checking on the dishes served, talking to the customers and seeing that they are happy.
- A print shop owner personally inspecting the important jobs that have been run and calling up the customers, to make sure they were satisfied.
- A sign manufacturer discussing specifications with a key client before starting a job, and later personally checking that the new sign meets the specs, rather than have the client discover any mistakes.
- A deli owner personally inspecting perishable products in the display cases for freshness, appearance and taste.
- A drugstore owner walking the aisles, checking the products on display and watching how the checkout employees treat customers.
- And so on.

In Big Business, quality control can be achieved only by establishing major internal programs, by requiring training, testing, supervision, inspections, statistical analyses and so on. Small businesses can seldom afford the costs of such special programs. If quality control is to be taken seriously, it automatically falls to the owner as a personal task. When the owner-operator makes it his/her personal responsibility to ensure that quality standards are maintained, the results will always be more successful than any large corporation can achieve.

You should think of your personal quality control efforts simply as a form of intelligent marketing. It takes much less effort and cost to hold on to a satisfied, happy customer and keep them coming back for more than to have to go looking for new ones after you've lost the old ones because of poor service or defective products.

Quality control is that simple, that obvious. A genuine no-brainer.

For those small businesses with a number of employees, the constant presence of the "boss person" poking around, sniffing, inspecting, checking and asking questions, keeps everyone on their toes and helps them understand, by personal demonstration, just what quality control is all about and why it's so important. It makes little impression on an employee to be told, "Keep up the quality." It has a far greater impact when the owner does it personally and says, "This is how I do it and this is how I expect you to do it when I'm not around. Otherwise I'm out of business and you're out of a job."

Being There

Logically enough, you the owner aren't going to be able to check on quality if you're never around.

Here's one of the classic mistakes. A start-up small business has successfully survived its hard first few months, with the owner there daily, from dawn until dusk. Things have shaken down nicely, daily routines have been established, sales are solid and the employees have gotten the hang of things.

But the owner has read too many management books on the art of delegating authority, without realizing that those books don't apply to small business. So he/she starts disappearing too much and too often, to work on marketing, expansion, or maybe just going to the beach. Things can come unstuck very fast, as soon as the employees catch on that this is going to be the boss's new work style, and that the previous style was just a temporary aberration.

You've got to *be* there, wherever "there" is.

If not all the time, at least most of the time.

If you have your small business well organized, so that you can free up some time for other priorities, that's fine. Just make sure that your absences are unpredictable, so that the employees never know when you may be coming through the door. And when you do stroll through the door, make sure the first thing you do relates to quality or customer service . . . to keep the priorities clear in everyone's mind.

Business Plans: One More Distraction

Every new entrant into small business is now told that they must first prepare their "business plan" for flashing at bankers, investors, the SBA, vendors, landlords, whoever, whatever. What, you don't have a glossy, spiral-bound four-color 100-page Business Plan? What are you, some sorta know-nothing business pervert? No way will you ever enter the Pearly Gates of Entrepreneurial Heaven; the Business Plan Border Patrol will gun you down at the entrance.

The business plan fad is the latest cottage industry, artifically created and specifically developed to exploit the growth of small businesses in the U.S. It's a spin-off from the résumé preparation business. Out of thin air, there's a trendy new product being hyped (with considerable quiet support from the banking industry, since it makes their life easier in analyzing loan applications). There are now entire books written on the subject, with fill-in forms,

SMALL TALK
Wendell E. Dunn Has Seen a Lot of Entrepreneurs—and a Lot of Mistakes

The Wall Street Journal: What are some of the common mistakes that would-be entrepreneurs make in the planning process?

Wendell Dunn: Well, the first one, and I'd argue the most common one, is simply failing to plan. We like action. We like doing things. Somehow, in planning and thinking about the future, we don't always get a sense of doing things, so there's a tendency sometimes not to plan. And when we do plan, sometimes we think about a document—the business plan—as if *it* were the business planning. But they're not the same thing.

The important part of business planning is that it's a continuing process. It doesn't end. It certainly doesn't end with the production of a business plan.

Another common problem is that, because people don't like to plan or know how to plan, they let somebody else do it. When you let somebody else do it—whether it's your accountant or your consultant or somebody like that—you wind up educating somebody else about your business. You don't get the benefit of that learning, and that's a real opportunity forgone. . . .

It's very important to not project wishful thinking, but rather to check and make sure the assumptions underlying not only your plan for the business, but also assumptions about your customers and your products, are grounded in reality.

Another common failing in planning is the business-plan format. There's a tremendous temptation to present information in accounting terms . . . and that's frequently done at the expense of understanding the underlying economics, like:

What's the cost of finding a customer? Of one widget delivered to a customer? What's it cost for the parts, the labor, and what's it going to cost the distributor? What are they planning to sell it for vs. what's the customer willing to pay for it?

Those kinds of things can be checked fairly simply. This is not rocket science. . . .

—Wendell E. Dunn, Adjunct Professor of Management, Wharton School, quoted in *The Wall Street Journal* checklists, report form layouts, presentation methods, the works. Plus software programs, audiotapes, videotapes, seminars, you name it. And naturally, these are all so glossy and sophisticated that there's no way in hell you will have the ability to pull together an adequate business plan on your PC's word processing program. Of course not. You're going to have to buy one of those expensive packages, plus contract the services of a business plan specialist. At least that's their marketing pitch.

Business plans have become the latest distraction from the serious business of starting your own small business. They have become one more waste of time and effort . . . and money, of course. Your time, your effort, your money.

They've invented a complicated new "requirement" for starting your own business.

The truth? Yes, of course you need to prepare the basic estimates and information contained in any standard business plan. *Because you need it for yourself.* No, no way do you need to package this information in some glitzy report. Your "planning" for start-up, operating and future expansion of your business consists of all the basic steps discussed in this book . . . all the estimates, legwork, homework, detective work, calculations and careful thinking that you must do anyway, for the most obvious of reasons: *to improve your chances of survival and success.*

You do all this planning, for yourself, because you must. For your own guidance. Because you have to do your homework if you want to improve your odds of survival and success.

You don't do all this work just to con some outsider. Particularly not some banker who is never going to lift his fat ass out of his executive chair to help you and your small business, in a month of Sundays.

You have to do all this preparation and planning, *because it's for your own good and your own protection.*

Now, when some really good reason comes along . . . say an investor is interested in talking to you, or a bank is serious about lending you money . . . then you can quickly bundle together the information you've already prepared, type it yourself (mistakes and all) on two or three sheets of paper, add a cover page entitled "My Li'l Ol' Business Plan," staple it (don't pay for binding) and hand it over, explaining with a smile, "This tells you what you need to know, it's all I've got right now anyway and I do not intend to prepare any more than this. I'm too busy running my business. If you like what you see and want to talk, fine, let's talk. If you don't like what you see, well I've just saved myself time and money."

So much for business plans.

Start Simple

Should you operate your new business as a self-employed small businessperson? Should you structure it as a corporation? What kind of corporation? Should you form a partnership? What kind? Should you prepare a shareholders' agreement? What kind? What are the different future tax consequences of each alternative? How many years ahead should you plan for? Five? Ten? Twenty?

You can spend a disproportionate amount of your start-up capital and available time just in studying all the alternatives and deciding how to structure your new business.

You will be warned of the need to consider most carefully the many tax and legal consequences of structuring your business in any one of many different ways. All this advice is sound, of course. What legal form your business takes *can* make a lot of difference to future tax liabilities, to possible legal liabilities, to your estate and family if you die, to your creditors, partners and shareholders, and to assorted other issues.

Trouble is, to study all this in detail and do it well, *before* you start up, will take up much of your time and a whole lot of your money, paid to our friends in the legal profession. Yet you really won't have and can't have the foggiest notion what your business will look like in a couple of years' time. If it's even still in existence, which the statistics say it may not be.

You have far more important things to be doing with your limited time and scarce money, in planning the first steps for your business activities and ensuring its short-term survival, than in worrying about its long-term tax structure. What use will that be if the business doesn't survive?

Basic common sense says: make it simple, do it fast, and keep it moving. Ask your accountant's (informal) advice on *the simplest, easiest, cheapest, fastest way of getting the business up and operating*. More often than not, this will be as a simple "d/b/a" ("doing business as"), and you'll be filing personal taxes as self-employed. If you *must* incorporate, use one of those $99.99 prepackaged incorporation services. Or maybe the $49.99 one will do just fine.

What you need at first is really only one thing; *to exist as a business entity,* so that you can start doing business: making contacts, signing lease agreements, contracting services, opening bank accounts, opening accounts with vendors, and so on. You can't do any of these things until you have created the form of the business.

So get going, get moving, get started. Rather than trying to plan the next twenty years of your business's corporate structure in such perfect detail that your legal fees are going to be in the thousands of dollars and your personal time wastage measured in months. While you remain paralyzed waiting for all this stuff to be defined, before you can make your first business moves.

Do the *minimum* necessary, not the *maximum*. Then ask your accountant to make a note to call you, exactly one year from the day you start operations, to set up a meeting to review your business's progress and its corporate and tax structure, and to discuss what changes might make sense, at that point in time. Only then, if absolutely necessary, might you call your lawyer and tell him/her what you want done. By then, you will know what questions to ask and what instructions to give.

You will have ample time to correct any mistakes and make any improvements at the end of that first year. Then, your business will be established, you will have acquired operating experience, you will know what you're doing, you will know what you want and you will be able to see your business's future much more clearly.

Being Organizationally Incorrect

You know all about political correctness: the pressures in modern society to conform to the many agendas of groups and individuals who want to ram their values and beliefs down your throat. To say the correct things, to act the correct way, to fit into the correct straitjackets. Being "p.c."

Well, that's really what this chapter has been about, hasn't it? What I call organizational correctness. Being "o.c." Which means following the agendas of all the experts who know what's best for you and your embryonic business . . . and who, not uncoincidentally, want to get their hands into your business pockets, in one way or the other.

To build something that works, you have limited time and limited money. The more of both that you waste on being organizationally correct, the less likely you are to survive the start-up period.

So give the bozos and the gurus the organizational finger. With a polite "Thanks, but no thanks."

Tell them where to put their business plans, their legal advice, their theories, their systems. Trust your own judgment, follow your gut feel, be self-reliant. Focus ferociously on the only thing that matters: making it work. Once it works, who cares how you did it?

Do it yourself. Do it your way. But do it.

LAND'S END KICKS OUT MODERN NEW MANAGERS, REJECTING A MAKEOVER
Mr. End Meets Sudden End

At Land's End Inc. . . . founder and Chairman Gary Comer, a former advertising copy writer, spent three decades nurturing his philosophy: "Take care of your people, take care of your customers, and the rest will take care of itself."

But Mr. Comer's idyllic vision was all but shattered in an abrupt boardroom coup–a shake-up he engineered. . . . At the core of the blow-up was a three-year-old experiment in modern-management techniques. . . . As the smoke clears, Mr. Comer is holding the reins even tighter, having replaced the outsider he had wooed to run the company. . . .

Four years ago, Land's End was grappling with unbridled growth. . . . Founded by Mr. Comer in 1963 as a seller of sailing gear, it had mushroomed into a major mail-order purveyor of clothes and home furnishings for men, women and children. Mr. Comer, who never finished college, decided the company needed some modern big-business management techniques.

He and the board recruited William T. End. . . . He quickly introduced systems and structures straight from the latest manuals of modern management. He installed a teamwork system and began encouraging employees to enroll in any of 20 short courses on topics such as memo-writing and career development. He launched the latest fad in reviewing employee performance, a New Age sort of method known as the Multi-Rater Assessment, which gathers comments from peers and underlings in assessing an employee's or manager's performance. Soon, an army of outside consultants arrived to poke around. . . . Mr. End also hired seven new divisional vice-presidents. . . .

The reorganization caused confusion, and had a troubling side effect: meetings. "I was going to meetings five days a week," says a supervisor in the quality-control department. "We spent so much time in meetings that we were getting away from the basic stuff of taking care of business." His normal workweek stretched to 55 hours from 45 hours.

Land's End was no longer the place it had been when the company was included in the 1993 book, "The 100 Best Companies to Work For in America."

"Turn every customer into a friend by delivering quality products, honest value and world class service," [said] a revised credo . . . displayed on company bulletin boards, buttons and banners overhanging its cavernous warehouse. But it didn't win Mr. End many friends. "We don't need anything hanging over our heads telling us to do something we're already doing," said [a 17-year employee].

Nor did employees cotton to the high-priced new consultants Mr. End brought in . . . among them a human-resources consulting concern. In just a few months, Land's End became one of its biggest clients, with the firm conducting some 40 seminars on topics like how to improve management-communication style. [Finally] Mr. Comer called Mr. End into a hastily arranged meeting and abruptly asked for his resignation . . . acccusing [him] of bringing "creeping bureaucracy" to the company and of "depersonalizing" employees with his numeric performance reviews. . . . His new chief executive, Michael Smith, 34, has spent his entire 11-year career at Land's End . . . where he first started working as a college intern . . . he doesn't have so much as an M.B.A.

–Gregory A. Patterson, *The Wall Street Journal*

8

SALES BLINDNESS:

Booby Traps in
Sales and Marketing

Obsession: A Problem, Not a Perfume

Sales and selling are *not* the problem. Markets and marketing are *not* the problem. This is *not* a chapter on how to sell, how to market, how to whatever; that's not what this book is about. Its purpose is not to teach techniques (you will easily find hundreds of useful how-to books on sales, marketing, promotion, advertising, etc.) but to focus your attention on each and every key "survival issue." Strangely enough, sales and marketing become one of these survival issues.

Not out of neglect, but the opposite: obsessive, excessive management focus.

Sales obsession can lead to sales blindness.
Sales blindness can lead to business extinction.

The good news is that most small businesses handle themselves well in their sales and marketing efforts. The need is obvious . . . what's a business without sales? . . . and it's a natural, top priority area for the owner-operator's attention. Almost all people in the small business arena have a natural, instinctive ability in sales. It goes with the territory. Entrepreneurs always have a little sales in their souls and a little hustle in their hearts.

If the small business you have chosen has a good product or service to offer, you'll find that sales and marketing are the most obvious, logical and natural part of your responsibilities as owner-manager. In most small businesses, what needs to be done to generate sales is clear, and your success in sales and marketing will mainly be determined by hard work, common sense and hustle. Not to imply that it's easy (it's hard work) but that it's not mysterious or highly complex.

What you need to worry about is when the sales function becomes all that matters to you and anyone else involved in your business.

Of course, marketing and sales are of vital, critical importance to any business. Of course, the earth is round and the sky is blue. Obvious.

Obvious as that may be, sales represent only one element out of many, in the overall "equation" of a business's performance. But in a small business it is usually the owner who takes personal responsibility for overseeing sales and marketing. Precisely because it is so vital. But this in turn can lead to overemphasis. Owner-operators of small businesses can become so anxious and obsessed over sales results and marketing activities that they lose their focus, suffer from "sales blindness" and fail to notice serious, less visible, potentially fatal problems in time to correct them.

The Business Body

Here's an analogy, to illustrate the problem.

A business is an organism, like the human body. Sales revenues are to a business what blood is to a human body . . . essential to start and sustain life. No matter what else is right or wrong with a business, if there's no sales income, there's no blood running through the organization's veins; if there's no blood, there's no life; if there's no life, the business is dead. Lights out.

To state the obvious: sales are the blood of business life.

Yet when a person dies, do they die from lack of blood? Only in the rare event that they bleed to death. Usually it will be from any number of other causes: trauma from accidents, cancer, heart disease, organ failure, infections, viruses, you name it. And, of course, old age.

Much the same applies in business organisms. They can be fatally afflicted, not just by the one obvious cause–not enough blood (sales) to survive–but more often by other assorted accidents or diseases of the business body, which can ultimately stop the heart from beating and the blood from flowing. When that happens, was it simply lack of sales that caused the business's demise? Often it was something else.

There can be other causes of business mortality: lack of oxygen *(cash)*, cancer *(poor product quality, poor management)*, obesity *(overpaid management; excessive costs)*, anemia *(lack of profits)*, gunshot wounds *(competitive sharpshooters)* and so on.

And, of course, old age . . . which is still the best way to go, both in life and in business.

Since few small businesses can afford doctors (i.e., consultants), they must rely on self-diagnosis and self-medication. That means having the self-discipline to look objectively at *all the potential ills* that can afflict the business, instead of a single-minded, simplistic fixation on sales levels.

Sales Obsession

Sales is the most visible, dynamic and emotionally satisfying activity in any business. Sales types are always the most extroverted, most enthusiastic, most talkative, most gung-ho. When sales are up, everyone in the business knows it and celebrates. When they're down, the gloom is everywhere.

Tracking sales results can become a dangerous obsession.

Sales results have an unhealthy habit of becoming the only scorecard by which everyone in the business measures if they are winning or losing. Other measurement sticks are often too nebulous or too technical or just plain boring–market share? gross profit? operating profit? net profit?–but everyone knows what *sales* means. Everyone cheers when the home team seems to be winning.

This is simple human psychology. Everyone likes to have an easy way of measuring their success. "Sales dollars" sound best, especially if they can be counted in the millions. Try working up a collective cheer for a monthly net profit of, say, $14,937.22. Not exactly a whiz-bang, blow-your-socks-off number, even if it's the business's greatest performance in ten years.

Everyone, especially in a small business, especially the owners, sees those sales dollars as a refreshing stream of cash flowing directly into the business's depleted bank account. You can't help but feel a warm glow, thinking of all those sales dollars cascading into the corporate cookie jar.

So what if the customers pay late? Or don't pay at all? Or sales costs are going through the roof? Or net profits are miserable? Those are just accounting problems for that nerdy bean counter down in the basement. We exceeded our sales goals, didn't we? What do bean counters know?

A lot, it turns out.

Sales Blindness Can Kill

You've heard of "sun blindness," caused by too much sunlight in the eyes, reflected off snow, sea or sand.

> **CAREFUL!**
> **GROWTH CAN EXPAND PROBLEMS**
> One of the main reasons small businesses fail is that they try to expand too quickly.
> It sounds strange, but sales growing too rapidly can destroy a company. . . . Before you think about expansion, consider:
> • Can I handle the increased overhead expenses?
> • Do I have the working capital and cash flow to support higher amounts of inventory and accounts receivable?
> • Can I measure the productivity gains?
> –Daniel F. Herz, "Small Business,"
> *The Miami Herald*

Well, sales statistics can do the same for businesspeople. As they tan themselves in the warm glow from their latest sales reports, they can end up with a bad case of "sales blindness."

The sickness is most prevalent in small businesses. Owner-managers can become blinded by the sales figures, not seeing what lies behind them, what they are concealing. Often they don't have the staff and other administrative resources required to generate the financial figures and controls needed to force them to take a calm, balanced look, not only at the sales figures themselves, but also at what those sales might be doing to the business's basic health. Just like high blood pressure, high sales may not be a sign of good health. High sales may themselves be generating potentially explosive problems.

These are tight, tough business times. The economic climate is unforgiving of business miscalculations. Mistakes must be detected quickly and corrected immediately. Your small business may develop some economic illness that could prove fatal if not corrected in time. Yet if you suffer from sales blindness, you may only dimly begin to perceive your business's illness when it's already too late and has become terminal.

Serious, even fatal, problems can be obscured by sales blindness.

- **Selling at Any Price:** During the start-up phase, a cheap and effective marketing ploy is to give away "for free" some of the business's product or service: through trade samples, taste testing, giveaways, free seminars, free consulting, no charges in the first month and so on. There are hundreds of variants on this technique, but they all lead to one end result: you're deliberately selling below cost to jump-start your new business. That's fine, up to a point; it's less than fine, beyond a point. Trouble is, you can start seeing these figures as real sales when they are only a quick marketing fix. Sooner rather than later, you will have to impose discipline on yourself and go cold turkey, to get off your marketing habit. Too often, new businesses cannot bring themselves to bite the bullet and charge what they should be charging, since it means an inevitable short-term drop in sales when reality kicks in. So the habit drags on, this marketing technique becomes a permanent crutch, sales blindness sets in and the business's basic profitability becomes permanently crippled.

- **Creeping Aging of Accounts Receivable:** Accounts receivable are in fact those sales that did not generate immediate cash in the bank, sales that really "happen" only when the customer finally pays up. One of the simplest, most elementary measures of your business's vulnerability is the average "age" of its accounts receivable. That is, the *actual* average number of days that customers are taking to pay up . . . not the number of days' credit you so graciously allowed them and they so ungraciously stretched way beyond the limit. When everyone in a business wants to please the customer and no one wants to get tough with the slow payers, you'll see (if you're paying attention) this average gradually creep up, like a patient running a fever. From, say, thirty days, to thirty-five, then forty, and so on. Suddenly, it's out of control, over sixty days, and all those stunning sales increases you were applauding aren't producing enough cold, hard cash to pay your business's bills. Yet you're actually having to shell out more and more precious cash to pay for additional materials and labor needed for the extra production that was generated by all those increased sales. A vicious cycle, if ever there was one. Result: a dangerous, maybe fatal, cash crunch, especially if you don't have a friendly (is there such a thing?) banker to loan you emergency funds.

- **Increasing Bad Debt Exposure:** You'll always have some customers who are potential "bad debts," otherwise known as deadbeats. However, you can still sell to them by keeping them on a very tight leash and watching their payment behavior like a hawk. The moment their payments are even one day late, you stop delivering and start pressuring for payment. You're running a risk but a controlled one, which you have calculated you can live with. So far, so good. However, that works only so long as you stay self-disciplined. In real life, there's always a strong temptation for the sales manager–or you yourself–to start gradually stretching the rules, as you see sales increasing. What if there's suddenly an economic recession, even a mild one? You can find that you're dangerously overexposed, with weak clients who are now in financial trouble and will probably never be able to pay your accumulated invoices. All those tempting sales you couldn't resist in the past have already been "booked" in your accounts as revenues, but now they'll probably only turn into hard cash the day pigs grow wings and fly. The lesson: sales showing in your sales reports don't necessarily mean you'll ever see that money in your bank account. Small businesses don't have financial safety cushions and can often collapse, just because of a few key customers who don't pay their bills.

- **Shrinking Gross Margins:** You or your sales manager may know that your business generates a satisfactory "gross margin" (the difference between the sales price and the actual costs of production). So it becomes tempting to use that as an excuse to give extra price breaks and discounts to big customers, to generate more sales–"Oh, we can afford to shave a little; the gross margin will cover it"–conveniently forgetting that the company needs the full dollar amount of that "gross margin" to pay for its sales, administrative and overhead expenses. Shave a little here, shave a little there, and when you finally start adding it all up, you've shaved yourself into a hole.

- **Ballooning Sales Costs:** It costs money to generate sales revenues: salaries, commissions, bonuses, travel expenses, advertising, promotions, etc. If the pressure to "sell, sell, sell" is excessive, these costs can easily start ballooning out of control. There's always the convenient excuse: "No problem. You see, we're spending money but it generates even more money in sales." That excuse often sounds all too logical to a salesperson: let's imagine that every dollar in additional sales is costing "only" 40 cents in sales expenses. Great, yes? That's 60 cents left over, yes? Unfortunately, no: your tame bean counter will probably show you that your business's gross margin on every dollar of sales is only 30 cents. Since you're paying 40 cents to "buy" more sales, you're actually *losing* 10 cents on every additional dollar in increased sales. Not exactly a formula for getting rich. And what if you're too small to have a good bean counter on your staff, to blow the whistle? Then who's going to blow it? The funeral parlor director?

> **SONOMA SALES JUMP; SO DO COSTS**
>
> Williams-Sonoma Inc. was the envy of the retail industry during [a] difficult holiday sales season. . . .
>
> The purveyor of kitchen wares and home furnishings enjoyed a sales boom that pushed its revenues ahead by about 50%.
>
> But every cloud has a dark lining. . . . Expenses of handling the addional sales cost $5 million more than the company had expected.
>
> "They just weren't prepared," said [a retailing analyst]. "By the time they saw the demand coming, it was too late to react. . . ."
>
> That surge meant the company had to hire more part-time workers than it had intended. Higher shipping costs . . . added even more to the company's expenses. And costs of expanding the company's distribution center in Memphis were also higher than projected.
>
> —Stephanie Strom, *The New York Times*

- **General Managerial Blindness:** And so on and so forth. You'd be surprised how often such things happen, even in large, established companies that should know better. Sales blindness is not just a sickness of small businesses. And remember, here we've only been talking about the serious problems that can be generated by sales themselves, when they're out of control. There are any number of other potential problems–financial, economic, operational and managerial–that a business can face from time to time, which can and will be overlooked until too late, if the owner-managers suffer from sales blindness.

Recessions Come, Sales Go

A variation on the sales blindness problem is the ingrained reluctance so many businesspeople have to face up to the inevitable fact that sooner or later the national economic weather will get rough, sales will consequently drop and the survivors will be those who realized what was beginning to happen, and cut back in time to weather the gathering economic storm.

You heard it right: *inevitable*.

ESPECIALLY DISMAL AT DOWNTURNS
Economists Are Way Off the Mark in Predicting Recessions.
History Shows That Upbeat Forecasts Are Unreliable. So Don't Be Complacent.

Whether they do their forecasts using large-scale computer models or on the back of an envelope, economists can do a good job predicting growth most of the time. But when it comes to calling recessions, their track record is dismal. Over the past 25 years, economic forecasters have missed four of the past five recessions.
—*Business Week*

RECESSION? WHAT RECESSION?
The Biggest Problem with Economic Forecasters Is That They Generally Can't Tell Us What We Most Want to Know.

When you turn on your television in the morning in search of the weather report, chances are you really want to know only one thing. . . . Is it going to rain, or not? . . . Likewise, when most people seek out economists, the single most important question they want answered is, When will there be a recession? Here the decisions dependent on the answer tend to be big and important, such as whether it is a good time to expand your business, buy a house, or take a new job.

Unfortunately, this one thing people really want from economists is the one thing economists can't give them. Economic forecasters, in fact, are very bad at predicting recessions. At any given moment, they can't tell you with much certainty whether a recession will begin next quarter, let alone next year. . . .

Hardly any forecasters warn of an imminent downturn, but the truth is that when the next one comes, they probably won't see it until it has already begun. To work the weather analogy one last time, it's as though weatherpersons could tell you whether it was going to rain only hours after the rain has started.
—Rob Norton, "The Economy," *Fortune*

JUST FOR LAUGHS

If an economist and an IRS agent were both drowning and you could only save one of them, would you go to lunch or read the paper?

Q. What's the best way to describe an economist? A. Someone who doesn't have the personality to be an accountant.

Q. Why did God create economists? A. In order to make weather forecasters look good.
—William Glasgall on the Internet, *Business Week*

Economics isn't called the "dismal science" for nothing. And the most dismal information that economists can give you is that the economic health of the U.S., or any other country, follows a regular cycle of ups (expansion) and downs (recession). On average, America's economic health has steadily improved in the past fifty years or so, but when the time comes for those inevitable periodic downturns, it always catches many businesspeople disbelieving ("This isn't happening") or unprepared ("Let's wait and see what happens").

Not that economists are great forecasters.

Economic swings depend on too many factors, national and international, for anyone to tell you confidently what next year's business climate is going to be. If economists could do that, they'd be better loved and much richer. They can't and never will. That's what makes them dismal.

Think of them as economic weathermen. Their long-term forecasts are for the birds. But short-term, economic science can often tell you when a bad storm is brewing (maybe) and where (roughly) it is about to hit. Also, they have some handy "economic indicators" (like barometric pressure readings), which can be helpful in telling you how much the storm may hurt your particular type of business.

The United States has been through nine recessionary periods in the past fifty years. That's an average of one every 5.5 years. But that's only an average; there's no fixed schedule for economic cycles. All you can be sure of is that another recession will be along in the next few years, just as surely as there are going to be spells of bad weather. But no one can give you an expected time of arrival.

When the next economic recession hits, each type of business will be affected differently. Some may sail through almost without a hitch, others may get badly battered. Here's where those "economic indicators" can be helpful in judging how severely the wind is going to be blowing in your part of town.

Reading Economic Barometers

If yours were a secure, established small business and you could find out that a spell of bad economic weather might be moving your way, it would be grossly negligent of you not to take basic safety measures in advance, just as you would batten down before a hurricane–reducing your staff, cutting inventories, building up cash reserves, canceling expansion plans, reducing credit terms, cutting superfluous costs and so on. Obvious, sensible precautions. Yet the biggest casualties in every economic recession are always large numbers of small businesses that were simply unprepared for a serious downturn in sales and thus suffered either severe damage or outright failure.

Why? Three reasons.

One reason is that many small businesses are relatively new. Their owners have not been through a recession before (at least not as small business operators); they underestimate the inevitability of it and the extent of potential damage.

A second reason is that the self-confidence and blind enthusiasm that helped them start their own business successfully can also make them overly cocky ("This can't happen to me").

A third reason is a reluctance to devote just a little time and some minimal mental effort to understanding elementary economic principles . . . it seems too complicated, too esoteric, too mushy and certainly too dismal. The unfortunate truth is that economics turns most people off. The details are dreary and boring, especially in this day and age when we only like quick, concise "bites" of information.

Believe me, please: it is far easier than you might imagine to understand the limited economic information needed to perceive that bad economic weather may be headed your way. You can extract all you will need from the business pages of your local paper (or business magazine or trade paper), the same way you use the local paper or TV to check out the weather forecast for the next couple of days. You don't have to be an expert weatherman to understand from the weather forecasts that you may get soaked in the projected rainstorms. And you don't have to be a qualified economist to deduce from the economic forecasts that your sales may slump if your customers are battered by an upcoming recession.

Each type of business activity has a few specific "economic indicators" that tell something, good or bad, about the way the overall business climate may be swinging and how it might affect that particular type of business. A little regular reading in trade magazines, for your particular kind of business–or just simply talking around–will teach you which are the most applicable. These "indicators" are regularly published indexes such as: consumer confidence, retail sales, housing starts, auto production, auto sales, interest rates, unemployment rates, credit card usage and so on. These indexes are like "cold fronts" or "warm fronts" in the weather forecasts, big numbers that give barometric readings for different bits and pieces of the national economy.

None of this information is perfect. None of it is foolproof. You can still get caught in unexpected economic storms, in spite of your best efforts.

But it sure as hell beats working in total ignorance of the economic weather fluctuations in which your small business has to generate its sales and survive.

Learning about and watching economic indicators can't guarantee your business's safety (nothing can), but it will certainly greatly improve your chances of beating the odds against survival.

Try it. It's easier than you think.

You Don't Need to Be Blind

Here's another way of saying it: sales blindness is simply managerial laziness.

If you're a corporate employee with a sales job, sure, all you care about is closing the sales and meeting your targets. Whether they're healthy sales or sick sales is not your problem. They pay you a salary to do just that, and nothing more.

If you're an entrepreneur, an owner of your own small business, you can't allow yourself the luxury of acting like a sales employee. Your primary concern has to be the overall health and survival of your business.

So it is your personal responsibility to be as concerned about the quality of your sales as the quantity.

Any idiot can deliver quantity sales.

It takes a smart entrepreneur to ensure quality sales.

A CAUTIONARY TALE OF SALES BLINDNESS:

PICTURE THIS! A FIRM FAILING FROM TOO MUCH SUCCESS

When Harvey Harris started selling elaborate cut-rate personalized calendars, he anticipated strong demand.

But not so strong that it would ruin him.

Recently, his Oklahoma City-based concern, Grandmother Calendar Co., went out of business. Mr. Harris blames the company's demise on an excess of success. "I'm a salesman, and a good one, that started this company up and it exploded and just went crazy," he told the *Daily Oklahoman.* . . . As the Grandmother Calendar case shows, conceiving a new product or a new twist on a product is only part of the challenge. The hotter the item, the more quickly and deeply an inexperienced entrepreneur can get into trouble.

Personalized photo calendars . . . have been around for years. What made Grandmother different—and apparently contributed to its demise—was the elaborateness of the product [with] all sorts of options. Mr. Harris offered calendar kits to retailers, greeting-card purveyors and mail-order catalog companies around the country. . . . Customers snapped up the calendar kits, which cost $20.

In the period leading up to Christmas, things began to fall apart. Orders came in much faster than Mr. Harris could fill them, so he diverted money needed for day-to-day expenses to expand capacity. . . . He leased more production space . . . bought additional equipment . . . new cutting-edge scanners. Output doubled to 300 calendars a day—but orders were coming in at 1,000 a day.

Equipment began to fail from overuse. Output from the scanners overloaded the printers . . . quality suffered. . . . In addition, the $20 for the basic item, which undercut most competitors by about $5, may have been too low, especially considering the complexity of the process.

As Christmas got closer, tens of thousands of orders went unfilled. Yet, some retailers say, Mr. Harris never breathed a word, encouraging them instead to keep selling the kits. That is, until things really started to get desperate. . . .

Looking back, Mr. Harris may have been insufficiently capitalized, having used his own savings and a loan from his father to get the business off the ground. Moreover, most customers paid by credit card, and the credit-card companies didn't pay Grandmother until the finished product was shipped. "Unless you have a deep pocket . . . you live and die by sales revenue," says the former president.

When companies suddenly get a big influx of orders, working capital often runs out, management is strained, and computer systems get overloaded, says [a consultant]. "It can all happen at once." And such was the case for Grandmother. By late last year, paychecks began to bounce for the 100 or so workers at the plant, most of whom earned only about $6 an hour. Paychecks ceased altogether in early January, and days later Mr. Harris ceased operations.

Now the Grandmother facility sits empty. Suppliers and creditors are trying to reclaim equipment, and the Oklahoma attorney-general's consumer-protection arm is investigating the company's demise.

Mr. Harris has been the subject of anger, ridicule, lawsuits and even death-threats. . . . He said, "I'm not an attorney. I'm not an accountant. I made mistakes and did not track receivables, payables, the funding. I should have made, well, better decisions."

—Louise Lee, *The Wall Street Journal*

9

THAT OL' BOTTOM LINE:

*Happiness Is Knowing
Your Profit Structure*

Profits, the Big Kahuna

Profits matter, right?

You won't hear any disagreement from people in small business. Sure, profitability matters . . . a whole lot. It's the fuel that drives each business. That's what people go into their own business to do . . . make money. And an entrepreneur makes money how? By making profits, not by cashing a payroll check. All the other personal reasons for any individual to start their own business may be fine, wonderful reasons, but they are all secondary, subordinate to that one overriding reason: *making a living out of making a profit.* If you don't have a profit, you won't have a business for long . . . nor a living.

So there's no disagreement. Yes, profits matter.

Logically, you would therefore imagine that understanding the basic nuts and bolts of how a particular small business "constructs" its final profit (or loss) figure would be very high on the owner's personal priority list. Like understanding the architect's drawings for a new home. How they put the building together is kind of important, since you're going to live there for a good many years. So of course you'd want to understand its structural basics. Naturally, the same thinking would apply to a business's P&L structure, right?

Well, you imagined wrong.

As a hangover from their prior existences as employees (in most cases), entrepreneurs all too often still think the whole "P&L thing" is just one more

> It's not how big you are.
> It's how much money you make.
> —John P. Reilly, CEO, Figgie Int'l.,
> quoted in *Business Week*

tedious bean-counting routine, to hand off to the accountant. So that they can go off and concentrate on entrepreneurial fireworks . . . which usually means sales and marketing, by the way (remember sales blindness?).

Big mistake. All successful entrepreneurs, however big or small their business, keep a constant, close and watchful eye on their business's profit structure and the results it produces. They work hard at understanding it, controlling it and improving it. For the very simple reason that their business lives depend on it.

So, for your own good, you must work at understanding the basics of profitability: its structure, its main components, its language, its numbers. Frankly, nothing could be simpler. It's only "accounting phobia" that makes many people run away from the responsibility. They're so convinced that they won't understand it, that they don't realize how easy it is and won't make the effort. You can't give yourself that luxury; the personal cost could be too high.

You do not need to be an accountant to understand what matters to you about your business's profitability. It's only simple arithmetic and organized thinking.

Once you understand, clearly and precisely, each key detail of your own small business's "profit profile"–the X ray of your profit's skeleton–you will know where to push the right buttons, either to increase your net profits or to protect yourself from losses.

P&L: Its Language, Its Numbers, Its Framework

One problem is imprecise language: "making a buck," "making a profit" and so on. Mushy phrases and loose language lead to mistakes and misunderstandings.

The language of business is precise numbers and clear terminology.

You never hear airplane pilots saying such things as: "We're nice and high now; we've got lots of fuel; we should get there in an hour or so; that's a strong wind blowing out there"; etc. In their world, everything is precise, measured and clearly expressed in gallons, m.p.h., p.s.i., hours, minutes, seconds, miles, feet, inches, whatever. There's only a very narrow margin for errors or misunderstandings when flying planes . . . the downside is all too down. Just as there is little margin for mistakes when managing your own small business. The P&L "language" must be precise.

The problem of terminology is not made easier by the fact that there is no "best" way of laying out the framework of your profit and loss statement. There are alternative ways of demonstrating the numbers, varying by type of business, size of business, complexity of operations, who prepares it, who it's for, and so on. Also, there are different schools of thought and different gurus (in the fields of accounting and financial analysis), each preaching their own preferred method.

Business owner-operators can find themselves with seriously confused notions about the whys and wherefores of their business's profits (or losses), only because they are using some standard textbook P&L format that is not made to measure to reflect the structure of their own unique "profit profile."

Getting your P&L framework straight has to involve you; you can't just rip out a page from an accounting textbook. You have to get personally involved in defining, clarifying and understanding every line and every column, in those precious one or two pages that will end up summarizing your business's internal Profit & Loss report. Get help if you need it, but never blindly adopt someone else's standard format, without making your own adjustments and your own "fine-tuning." So that, like a suit, the final format is made to measure and fits snugly on your small business's framework. You are the designated "end user" of your business's P&L statement, not your accountant.

As your company grows and changes, make sure that this framework keeps getting adjusted along with your growth. Again, think of a suit: after a couple of years, it may need adjustment.

If you can reconcile your monthly bank statement, you can do this work. It's mostly common sense. You will not find it especially complicated. Your outside bookkeeper or accountant should work on this with you, *but it's a joint effort.* You know your company and where it's headed; they don't. The only reason so many businesspeople are afraid to get involved in this area is that they think of it as being highly technical accounting stuff. It just isn't. At least not what we're talking about, which is *your internal P&L format*–your business's monthly and yearly "report card," which will show you the details of each of the key nuts and bolts that, all together, go toward making up your business's overall "profit profile."

Technical difficulties start cropping up only when more complex "adjusted" versions are prepared for the IRS, for financial analysts, for bank credit officers, and other outsiders who need to see "sanitized" versions.

You may need to fool these outsiders a little (hey, it's only business), but you must never fool yourself. Your version, your personal P&L report, must show you the cold, hard reality of your business's profit performance: in precise numbers, clear language and a logical, step-by-step structure.

So that you're not flying blind.

Visible Bucks versus Invisible Bucks

Entrepreneurs know that they are operating their own business to "make a buck." But often they can't help seeing those bucks they need to make as the ones that come in through *sales* . . . the Big Bucks. Those they can actually see and handle–bank notes in the cash register, client checks in the mail, deposits into the business bank account. Those are the bucks they're going to use to pay the rent, utilities and phone bills the following morning.

So they watch them very closely. Sometimes too closely, to the exclusion of possibly more important matters.

It's psychologically understandable. One sympathizes. Many small business owners have suffered through terrifying "cash crunches," when their backs are to the wall, their survival is at stake and they are desperate for a few miserable dollars in sales to materialize out of the blue, so that they can meet the payroll and pay the suppliers.

Those are *sales bucks*. They are the lifeblood of your small business. Without them, you don't have a business.

But the *profit bucks* are just as important. They are the oxygen in the business's blood. Your body can have all the blood it requires, but if your blood is starved of oxygen, death will result, no matter how much blood there is.

Businesses must make profits to survive and grow. True, they can survive (uncomfortably) on zero profit ("breaking even"), but what they cannot do is survive for long, if they are losing money.

Obvious enough, right?

May seem obvious, but this is where far too many new entrepreneurs trip themselves up and fall on their faces. You can see, touch, feel and smell your sales dollars–your *visible bucks*–but the real dollars you are making (or losing) in profits (or losses), are your *invisible bucks*. You only see them on pieces of paper weeks, maybe months, after everything has been added and subtracted. And they'll stay invisible, unless you go looking for them.

Depending on your degree of confidence in your own bookkeeping, you may not take those pieces of paper too seriously. Or you may be too busy with sales. Or you may be too bored by those columns of figures. Or you may

From an Interview with Wendell E. Dunn:

A [frequent] mistake is thinking in terms of sales and units, rather than profits and cash flow. Cash is the lifeblood of a business. If you run short on cash, you're going to be in real trouble, real fast.

Similarly, it's profit that you're interested in, not just sales. Profit is related to sales and unit volume, but it's also an issue of margins, which brings in the issue of pricing.

So if you look only at the sales issues and not the underlying economic issues–the cash flows and profits–you're going to be in real trouble.

—quoted in *The Wall Street Journal*

want to avoid looking at what you suspect might be unpleasant news.

All too often that's the story of small businesses that lose money and then have to fold: "I didn't check the numbers, I just didn't see it coming."

That's a dumb way to go. It's one of the most basic responsibilities of any businessperson to make sure that they always have accurate, up-to-date, easy-to-read profit and loss figures (sitting on their desks, not buried in the filing cabinet) and that they examine them regularly, personally, so that they can see immediately what's going right, what's going wrong and where, and then take corrective measures, before it's too late.

If this is to happen, the boss person, the owner-operator, must proclaim at the top of his/her voice, *"These numbers on these pieces of paper are of life-or-death importance,"* must sincerely believe it and must force everyone else in the business also to believe it. Threaten death and dismemberment of disbelievers (or at least firing), if need be. Because if the boss shows a lack of personal interest in the P&L figures, no one else in the business will care either. Because, let's face it, most people don't enjoy studying numbers and need to be forced to do it . . . it doesn't come naturally. They'd rather go play in sales.

None of this will happen unless you make it happen.

It takes self-discipline, conviction and leadership. First, to guarantee that the P&L reports are produced correctly and on schedule, like clockwork. Second, to make sure that they are carefully studied and analyzed, immediately when they become available, to discover what the numbers are trying to tell you. Third, to see that the end result of this internal work is fast management action, to correct any problems that the numbers are highlighting . . . otherwise it's all just a paperwork and numbers game. That's not what you went into your own small business for. You became an entrepreneur to make profits.

So What Exactly Is "Profit"?

Start off by getting your language straight.

Anyone operating their own business should have an absolutely clear understanding of what that word *profit* (and of course *loss*) really means, relative to their own business. Yet very often they don't. That's a little like not knowing what m.p.h. means or what the gasoline gauge shows, when you drive a car. It's kinda basic.

Start off by blaming the IRS. That's always good for a round of applause. Although, to be fair to the IRS, the real villain in this case is Congress, which makes the tax laws the IRS has to police. But let's not get into *that*.

The reason for much of the confusion is that there are many different accounting rules and financial methods for calculating your business's taxable net profit. Because businesses pay income tax on their "final" net profit, and because there are an unbelievable number of arbitrary rules and regulations, established by the government, to allow an equally unbelievable number of deductions, loopholes and "adjustments," your business's official financial statements, which are shown in your tax returns, are pretty much useless for telling you anything clear and reliable about your *real* profit.

Add to all this the miracles of modern "creative accounting" and the final profit (or loss, if your accountant is a true creative artist) shown in your annual tax statements can become even more meaningless for management purposes. It's merely a final number, for tax calculation purposes only.

What your accountant prepares for your personal (if you're self-employed) or corporate (if your business is incorporated) tax returns are your *financial statements, tax returns, official books* . . . there is a choice of labels. Some businesspeople like to get heavily involved in this area and enjoy playing technical accounting tricks and tax avoidance games. That can be a valid business objective for those who really know how to play such games and it can make a big difference in your tax bill. But I don't recommend you try it; it's a specialist's game. You'll have to work hard enough just managing your small business well. Stick with what really matters, the real profit performance of your business, not with the fabricated profit figure showing on your tax return. Let your accountant play those tricks for you.

The figures on your business's official financial statements and tax returns cannot help you in managing your business. *They are not true numbers; they cannot and should not be used for managing your business.* Their only purpose is managing (i.e., reducing) your taxes (or keeping your shareholders off your back, or fooling your creditors).

To get a perspective on these playground antics, just take a look at the quarterly and annual profit results divulged by companies whose stocks are publicly traded on the Stock Exchange. Those numbers are so doctored, tweaked, adjusted, corrected and cosmetically enhanced that they are managerially meaningless.

Managers in such companies have their own, reliable internal numbers to show them what is truly happening in their operations. They would no more use their own company's public financial statements for management decisions than the astrology columns in the newspaper.

The true numbers you must use for understanding and tracking your company's profits, costs, sales and other key pieces of information must be prepared internally–quickly, simply and consistently–preferably in the form of the monthly figures in your MIS (Management Information System). More about that later. For now, let's stay focused on profit structure and its component parts.

Profit . . . The Basic Structure

There is a simple, basic structural "skeleton" for organizing and understanding the key profit and loss components in any business. Grasp that and hold on to it. There are many variations and refinements to confuse matters, but the basics are always fundamentally the same.

In any small business, *stick with these basics when you start.* It'll be hard to go wrong. Get more sophisticated later, when your business is successful. Then you will be able to add improvements and refinements . . . and you will also be able to afford more professional help.

In your small business, if from the start you can have each of the following "basic" lines, clearly, correctly and separately displayed in your monthly P&L report, it will keep you honest (with yourself) and you will thus already be ahead of the game, in understanding and controlling your profit.

Start with:
>**Gross Revenues** *(sales, fees, commissions, royalties, etc.)*

Then show separately and deduct:
>**Direct Costs of Goods** *(for a reselling business)*
>**or Direct Costs of Materials and Labor** *(for production)*
>**or Direct Costs of Services** *(for service)*

Thus giving you your:
>**Gross Profit Margin** *(i.e., your <u>real</u> revenues)*

Then show separately and deduct:
>**Each Operating Cost** *(payroll, rent, utilities, marketing, sales costs, services, maintenance, etc., etc.)*

Thus giving you your:
>**Operating Profit** *(i.e., your <u>working</u> profit)*

Then show separately and deduct:
>**Each Overhead Expense** *(owner's remuneration, insurance, accounting, loan interest, etc., etc.)*

Thus giving you your:
>**FINAL NET PROFIT (or LOSS)** *(i.e., your "<u>bottom-line</u>" profit [or loss] from the business as a whole, <u>before</u> calculating any income tax due)*

Simple, obvious, kids' stuff, huh?

Maybe. But I've seen bright, bushy-tailed folks with college degrees in accounting and finance, MBAs and other assorted impressive credentials lose their shirts and their businesses, only for the simple, idiotic crime of neglecting to pay constant, careful attention to each of the above lines.

Instead, they fell madly in love with Line One, Gross Revenues. The other lines were just plain boring, not the stuff hotshot entrepreneurs waste their talents and time on.

So they got "sales blindness" and paid the price.

Make sure you have an internal P&L report every month that looks something like the one above. It'll keep you honest.

Let's take an example. Let's assume the Entrepreneurial Dreams Inc. business has the following "profit profile" for an average year:

	Sales Income	$200,000	100%
minus:	Cost of Goods	$100,000	
equals:	Gross Profit	$100,000	50%
minus:	Operating Costs	$50,000	
equals:	Operating Profit	$50,000	25%
minus:	Overhead Exp.	$40,000	
equals:	**Net Profit**	**$10,000**	5%

Let's play with an assumption, to illustrate the relative importance of each line and the interconnection between them.

If our sales-blind owner-manager increases sales by $10,000, the extra gross profit would be $5,000 (50 percent). So the final net profit would increase to $15,000.

Nice.

But if the blindness at the same time permits operating costs to increase by $5,000 and overhead expenses by another $5,000–totaling the same $10,000 as the sales increase–do we get a "wash"? No. Net profit would *drop* from $10,000 to $5,000 *in spite of the sales increase.*

Not so nice.

In this illustration, to compensate for a cost increase of $10,000, the owner-manager would have to increase sales by $20,000 just to maintain the same level of profitability.

Each "line" in your company's basic profit profile represents a descending step, beginning with those nice fat sales numbers we all love to see, then steadily slimming down, step by step, until you hit the ground, the bottom line, where the $10,000 in net profit for the year is the *really* good news. *Not* the $200,000 in sales.

The $200,000 are the visible bucks. The $10,000 are the invisible bucks.

Everything interconnects: any changes in any one of those lines, for better or worse, will *automatically* change the bottom line too.

"Bottom-Line Thinking"

That horribly overworked and overused phrase "bottom-line thinking" is nevertheless of fundamental importance. As owner of your own small business, if you think bottom line, you will follow a mental discipline of always thinking out your business's problems and opportunities in terms of "What will this do to my final net profit?"

That's bottom-line thinking.

So your sales have dropped 10 percent but you have also reduced your staff by two people. Is that good news or bad news? You can answer that question only after evaluating exactly what those two changes will do to your bottom line. Such "what if" calculations, which would have been time-consuming and complicated for a small business some years ago, using a calculator and handwritten columns of figures on ledger paper, have become stunningly easy to perform today, with the use of personal computers and spreadsheet software programs . . . more about them later.

Your bottom line–your final net profit–is why you went into your own small business. Never forget it. It's your only financial reason for being an entrepreneur. So make "what if?" calculations one of your standard management habits.

You did *not* go into your own small business on an ego trip, to flash your stuff as a hotshot salesperson or marketing genius. If you're talented in those areas, so fine–that will be a major asset to your small business. But it won't mean diddly-squat, if your sales and marketing abilities cannot translate into a healthy bottom line. A corporation may once have paid you a handsome salary as an employee, for those sales and marketing skills; profits were someone else's problem. Now, your own small business will be a far tougher taskmaster with you than your ex-employer could ever have been. It will force you to use those skills not for show but only to improve the bottom line.

Otherwise, what's the value of all that talent?

The bottom line is the only true thermometer reading of your business's operating health. The stronger the net profit figure on your bottom line, the healthier your business will be and the likelier it will survive and prosper. If your bottom line is consistently weak or negative, your business has serious health problems that require medical attention. If you ignore them, the fever will persist and your business's health will steadily decline.

Fat Profit Margins: A Thing of the Past

The need for every business owner-operator to possess a solid and intimate knowledge of the business's overall profit profile and of each individual line in the P&L statement, is far more important today than it ever was in the past.

The competitive and cost pressures of the '90s make it tougher than ever to produce a comfortable "profit buck" in almost any business. And it's often harder for small businesses than large ones. The only reliable defense for a small business owner is to be well informed and up-to-date, on each and every line in the P&L and to "turn on a dime," moving quickly and efficiently to face potentially serious problems that are beginning to show up.

The good news is that if they do this right, small businesses have a considerable advantage over bigger, more cumbersome companies. They can see the problems more clearly, study their options faster, decide for themselves more quickly on what needs to be done and take corrective action immediately. Speed and flexibility are their weapons in the competitive battle.

Business life was simpler, once upon a time. Successful small businesses grew and prospered before and after World War II, with little more than the conventional annual P&L and balance sheet, prepared by the company's accountant in the standardized form. The owner was a hardworking salesman, engineer, store owner, mechanic, architect, manufacturer or whatever, who got on with what mattered: running the business. If he (yes, ma'am, it was all male in those days) had any questions about profits or costs, he'd ask the accountant. He knew his company was making money and how, knew nothing was going to change dramatically from month to month, and didn't necessarily need to understand each of the details of the company's profit structure and key costs. That was the accountant's problem. That's what he got paid for.

Businesses still failed in those days. But once they were reasonably secure, they were pretty much assured that success would continue, so long as they kept doing their basic stuff, the same old way. Conditions did not change that rapidly. Costs were pretty stable, profit margins were fat and comfortable, customers were loyal, suppliers were reliable . . . life was good.

> The margins in retailing have steadily gone down, because the mass merchants are forcing that.
> —Stanley Logan, Arthur Andersen, Chicago, quoted in *The Miami Herald*

Maybe it wasn't always quite that easy, but it certainly wasn't as hard and complex a business environment as it is today.

In today's business jungle, change is constant, competition is fierce, customers are volatile, prices are under pressure, costs escalate. It's a business world that is constantly moving and shaking and changing, at a pace that would have been unthinkable in those days. This process of dynamic change means that every component, every line in your business's profit structure, is under constant pressure. Since your profit margin is thin enough to begin with, a pinch here and a squeeze there, and you can easily find yourself in the red, bleeding to death.

Here are a few illustrations of unhappy things that can happen:

- **Sales:**
  Competition can be intense and fast-moving. A sudden aggressive move by a competitor and the loss of a couple of good clients, and that steady monthly stream of sales revenues could drop. If your profit margin is already thin, even a 5 percent drop in sales could flip that bottom line into a negative figure. If your internal reports are showing you your sales figures, every week and every month, and comparing them against what you sold last month and last year, you'll detect the problem quicker and correct it faster.

- **Selling Prices:**
  Even though some of your costs may have increased, your business may be one of many where competition is so fierce and customers so aware of what they are paying that you cannot "pass on" your cost problem to the customer simply by raising your prices. Customers probably won't accept your increase and you may price yourself out of your market. You will have to find other solutions, maybe by improving your marketing and thus selling more, or by cutting some other costs.

- **Supply Costs:**
  Large corporations often have considerable clout over small suppliers, allowing them to refuse price increases. Small businesses never do. You can get jumped overnight by a price increase from a key supplier and you'll have to grin and bear it. By knowing every small detail of your profit profile and taking a creative look at the direct costs of your product or service, you may find cost solutions. Maybe by switching to a cheaper supplier, maybe by using lower-grade materials, maybe by

using less labor. The "business self-knowledge" gained by constantly studying your profit structure will help you discover solutions that you would never have thought of if you hadn't had this knowledge.

- **Payroll Costs:**
  "People costs" can keep creeping up, especially for small businesses. Big companies can and do regularly beat their employees over the head, but small businesses are much more dependent on their few employees and risk losing the good ones if they apply harsh measures. And it's not only payroll; it's payroll taxes, health plans, child care assistance and so on. They all add up. Your detailed knowledge of your own profit structure can help you devise a workable incentive or bonus plan that offers your employees a base salary, plus some form of additional incentive payment. When the bottom line is healthy, everyone benefits . . . when times are tough, everyone suffers equally. Your employees can trust such a plan, since they also know that the business's profit figures are honest, understandable and reliable; after all, you use those same numbers to guide yourself.

- **General Costs:**
  Other miscellaneous costs (rents, insurance, electricity, telephone bills, local taxes, etc.) can unexpectedly get out of line with the business's profit realities. The quicker you become aware that you have a new cost problem that is beginning to eat away at your profitability, the quicker you can look for some other cost to cut or some way to increase income, thus compensating for the damage and keeping that precious bottom line intact.

- **Unexpected One-Time Expenses:**
  Sooner or later, every business gets jumped by unexpected "one-time" expenses. You think you have all your regular costs and expenses clearly defined and tightly controlled. Suddenly, bang, out of nowhere . . . a huge bill for lawyer's fees, an unexpected tax assessment, whatever. The only way to manage this is to open a special cost category in your profit controls with an estimated "allowance" for such unpredictable events, so that you have a built-in safety cushion for bad news, when and if it happens. You can most appropriately label this your "Shit Happens" account; sooner or later, it usually does.

Profit Self-Knowledge = Creative Business Solutions

The bad news is that it's a tough, rapidly changing, competitive jungle out there. It's harder on small businesses than big ones. Small ones have a difficult time making a decent profit. They don't have much weight to throw around when confronted with unexpected cost increases or sales declines.

The good news is that small businesses can compensate for their size disadvantage by working smarter and faster than the big guys. If they fully understand every key segment and line in the P&L structure of their business, when the unexpected happens–and it always does–they will be able to devise creative solutions and implement them fast. Because they will already know where the problem lies and can immediately estimate the profit impact of any solutions they dream up.

Without this profit self-knowledge, you're managing in the dark. You have no way of measuring the impact of the problems or seeing the solutions.

Cursing the darkness won't solve matters.

Light a candle instead. Get your internal P&L reporting in place and in good shape. It will cast a bright light on both problems and solutions.

Think bottom line. Always.

10

THINK WORKING CAPITAL, CALCULATE CASH FLOW:

Stay Liquid . . .
Stay in Business

It Ain't Necessarily So

Profits don't necessarily mean cash in the bank.
Losses don't necessarily mean no cash in the bank.
Cash flowing in doesn't necessarily mean a profitable business.
Cash flowing out doesn't necessarily mean a lousy business.
Negative working capital doesn't necessarily mean no spending money.
Positive working capital doesn't necessarily mean any money at all.
Confusing?
Very.
Step #1 is: Don't panic. You're in good company.

You're not the only one somewhat confused. Large corporations declare bankruptcy every month, like clockwork, because their CEOs, CFOs, COOs and UFOs (Unwise Financial Officers) also didn't quite get it . . . or simply didn't give a damn. Except that their bankruptcies cost shareholders and creditors (small businesses like yours) hundreds of millions of dollars. If you were to make the same miscalculations, your bankruptcy would be pocket change in comparison . . . and you would suffer personally, far more so than any of those assorted Os. They have their severance agreements and indemnity deals. You don't.

So, step #2 is: Don't follow their example.

Let's start with some clarifications:

1. Your P&L shows a "paper" profit or loss. That has nothing to do with the amount of cold, hard cash churning in and churning out of your business, nor the speed with which it churns. It simply means that, when you finally pay everything you owe and have finally received everything you are owed, the end result will be that bottom-line figure–a profit or a loss. That could be tomorrow; it could be a year from now. Depends on the cash flow patterns in your particular type of business. Which are often totally out of your control; they are what they are. (Do you want to hear gossipy little stories about the six to nine months it takes for major bookstore chains to pay for the books they buy from publishers, especially small ones? Some other day.)

2. Your "cash flow" report couldn't care less if you're making a profit or a loss. All it needs to show you is the cold, hard cash flowing into and out of your business, day by day and month by month, as a result of the activities and transactions reflected in your P&L. It deals strictly in the cash reality of what comes in and what goes out, every day.

3. Your "working capital" fund is your operating piggy bank. It's the money grubstake you must have permanently invested in your business (or loaned by a bank) to bankroll your starting position at the cash flow blackjack table, plus any additional amounts needed over time, if your cash flows out, rather than in.

To summarize: Your profit or loss is one thing. Your cash flow is another thing. Your working capital yet another thing. Yet all three are umbilically interconnected and permanently interacting with each other. You can never look at only one of the three elements in complete isolation; you must simultaneously check what the other two are up to. They may be plotting surprises, nasty ones.

Uncomplicate and understand these three financial elements, within your own small business, and you won't risk becoming one of those UFOs.

Don't Die of Cash Thirst

Profitable, well-managed, beautiful little businesses can and do die the dumbest of deaths. They die of thirst . . . cash thirst.

Another analogy: Everything's fine with your business body–perfect health, great shape, working like a dream. You're taking a long hike in a hot desert, your need for liquids is greater than normal, you didn't plan your trip properly, you didn't load enough water in your water pouch and you're still many miles from the next water spring. Unless help comes along, you're vulture snack food.

The water, of course, being cash.

Small business owner-operators can find themselves in this most frustrating of all small business binds. The business is doing fine, it's producing healthy profits, but there just isn't enough money to pay the bills and stay alive. And they can't understand why this is happening.

Although this problem can and does arise in all types and sizes of business, as usual it's the green, wet-behind-the-ears small businesses that are most vulnerable to the destructive effects of an unanticipated cash shortage and most likely to have to fold, if and when this happens.

Why?

Because bigger, longer-established companies have built up "banking relationships" over the years. The banks they deal with have seen years of money flowing steadily into the account, have looked at years of healthy profit and loss statements, and years of lunches, dinners, cocktail parties and generalized schmoozing have made everyone buddy-buddy. So, based on a quick phone call, the friendly banker lends the friendly client the friendly money needed to overcome the business's unexpected cash shortage. The bank knows it will get paid back. No one thinks nasty, offensive thoughts about the client's managerial competence. Cash crunches can happen to the best of businesses; we all know that. *No problem, ma'am, the money'll be in your account this afternoon.*

Now let's take a look at *your* case. You have no "relationship" to wave around in the bank lobby. Your small business is much younger; it's only been around for a year or so. But you, the owner-operator, know every single detail of the business. You can show that operations are on track and profitable. Your accountant can prove that the numbers are rock solid and that the cash crunch is only temporary. So you're confident the average commercial banker will lend a sympathetic ear, plus the small working capital loan that's needed for you to get over the hump?

Fat chance.

Not only will the loan be denied, you'll spend a lot of time, money and effort in preparing and presenting your

DEEP POCKETS

1. Be sure you have enough operating capital!
2. Be sure you have enough operating capital!
3. Be sure you have enough operating capital!

This is the answer to the question, "What are the three most important things a new owner can do to ensure the survival of his or her venture?" Many beginning entrepreneurs have a good idea but are not aware of the time and effort required—not to mention the pitfalls encountered along the way—to turn the idea into a successful business. Remember, you must be able to pay the bills and meet the payroll while you are out selling yourself and your idea. . . . It may take longer than you planned.

—Dale Mathews, *Your Company*

detailed, documented case, only to be told at the very end that, well, it doesn't look bad, but . . . you have no proven "track record" (meaning you haven't been in existence as long as they'd like); your business has no unattached fixed assets to put in hock with them (you're still paying off start-up loans on the initial assets you needed to get started); your personal guarantee's not so hot (because everything you own you invested in your company's start-up, and your personal credit cards are maxed out); and (under their breath) what kind of immature, incompetent manager are you anyway, to have miscalculated your working capital needs?

It isn't easy being green, to borrow Kermit's phrase.

Brighten up. At least now you know that outside financial help will probably not be easily forthcoming, if a cash crunch catches you by surprise, and you won't be counting on that fictional figure of the friendly banker. Now you'll be far better motivated to pay serious attention to how working capital and cash flow problems can arise and how they must be avoided, so that you *won't* need to go groveling to that less-than-friendly banker.

Don't expect friendliness from friendly bankers and you'll never be disappointed.

Fixed Assets Can Eat Away at Working Capital

First, let's look at your initial investments in *fixed assets and start-up costs,* since they will be first in line for your money, before your *working capital* needs.

Fixed assets are where you first start spending your limited investment capital for your new business; you only start spending the working capital portion when you are ready to operate. Right there, you have one of the prime reasons why many new small businesses crash and burn on takeoff. Whatever mistakes and miscalculations you make on your fixed assets will often mean that there will be less money left over for working capital, when you finally start to operate the business.

In theory, you should calculate your future working capital needs precisely and make sure that you have those funds, separate and available, when business operations finally commence. In practice, working capital funds are often whatever money you are lucky enough to have left over, once you've finished making your fixed asset purchases.

Fixed asset investments are not, in themselves, the prime cause of cash crises and liquidity problems. Either you have enough initial funds to buy the fixed assets you need, or you don't open up. And once you've made these initial investments, nothing much changes in your first years, at least not with the same volatility as can affect working capital and cash flow.

In real small business life, all funds are usually lumped together in one pool of money in one bank account; you don't have separate piles of money, each with their own little label *(My Fixed Asset Money; My Working Capital Kitty; My Fallback Fund)*. Too often, start-up businesses are tempted to rob Peter to pay Paul; they may use part of their supposed working capital funds to pay for overruns on fixed asset purchases, thus depleting their piggy bank cushion and increasing their vulnerability to the very first cash crisis that comes their way.

Your business, whatever its nature, will require an investment in certain fixed assets. This label covers all the basic, fixed investment needed to start up and operate. If you're talking of a small, home office freelance writing activity, you may be looking at, say, $5,000 in fixed assets (computer, printer, copier, furniture, telephone, fax, etc.). If it's a small retail store, you might be needing fixed assets of some $50,000 (remodeling, decoration, furnishing, shelving, counters, external sign, cash register, office equipment, air-conditioning, etc.). If you are setting up a full-service, freestanding restaurant with complete kitchen facilities, your fixed assets could easily exceed $500,000 when you've finished adding up all the investment requirements for parking area, external improvements, dining area, bar area, kitchen, etc.

Unless you start expanding and making additional investments, your fixed asset investments should not be the cause of ongoing financial problems, as long as you did things right at the beginning. When start-up entrepreneurs have problems with their fixed assets, the problems happen at the start.

They don't do their homework. They don't plan out and specify in careful detail all of their fixed asset needs, and estimate correctly the probable costs.

By the time they are ready to start up, their total fixed asset investment has exceeded what they had originally expected to spend. They then have to scramble to find additional money or to assume larger debts, before they have even started to operate.

Or they may make mistakes in their technical plans and discover, shortly after start-up, that they need different equipment, say, or must add more fixed assets that they had not known they would need.

All this happens more often than you might imagine–the "stuff-we-forgot-or-miscalculated" category of fixed assets. Since most new businesses start with limited funds, such miscalculations can be a major financial head-ache and a dangerous management distraction, at the worst possible time, when the owner-operator should be concentrating on critical start-up operations, not on scrambling for more money.

Do Your Investment Homework

The advice is painful and obvious. If you wish to avoid such unpleasant surprises: *do your homework, do your homework, and do your homework.*

Planning to set up any new small business always requires a considerable amount of hard, plodding legwork and laborious homework, in studying and listing everything that is going to be needed. There are no shortcuts in this kind of planning phase. It's the same as the architectural drawings and materials specifications for constructing a home . . . you must think out every nut and bolt, every detail and cost, ahead of time.

A reminder: Never forget *start-up costs.*

Start-up costs must be thought of as a form of fixed asset, even though they don't exist in a physical sense. Start-up costs are what you invested in miscellaneous expenses in getting your business ready to operate, the one-time costs you incur before you are ready to operate. Such things as legal costs, travel expenses, realtor commissions, broker's fees, research, printing and so on. Often these are relatively minor costs, but there can be a lot of them; they all add up and can end up totaling a substantial amount of money. Which you should also have planned for, in calculating your fixed asset investment budget. If you didn't, this will be one more item to add to the "stuff-we-forgot" additional funding.

New businesses' investment needs are almost never overestimated but, regrettably, almost always underestimated. You will probably not be a shining exception to this rule. The sensible solution is, when you have completed your homework and your detailed planning, to add an arbitrary 10 or 20 percent or more to your total estimate of fixed asset investments, as a "reserve for unpleasant surprises" account. You'll always need it.

Unless you calculated well and conservatively and raised all the money you estimated you'd need, the bad news can start happening when your start-up bills have all come in. Only then do you add it all up and see that you have spent more than you budgeted for, in start-up costs and fixed assets. So what do you do? You short-change your working capital reserves, using the justification: *No problem, there'll be all kinds of money pouring in, now that we are operational. This shortfall will quickly be replenished.*

Dream on. Do that and you'll be raiding your own piggy bank, possibly putting your entire venture in jeopardy a few short months later.

Working (Operating) Capital . . . Your Piggy Bank

Everyone uses the term *working (operating) capital,* but often there is not a clear understanding of what the label means. Loose terminology can lead to loose thinking. Which can make matters worse, if you run into cash problems. So first let's get our language and our thinking straight.

Working capital is a label used by financial analysts, accountants and tax consultants in a number of different ways. They each have technically complex definitions and rules on what to include, exclude or adjust. Don't let any of that bother you. None of it is relevant to what you need to understand, which is the basic function of working capital in your business.

Your small business's working capital can best be described as the cushion of money and "near money," needed to keep the business operating smoothly day to day. Different types of businesses have different types of working capital needs, but a reasonable common definition would be to say that your business's working capital is the end result of:

ADDING:

Your "liquid asset" accounts, such as:
- Cash in your bank accounts
- "Near cash" investments (funds, shares, bonds, CDs, etc.)
- Short-term debts owed to you, by customers and other debtors (accounts receivable)
- Your stocks of merchandise, materials, etc. (inventories)

SUBTRACTING:

Your "short-term liability" accounts, such as:
- Bank loans and other loans that must be repaid in the near future
- Short-term debts owed by you, to suppliers and other creditors (accounts payable)
- Taxes owed (short-term), of all types, shapes and sizes

(Note: Consider "short-term" as being between thirty and ninety days, i.e., about the time you might have to turn everything into only cash and to pay all debts)

If the sum total of all this is a positive number, your business has a "positive working capital" balance. A comfortable position, since you are not likely to get caught in a cash squeeze, at least not in the near future. If you come under pressure to make immediate payments, normally you have ready funds available to cover the demands. The downside is that your business will need more investment capital to finance that working capital.

If the sum total of all this is a negative number, your business has a "negative working capital" balance. Not necessarily a comfortable position; if you ever get caught in a cash squeeze and need to make immediate payments, you may not be able to find the money quickly enough to cover the demands. The upside is that such a business will require little or no investment for working capital; in effect, your suppliers are financing your business.

Having positive or negative working capital is not necessarily either good or bad news, in itself. Some businesses can live happily (if a bit nervously) with a negative position, if they have learned to manage their daily cash flow tightly and efficiently. Others with positive working capital can get into trouble, because they relax too much and pay no attention to their cash flow.

Ultimately, whether your working capital position means good news or bad news will really depend on what is flowing in and out of your business every day: your cash flow.

Positive versus Negative Cash Flows

Cash flow is easy enough to describe: it's the difference between the money regularly flowing into the business (usually from cash sales and customer payments of their invoices) and the money regularly flowing out (usually for paying suppliers and other current debts).

You would naturally think that a business's ability to accumulate (or dissipate) cash is directly related to its ability to make profits (or losses) on its "bottom line." A profitable business would generate cash; an unprofitable business would need cash. Right?

Seems logical but it ain't necessarily so. The world of business cash flow can sometimes be strange indeed.

Long-term, of course, no business can survive if it's consistently producing bottom-line losses. The losses would steadily eat away at whatever working capital cushions the business possesses; one fine day the money would inevitably run out.

But short-term, and sometimes for years, a business can be showing a

PAYING FOR GROWTH

There's a hard lesson we all have to learn when we go into business. The lesson is that you live or die on cash flow. Sales are nice. Profits are even nicer. But it's cash flow that determines whether or not you survive.

Where most first-time entrepreneurs trip up is in failing to understand that more sales almost always mean less cash flow—and less cash flow means trouble.

–Norm Brodsky, "Street Smarts," *Inc.*

bottom-line loss yet at the same time growing rapidly and actually piling up more and more cash as it grows. Sounds crazy–*losing money yet producing cash*–but it can happen.

These are "positive cash flow" businesses. Typically, their sales are made for cash payment (or better yet, paid in advance . . . ever notice how magazines are always pressing you to renew your subscriptions many months before the expiry date?) but their biggest expenses are only paid months after their sales are made. In that kind of business, your accounting might be showing that your expenses are too high and you are losing money on each sale, but *as long as you keep growing fast,* more cash will be coming in than going out. Not a game for the faint of heart . . . just try standing still for a second or, God forbid, suffer a drop in sales. The cash tide would instantly swing against you; you would be swamped with outstanding bills and have no cash with which to pay them.

We'd all love to own a positive cash flow business.

But a profitable one.

However, it's the destiny of many small businesses to be "negative cash flow" businesses, where the process is reversed . . . they're possibly making a decent profit but have a negative cash flow profile and thus need additional investment (or loan) funds to bankroll their higher working capital needs. This can happen because most small businesses are unable to get tough with their customers; they grant them overly generous payment terms, or tolerate late payment, or both. But their suppliers are often big companies that require them to pay cash or allow them only very short payment terms.

You'll find examples of healthy small businesses, growing and making decent profits but, mathematically, the more they grow the more working capital they require, because they have a negative cash flow profile. Someone, whether the owners or a bank, will have to finance that extra working capital temporarily, until enough real profit has rolled in to pay off the extra financing.

The best of all economic worlds, of course, is to own a business that is both profitable *and* produces a positive cash flow. If your small business is one of those gems, love it and never leave it.

Cash Flow Profile Determines Working Capital Needs

You have to be aware that your small business's needs for more or less working capital funds, when it first starts up and later as it grows, will be decided by its cash flow profile. Depending on that profile, your small business may require a lot of working capital or only modest amounts or–best of all worlds–have negative working capital, meaning basically that you are using your suppliers' credit as if it were a permanent, interest-free bank loan; a great game, but only for those who know how to play it well. Too risky for those who don't.

Therefore, understanding the basic characteristics of the business's cash flow profile is essential for any owner-operator. It's equally as important as understanding your P&L profile. It's not that complicated, once you've done your homework.

This cash flow "self-knowledge" will allow you to estimate: (1) how much working capital your business is going to need when it starts up, and (2) how much *extra* working capital it will need (or not) as it grows. It's that second part that often trips up newcomers to small business. The new entrepreneur may start off with a comfortable cushion of initial working capital, but may not realize that, unlike the other fixed asset investments in the business, working capital is a fluid "moving target." It may increase or decrease, at faster or slower rates, as the business evolves and grows, depending entirely on its cash flow profile.

There are many different ways that cash can flow into and out of any particular business. Those individual characteristics are what make up its cash flow profile. This profile can vary widely, depending on the type of business, the nature of the trade and other individual quirks and peculiarities.

It is of critical importance to know, *before you start,* what the working capital needs of your particular business will *probably* be, in its first months of existence, and have the necessary funds available to finance it. "Probably" is the best you're going to do; you can't aim for perfection. Working capital needs are always much harder to estimate than fixed asset investments. Fixed asset investments are what they are, at least if you did your homework right. Working capital needs are a direct reflection of your cash flow profile . . . and your cash flow profile is a direct consequence of your sales performance and supplier relationships . . . none of which you can forecast with any great precision, especially when you are new to the business.

Intelligent guesswork (plus reasonable margins for errors and the unexpected) is the best you will be able to do. Don't try for perfect estimates; it's an uncertain world. When estimating working capital needs, nothing *ever* works out exactly the way you project it. Your final working capital needs will end up being determined by many different

SMALL BUSINESS OWNERS FIND NEW WORRIES
Concerns Despite Overall Optimism
   Cash flow remains a top concern. . . . While cash was previously in short supply because of flagging sales, it now is scarce because of rising needs to fund increases in receivables and inventory.
                   —Michael Selz, *The Wall Street Journal*

factors, like how much credit (if any) you can get from suppliers, how much credit (if any) you need to grant your customers, how much inventory of raw materials and merchandise you will need to carry, and so on. And remember: what you're told when you are doing your research may turn out to work quite differently in practice.

It's a moving target and an uncertain world.

Allow a wide margin for errors and miscalculations.

Examples, to Hammer the Point Home

Many businesspeople struggle to understand the interplay of working capital versus cash flow versus profit/loss within their new (or even old) businesses. Not that it's especially complex. It isn't; basically, it's simple money arithmetic. But, to impatient, action-oriented entrepreneurs, who just want to get off and running with their show and start doing their business stuff, it's a nebulous, mushy, conceptual, hard-to-nail-down way of looking at how money flows around and into and within and out of a business.

Yes, it can be irritating, boring work. Sometimes nothing is what it seems. None of it's clear and obvious at first glance (unlike sales figures, payroll checks, rent payments, etc.). By definition, entrepreneurial types are exactly the ones who have the least tolerance for the kind of slow, analytical, investigative thinking that is required to get their hands around this subject.

It's bean-counter stuff.

But it's killer bean-counter stuff.

It's why far too many entrepreneurs bomb out. I'm here to tell you about *all* the key survival priorities in small business start-ups . . . even the ones you may not want to hear about. Sorry, folks, but this is one of them. A big one. All too often, when businesses fail, it's only because of something that went wrong with working capital or cash flow, primarily because the owner-operator just didn't want to know about it.

And don't think you can run away, by delegating this to your accountant. Yes, you can certainly ask your accountant to help with the calculations. But that's the easy part. The hard part is: *What does this all mean? Now? Three months from now? What can I do about it?* And so on. So I have invented two extreme hypothetical examples, as a way to illustrate what we have been discussing so far in this chapter. They will give you a better feel for the end result of all this stuff. These are not real-life examples; they're deliberately simplified and exaggerated, just to show the differences.

Let's play for a moment with two imaginary start-up businesses: the

ABC Gadgets Factory and the XYZ Novelties Store. Both have been in business for two years, successfully, and both have annual sales of about $1 million. Very similar, right? Not when you look at their cash flow profiles and working capital needs, they're not.

ABC, a small manufacturing business, imports its electronic components from China, has to pay for them months in advance of delivery and has to hold large inventories in the factory, because the deliveries are so unpredictable. Its gadgets are new to the consumer market, so when it finally gets to sell them, it has to give its retail customers overly generous credit terms.

XYZ, a small retailing business, spends big money on heavy local TV advertising, offers aggressive discount pricing and its store is always packed with customers, buying novelties. Stocks of merchandise are always low because its suppliers ship goods within two days. Customers all pay cash, but the business pays its advertising bills and its main suppliers on ninety-day terms and stretches payment even longer, by mailing checks late. Suppliers don't like it, but they tolerate the extended payment terms and payment abuses because purchase volumes are high and XYZ is a good customer.

Very simplistically, their main working capital accounts might look something like this, if compared side by side:

	ABC Gadgets	*XYZ Novelties*
Cash in Banks	$20,000	$120,000
Receivables (from customers)	$100,000	Zero
Payables (to suppliers)	Zero	($370,000)
Prepayments (imports)	$40,000	Zero
Stocks (parts)	$20,000	Zero
Stocks (finished goods)	$20,000	$50,000
Total Working Capital:	$200,000	($200,000)

So ABC, the manufacturing business, in addition to its high initial fixed assets investment for its factory, manufacturing equipment and other start-up costs, *must also budget for at least an additional $200,000 in working capital.* Whereas XYZ, the retailing business, *has negative working capital of about $200,000,* represented by other companies' money, pumped into and permanently held within the business. If it only required a fixed investment of, say, $200,000 to set up another store and if they got up and open very fast, XYZ might find it could actually get another store opened, with *zero* total investment; the negative working capital would finance its fixed assets needs!

ABC and XYZ are exaggerated, simplistic illustrations, of course, but they're here just to show how widely the working capital needs can vary, *only because of major differences in the cash flow patterns*. The working capital needs and cash flow patterns are totally different between the two similar sized businesses. So this has dramatically different consequences on the amount of start-up capital needed by each business.

Continuing the illustration: how might they compare, profit-wise?

ABC, the manufacturing business, may make excellent profits and have a net profit margin of, say, 10 percent on sales (that is, $100,000 per year), but it will always be scrambling to find cash to pay its bills, because of its heavy working capital needs. XYZ, the retailing business, discounts its sales prices aggressively and may end up with, say, only a 1 percent margin (that is, $10,000 per year) . . . but it will have a large and comfortable cash balance in the bank. You may even see the owner happily driving around in the latest model Porsche, kindly financed in effect by the business's suppliers.

So who's better off? The owner-operators of ABC or XYZ?

Who can say? That all depends on what the owners want out of their businesses (and lives), how much risk they can live with, where they think they are headed and how they manage their finances and growth. ABC, the manufacturer, may grow steadily, gain the muscle to improve trade credit and reduce customer credit, thus becoming *both* highly profitable *and* loaded with cash. XYZ, the retailer, may push its power tactics too far, suddenly lose important trade credit terms from an exasperated major supplier and come crashing down in flames overnight.

The key point to these illustrations is this: working capital funds and cash flow patterns are both of critical importance, in planning the total investment needs of a new business, both at the start and as it grows. This can be neglected or badly miscalculated when making the initial estimates of investment requirements, because no one knows quite how things are going to pan out, until the business actually gets started. There could be too much of a "wait and see" attitude, which might lead to a major financial crunch, at a time when the business does not yet have the necessary financing to save itself.

And another one might bite the dust. Needlessly.

Changing Patterns, Changing Cash Flow

Once a business is established and stabilized, with its financial characteristics having settled into fairly routine "patterns," the working capital needed by the business to sustain itself and keep growing *will depend on the nature of those patterns.* All too often, start-up entrepreneurs have their attention so heavily concentrated on day-to-day operations that they do not take time out to step back, refocus and take a fresh look at those patterns, now that they have become clear and predictable, and make up-to-date calculations of what is really happening, and what will probably happen in the near future, to their business's cash flow.

The patterns to look for are such things as: What credit terms have they *actually* been able to squeeze out of their suppliers? What terms did they *originally* project? Are they substantially different? What credit terms have they *actually* had to give their new customers? Are they better or worse than their *original* projections? How much inventory are they *actually* having to carry? Is that radically different from their first estimates? By how much? And so on.

One thing you can always count on: What is *actually* happening will *never* be precisely what you first estimated would happen. Estimates are only estimates. Often they are only guesses or wishful thinking; they are never 100 percent accurate. By going through this refocusing process, with reliable, up-to-date input, you can now make sound cash flow projections for the foreseeable future . . . say, the next three to six months.

You do this for one reason only: to avoid getting jumped unexpectedly by a cash crunch, just because your original underlying assumptions about cash flow are no longer valid.

Cash crunches are bad for your business health.

Preventing Financial Crises

If your new cash flow projections are encouraging and you can see that you are not going to need extra funds or, better yet, will have extra cash flowing in, well and good. Congratulations. You did your homework, you know that you're going to be comfortable on the cash front, so you can now concentrate your management attention on other priorities, without constantly looking over your shoulder to check if the cash crunch monster is sneaking up on you.

But if things don't look good . . .

If the projections seem to be forecasting bad news and you can see a cash crunch about to clobber your small business, *there's still time to do something about it.* Reduce inventories quickly, cut orders to suppliers, negotiate onetime credit extensions with suppliers, crack down on overdue clients, increase your personal credit card limits, whatever. Even get lucky with an enlightened banker. Preventive action is always possible, if you have advance warning and you can see the noose before it starts tightening around your neck.

About the worst thing that can happen to any business is suddenly to find itself in a full-blown financial crisis. That's one of the most shattering events that can happen to a small business. The owner-operators hit the panic buttons, the panic spreads to employees, suppliers detect something bad is happening, they start holding back on deliveries, routine operations start screwing up, service to customers declines, sales start dropping . . . all this in a downward spiral of panic, sucking everything with it.

It's like wildfire. It can consume and destroy a good business, lacking adequate financial support, in a matter of days or weeks. It happens over and over. And the sad thing is that, with a few weeks of advance warning, simple, sensible countermeasures might have been taken, quietly and calmly, and the crisis averted . . . and no one outside the business need be any the wiser.

So, please, take my heartfelt advice. Make damn sure an indispensable part of your Management Information System (coming up shortly) is a *cash flow projection,* for at least three months ahead. Using your PC, it's a simple process to input new data and make new calculations on a spreadsheet program. It'll take you some time and effort to "construct" your first model spreadsheet, but from then on, it'll be easy to keep adjusting it when necessary.

This may not only save your ass one fine day but it will also certainly help you sleep better at night.

In short: there are no acceptable excuses for not making regular cash flow projections, once you can see the basic financial patterns of your business.

Speeding Cash Flow

Squeeze, squeeze and squeeze again. That's the cash flow message for the '90s. Small businesses let the "small" get to them, and often develop inferiority complexes. They hang their heads in shame and humbly take whatever is handed out to them.

You'll be surprised what a little self-confident, aggressive, in-your-face attitude can do to improve your cash flow.

- **Payment Terms to Customers:**
  Never be afraid to ask for tough payment terms; it often works and even if it doesn't, you've established a good base position for bargaining. Whenever possible, request deposits or partial advances against future orders or service contracts. If not, always try to get cash payment on delivery. If not, try to get some advance, any advance,

against delivery. If your terms are sixty days, shorten them to thirty days; if they're thirty, go to fifteen. Never offer credit to new clients; wait for the customer to ask. Play each customer for what you can get . . . you don't need to be consistent or even "fair." Even be prepared to lose a few sales, if overall you can improve your cash flow; there may be some slow-paying customers you'll be well rid of.

- **Getting Paid on Time:**
  The bigger the customer, the more muscle they have to pay you when they please. It has become standard practice these days for many large companies to pay their bills when it suits them, regardless of the terms on the invoice. The best advice is: Don't give in. Persistence pays. Be as insistent and tenacious as possible, even at risk of losing the customer. You may not get paid on time, but you will certainly be paid well ahead of the other vendors who don't have the guts to make noise.

- **Payment Terms from Suppliers:**
  If you're timid, suppliers will be more than willing to leave you with the

---

WHEN A CHECK *ISN'T* IN THE MAIL

And you thought all you needed to be your own boss were clients. Once you've lured the job orders, what could be so difficult?

Try collecting overdue payments.

It's a widespread problem for small service firms. So listen up, all you downsized corporate executives starting practices as management consultants, marketing specialists and systems experts.

You can attract many clients with bargain rates and boutique expertise. With low overhead, you can make a good living.

That is, of course, if an unexpected interruption in cash flow doesn't sink your firm. . . .

Just a couple of changes in the wording of an agreement could make all the difference. . . . Don't write it in a way for the client to be happy, which is a very common mistake. When you really want business, there is a tendency to be as flexible or congenial as possible. . . .

Any contract should include what both parties expect to achieve. *Getting paid on time is another part of the bargain. SPELL OUT THE TERMS.*

Persistence Pays

Suggested four steps:
- **The "nudge,"** or notification. Maybe they simply forgot to pay and need a polite reminder.
- **The discussion.** By now, they know payment is overdue. Find out what the problem is. Focus on working something out.
- **The push,** or firm demand. After 45 to 90 days, it's time for a different approach—or time to let someone else try.
- **The squeeze.** Other alternatives exhausted, you turn to a collection agency, lawyer or small claims court. Remember, laws protect debtors from harassing and deceptive practices.

—Susana Barciela, *The Miami Herald*

same miserable restricted terms they gave you when you first started buying and had no credit history with them, even though by now you may have established an excellent payment record and your volume of purchases has doubled or tripled. They'll never offer to improve terms; you have to put on the pressure. Get politely aggressive, get gently pushy. Ask for another thirty days and settle for fifteen. Ask to pay your bills monthly instead of weekly. Any extra time you get to pay, however small, is extra money into your cash flow.

- **Making Payments:**
  Automatic electronic bank transfers may be the modern way to do things, but they can also be the dumb way to do things, if you are squeezed for cash. The bank will always execute your orders on time. You lose your flexibility to play for a little extra time, when a bad month comes along. Often, without hurting your payment record in any way, you can pay by mailed check and gain a few extra days, before they hit your bank account. So what if it's a little extra work?

- **Paying Late:**
  By carefully reading supplier invoices and statements, or asking innocent questions by phone to their accounts payable department, you will discover what their "tolerance level" is. You may find that small delays of five or ten days are not even recorded on customer files. This information can be invaluable, when you need a little leeway.

- **Speeding Up Bank Deposits:**
  Businesses will sometimes leave cash receipts in the register or the safe for a few days, until someone gets around to going by the bank. Incoming checks can often sit for days on someone's desk until they are processed and deposited. Credit card transactions can also be delayed in processing. You should have zero tolerance for such laziness . . . especially if it's your own.

- **Reducing Inventories:**
  If you are ordering monthly when you could be ordering weekly, you are probably carrying too much inventory, on average. Sales representatives, even the good ones, will always try to increase the order size. Squeeze back. Order little and often is usually the best policy for a small business. Again, so what if it's a little extra work, placing four orders a month instead of one?

SMALL-BUSINESS OWNERS RELY ON SUPPLIER CREDIT

Credit from suppliers is the most popular source of financing for small-business owners, a Dun & Bradstreet survey indicated.

[The survey] found that 65% depend on credit from suppliers, while 40% use credit cards and 35% rely on commercial bank loans for funding.

Among women business owners, 50% said they use personal credit cards to help finance their business, compared with 36% of male business owners.

—*The Wall Street Journal*

These are just a few of the more standard ploys. You'll often find others, if you look for the pressure points in your own cash flow profile. All these little squeezes can add up, mathematically. If your small business is selling, say, $20,000 per month and the sum total of your squeezes ends up representing the equivalent of fifteen days of sales, *that's $10,000 in real money you just injected into your cash flow.*

Such an amount could make the difference between survival or failure in a small business, especially if there's no friendly banker to come to the rescue.

First Understand It, Then Control It

Now, that wasn't *too* painful, was it?

You've just finished examining the one area that brings the most grief to business owners: understanding the differences and connections between *profit and loss, working capital* and *cash flow,* and learning what can be done to protect the business's liquidity.

In the following chapter, we'll be talking about how to control this and other key areas, through the use of your own internal Management Information System.

But you can't get to work on controlling and managing your working capital and cash flow if you don't first understand the process. And too many entrepreneurs just don't get it, because they are more interested in the purely business activities—often to their regret, when their businesses collapse strictly because of liquidity problems that might have been avoided.

Feel free to read the chapter over again, just to be sure you've gotten it. There's no charge.

RAIDING A COMPANY'S HIDDEN CASH
Mining an Overlooked Trove: Working Capital

Talk about stretch targets: Could any corporation operate without working capital? The answer may surprise you. A fast-growing number of companies are setting that audacious goal.

But c'mon–zero working capital? It isn't a fantasy. . . . Two diversified manufacturers boast negative working capital in some of their businesses. . . .

"Working capital is the grease that keeps the [business] motor running," says [a consultant]. It consists of inventories–raw materials, work-in-process, and finished goods–as well as a company's receivables [what other companies owe it] minus its payables [what it owes other companies]. . . .

Reducing working capital yields two powerful benefits. First, every dollar freed from inventories or receivables rings up a one-time $1 contribution to cash flow. Second, the quest for zero working capital permanently raises earnings. Like all capital, working capital costs money, so reducing it yields savings. . . . It increases profits over the years, by lowering overtime, storage costs and other expenses–savings that persist year after year. . . .

The most important discipline that zero working capital necessitates is speed. . . . It requires that every order and part move at maximum pace, never stopping. . . . As velocity rises, inventory–working capital–dwindles. . . .

–Shawn Tully, *Fortune*

DID BARNEYS OVEREXTEND ITSELF?
Late Payments to Suppliers

[When] Barneys opened the largest new store in New York City since the Depression . . . [there were] a stream of reports of late payments to suppliers. Rarely does the chorus of complaints . . . get as loud as it did in the case of Barneys.

Some small designers say late payments last year almost put them out of business, leaving them short of cash to buy fabric and other material, needed to prepare their [next season's] lines. . . .

Many designers, especially smaller ones, are so eager to have coveted floor space in the most fashionable stores that they put up with slow payments. How slow is slow? With terms of net 30 [the full amount owed within 30 days of shipping], designers expect most stores to pay 30 days later than that, or 60 days after shipping. While 60 days is late, it's considered to be a standard lag.

Yet . . . the problems some designers encountered trying to extract payment from Barneys were extraordinary. Payments stretched to six months late for many designers. Soon after the new store opened, payments seemed to stop completely for some small vendors. Even worse, suppliers seeking information about delinquent payments say they left dozens of messages that went unanswered or couldn't get through because answering machines were full.

A pottery designer conducted a sit-in at the Barneys office when no one would take his calls. "I ended up being owed a quarter of my yearly income," he said. "It finally got to be well beyond the emergency stage. I had been living off loans from friends and family for three months or so." Armed with a duffel bag filled with sandwiches, reading materials and compact discs, he parked himself in the lobby and called the Chief Executive's secretary and told her, "I've come prepared. I'm here for the long haul."

A few minutes later, his check appeared.

–Amy Spindler and Stephanie Strom, *The New York Times*

11

GOTTA HAVE INFORMATION:

*Flying Blind
Causes Crashes*

Instrument Panel Not Included

Good. So you've bought the exhortations on "business basics." That you cannot and must not risk overlooking key bits and pieces of information, which will tell you about the state of your business's health in time to do something quick and constructive about both problems and opportunities. You aim to be one of the survivors. You want to set up the business and manage it tightly and efficiently. You intend to keep your owner's eye closely focused on its vital signs–sales, costs, profits, working capital, cash flow, stocks, etc.

You've decided you're not going to run your business by the seat of your pants. Bravo!

As you know, seat-of-the-pants management is a major cause of entrepreneurs losing their shirts . . . and often their pants as well.

Having made these important resolutions, you now spin around and ungraciously confront the author: "So fine. You've convinced me. I'm now the pilot of my own small business plane. Just explain one thing: Who in hell is going to provide me with this kind of internal information about my business, every week and every month, so that I can see what I'm doing and where I'm going? Where's my business instrument panel? This plane came stripped."

Good question. So now the time has come to discuss your MIS: your Management Information System.

SMALL BUSINESS OWNERS FIND NEW WORRIES
Concerns Despite Overall Optimism

Failing to manage costs can be lethal in good times as well as bad, says Nancy Pechloff, director of Arthur Andersen's Enterprise Group. "It's so easy in a flurry of expansion activity to lose control of expenses, especially for owners who are used to managing by the seat of their pants."

–Michael Selz, *The Wall Street Journal*

Digging for Management Information

Too often, entrepreneurs have a weakness for winging it, for managing by the seat of their pants, for flying blind . . . instead of paying regular, disciplined attention to what the "performance numbers" are signaling about the state of their business's health. They don't look for "feedback" information that will give them a clear picture of what's beginning to go right and what's beginning to go wrong. Particularly what's going wrong.

Some are simply undisciplined or lazy, and just can't be bothered with the detail work. In which case, they deserve to suffer the consequences. You can't give yourself such personal indulgences when you're runnning your own business. You must do the grunt work as well as the fun stuff.

However, most often it's not willful negligence. It's not because they don't *want* to check the vital signs. It's because they simply can't *find* them. The management information they need to study is not conveniently available right there on their desks (or computer screens) at the right moment, on the right day of the month, in an easy-to-read form and in a language they can understand without being a trained accountant or qualified financial analyst . . . which very few entrepreneurs are.

It's a serious matter, which they have little experience in dealing with.

The root of the problem is that all important information about a business's financial state and operational condition has to be "condensed" from the large amounts of minor details, pieces of paper and individual computer entries buried in the business's bookkeeping, filing and accounting systems. Only after these many small details have been reassembled into "big numbers" that tell you something important–like a pilot's instrument panel, showing air speed, fuel levels, course setting, cargo weight, weather conditions, etc.–do you end up with what is normally labeled "management information."

Management information doesn't grow on trees. It doesn't happen naturally, as a part of your normal business activity. It requires a conscious, calculated, creative effort by the owner-manager to generate the information and turn it into a routine system.

Here's what normally happens:

Daily business operations involve tens, hundreds or even thousands of individual "transactions" and their related pieces of paper (or computer entries): sales invoices, daily cash register tapes, bank deposit slips, check stubs, purchase orders, suppliers' invoices, records of incoming merchandise, job completion slips, accounts payable, shipping records, outgoing orders, accounts receivable, stock control cards, employee time cards, payroll calculations, payroll checks, payroll tax calculations and so on.

Even in a small business, altogether that's a fair pile of paper.

This flow of individual daily "transactions" has to be organized by some systematic office routine, or it will quickly degenerate into a chaotic, disorganized mess, endangering the entire business. So filing systems, recordkeeping systems, office managers and accountants do their best to organize and control this flow so that those individual transactions all follow their *natural, traditional path.* Which is into the *bookkeeping and accounting systems,* where every item gets separated into different categories of the business's "chart of accounts." The chart of accounts organizes the transactions into their individual pigeonholes, for preparing the final accounting documents and statements.

Bingo.

So all the key, critical, essential bits and pieces of financial and operational information, which could and should be telling *you* exactly what *you* need to know to pilot *your* business, just got themselves nicely organized and slotted away, for the convenience of the accounting system and of the IRS.

Not for your convenience ... you, the owner-manager, the businessperson with the management monkey on your back and the daily decisions to make.

You might compare this to a hospital where monitoring devices have all the necessary information on the patient's temperature, blood pressure, heart rate and other key vital signs, yet the surgeon can't find this information on a computer screen or printout when he's about to perform heart surgery.

Your Accounting System . . . Learn to Love It

Accounting is a pain in the butt . . . but an *essential* pain in the butt.

Therefore, you must train yourself to love and respect your own accounting system (though not necessarily your accountant). You can't (or shouldn't) operate a business, however small, without one. Even if it's only a $49.99 software package on your PC.

Never expect your accounting system to give you all the management information you need. It won't. It can't.

There's no way a standard, basic accounting system and its different component parts will be able to tell you, as the company's owner-operator and key decision maker, everything you need to know, when you need to know it and how you need to know it, in a quick, easy-to-understand manner.

That's not its purpose.

Accounting systems (and their connected bookkeeping and filing systems) are essential: (1) as a basic, efficient, foolproof mechanism for keeping each and all of those individual daily transactions well organized and under control, preventing them from degenerating into chaos; (2) as a "common financial language" accepted by the IRS, bank loan managers, shareholders, financial analysts, auditors and other assorted bean counters, to demonstrate the basic economic picture of your business; (3) as one key source, from which you will ultimately extract some (but not all) of the key management information you so badly need, and thus help construct your own MIS.

So you have to have a good, basic, reliable acounting system, whether you like it or not.

However, detailed accounting is not a language most small businesspeople have the patience to learn and understand. Their attention is focused on the dynamics of managing the business. Rightly so. It's an advantage if you do understand accounting, but it certainly isn't essential. Managing your business profitably is essential.

So the building blocks for your MIS are buried in the guts of your accounting system (and other recordkeeping and filing areas) and are available mainly in "accounting language." They're there, all right. They're just not organized, summarized, analyzed and logically presented the way busy managers would like to see them.

To build yourself an efficient control panel for piloting your small business plane, the informational gold nuggets that you want displayed on the panel first have to be mined out of the accounting and bookkeeping systems, brought to the surface, processed, cleaned up, filtered, condensed, polished and attractively presented.

Only then will you have your MIS.

Controllers: A Big Business Luxury

So how is all this handled in Big Business?

Large corporations have a smart, well-qualified, highly paid executive, with the title of Controller, who is a kind of enlightened chief bean counter and multilingual corporate housekeeper, who speaks three languages: accounting language, financial language and management language.

The controller understands the fundamental need for both an efficient, traditional accounting and financial controls system, *and* the rapid-fire, key information "feedback" needed by corporate managers to guide their important decisions on the business battlefield. The controller manages the entire "flow" of financial and operational information within the corporation, so that one part of it continues to follow its traditional route to its designated accounting and financial destinations. But another part of it gets *converted, analyzed, simplified and compacted,* then communicated to key managers daily, weekly and monthly, in the form of reports, memos and information sheets . . . all these, together, making up the corporation's MIS.

And how is all this solved in small business then?

Therein lies the problem. Your problem. A serious problem.

The problem is that it usually isn't solved. It's neglected.

Which is why too many small businesses fly blind and crash, needlessly, simply because their owners could not read the vital signs at the vital moment. Small businesses rarely, if ever, can afford to hire qualified controllers. Even their accounting is usually performed by external services, offering standardized packages.

But instead of finding an alternative way of handling the controller's function, they do nothing.

Doubling as Your Own Controller

The solution? You guessed it. More work. For you.

You, the long-suffering, overworked, stressed-out small business owner-manager, will have to double as your own controller.

Relax, it's not that bad. This really is not as hard or as time-consuming as you might fear. It's certainly not complicated. It does not mean you have to become an administrative genius. Like so many of the priorities discussed in this book, it's more a matter of convincing yourself of the vital importance of certain MIS tasks, of assuming responsibility for them and of ensuring, somehow or other, that they get taken care of. You may actually end up doing little or none of the work yourself, but you are the only person in the business to feel in the gut the critical importance of your MIS. Because an MIS exists for the use of top management, and in a small business the owner is the one and only top manager . . . *thus you have to be the one to make it happen.*

So how do you double as your own controller?

You study and think about and become familiar with your business's profit profile, cash flow profile and operational profile. You decide what key pieces of information must be essential components of your internal MIS. You determine if you need them weekly, monthly or yearly. You set deadlines for the different pieces of information to be produced. *And you make damn sure that someone produces them . . . even if that someone is yourself.*

None of this has to be sophisticated. Your MIS does not have to be polished or impeccably produced. At the beginning, it can be a couple of pages of handwritten notes on a paper spreadsheet, if need be. It's only for your use, not for external viewing. It just has to get done, regularly and methodically. When things go wrong with management information, nine times out of ten it isn't because something was done wrong . . . it was because nothing was done.

Owners of small businesses are invariably busy with pressing day-to-day problems and management responsibilities. They can always come up with good excuses to delay or overlook MIS work . . . *it can wait until tomorrow.* Unless you set your own priorities and establish your own deadlines, it just won't happen. It's just too easy to keep postponing.

By making this your personal responsibility and making it happen, you'll be creating a makeshift but workable instrument panel for your small business plane. You'll be assembling it yourself in your workshop and you'll be using it to guide your business through safe takeoffs, flights and landings. As you grow, you'll keep tinkering with it, making improvements, adding new pieces of information here, discarding outdated sections there.

So you just got promoted to controller of your small business.

Congratulations. It's an offer you can't refuse.

Thinking It Out, Setting It Up

There are technical books, seminar operators, software experts, systems analysts and business consultants, all anxious to offer you (for a fee) a bewildering selection of alternative methods for organizing your MIS (Management Information System), MIPAC (Management Information Planning and Control System), MAS (Management Accounting System) and other esoteric acronyms.

Some are excellent, some are good, some are less than good, but all of them essentially do more or less the same thing.

They organize the bits and pieces of scattered information already somewhere in your system (sales statistics, bank transactions, purchases, payments, payroll, production, etc.); they generate some that may not already exist; they reassemble, summarize, analyze and simplify them in different ways; they compare them against previous periods and against your own plans; and they then "publish" them internally, in the form of regular (weekly or monthly) information reports, which highlight the key information the business's managers should be looking at and thinking about.

But most small businesses cannot and should not pay for such specialized outside help.

First, simply because of the cost . . . it's usually far too expensive. There are cheaper ways of getting better results.

Second, because the sophisticated systems these folks offer are usually massive overkill, in the first years of a small business's life. These are the survival years. You need to focus your attention on only a small number of vital pieces of information and will only be distracted by other superfluous stuff.

Third, precisely because your information needs are so basic, you can do it yourself.

So, unless you have money to burn, you will have to do this yourself, probably with some help from your outside bookkeeper or accountant. What it mainly requires on your part is hard thinking about the three main facets of your MIS:

- Operations: Sales, production, purchases, stocks, etc.
- P&L: Income, costs, expenses, profit margins, etc.
- Cash Flow: Payments made, payments received, cash in bank, etc.

Businesses vary greatly. The more tailor-made your MIS, the more useful it will be to you. So you must think through everything your business does (or plans to do) and determine the key "building blocks" of your MIS. When you've finished this process, you will have assembled a rudimentary but workable shopping list of your key information needs. If yours is a small, home-based business, this shopping list will be very short and sweet; you're going to pull together the basic information yourself, maybe with a little help from your bookkeeper and the use of one of the "office suite" PC software packages. If your business is larger, you'll probably be working with your office manager or outside accountant, to decide who does what and how these information reports will be prepared, on a routine basis.

None of this will happen if you don't make it happen.

When you've finished and your final MIS package becomes a reality, you might paste a big warning label on the file folder: *"This MIS Contains Vital Business Information–Ignore It at Your Own Peril."*

If It's All So Great, Why Isn't Everyone Doing It?

Now it's your turn to question: "If good management information is so important to one's business health, why doesn't everyone have it and use it?"

Good point. And you're right . . . quite a few don't.

How many smart, well-informed people do you know who eat high-calorie fatty foods, are overweight, don't exercise, smoke cigarettes, drink too much, are TV couch potatoes and have an endless assortment of other lousy personal habits . . . in spite of knowing that this will probably end up killing them long before their due date?

Same thing.

Or did you think that laziness and bad habits exist only in people's personal lives, never in their business lives?

Just because good business habits and essential management disciplines are important for your business, maybe even key to its survival, doesn't mean you're gonna do what you oughta do. That's the reason I keep throwing the "death threat" at you, just to focus your attention. Don't those diet/health/exercise books constantly remind you you're headed for a massive coronary attack?

But, let's face it, the good, healthy stuff we're talking about–information, control, profit profiles, cash flows, reports and so on–can be pretty damn boring. Routine administrative stuff, rather than managerial fireworks. Like working out on the StairMaster or taking a five-mile run.

The work involved in thinking this stuff out and making sure everything is properly done in organizing your business's MIS can be pretty dreary at times. There's no way to make it sexy stuff. It just ain't. None of it compares to the adrenaline rush of goosing up sales, of closing profitable deals, of being a business hotshot.

So let's tell you a little secret about business hotshots and gunslingers.

The successful ones either do this dreary stuff themselves but never talk about it (it's bad for their hotshot image) . . . or they have already become successful and can now give themselves the luxury of employing their very own tame, well-paid controller to do all the grunt work. Either way the necessary MIS work is actually getting done, and well done . . . you just don't hear about it.

Do you think Donald Trump, Ted Turner and Sumner Redstone all run around casually cutting those fantastic deals, based just on entrepreneurial flair

MEASURE IT TO MANAGE IT

Employees of C.R. England, a long-haul refrigerated truck company in Salt Lake City, have had to adapt to a world that's anything but loose. Strict centralized control is maintained by a computerized system that monitors roughly 500 procedures a week, everything from arrival times, to billing accuracy, to how well a trucker feels he is treated by the company's repair shop.

Says the VP for technology: "We want to run this place like the cockpit of a jetliner, where you have hundreds of different instruments before you at all times and know exactly where you are. . . . I don't think anyone likes to be this closely monitored. But most people start using the information as a learning tool."

Says [a consultant]: "I don't see anyone within leagues of where they are. C.R. England captures information on everything and recycles it back through the engine to improve performance."

—*Fortune*

and business instinct? No way. They have private armies of bean counters and rocket scientists, locked in their basements, shackled to their PCs, crunching numbers, and constantly feeding them all the key information they need for making those snappy business decisions.

The hotshots who try to shortcut this process may look like hotshots for a few months, but they usually end up broke.

The single most important characteristic that separates the successes from the failures in small business is *self-discipline* . . . the self-discipline of the entrepreneur. You need self-discipline to plan, set up and maintain your MIS–and to overcome the occasional attacks of boredom.

The math required for MIS work is basic high school stuff, and your spelling and grammar can be as bad as you wish; it's only the numbers that matter. But your brain has to be in good working order and you have to possess the personal drive and motivation to put that brain to work, on thinking through your MIS priorities.

In the end, if you take all this seriously, set up your own MIS and maintain it properly, you'll find it becomes an easy routine to follow, like brushing your teeth daily. You'll be flying with a complete, fully functioning instrument panel, with all its gauges working, and your odds of surviving will have improved tenfold. You'll always have an edge over less well-armed and well-informed competitors.

The Language of Hard Numbers

Your MIS tells you what's going on in your business *in numbers*– dollars, cases, units, tons, pounds, percentages, ratios, hours, people, whatever. This forces everyone in your business, starting with yourself, to adopt a mental

---

BARING THE BOOKS

At the end of its first fiscal year in 1984, SRC had lost $61,000 on sales of $16 million.

"I felt the only way to turn things around was to get people to think like owners," says Jack Stack, 46 [the CEO]. "I needed to teach anyone who moved a broom or operated a grinder everything the bank lender knew. That way they could more really understand how every nickel saved could make a difference."

"At first it wasn't easy for everyone to understand the numbers," concedes [a machinist]. "But we've been over and over and over the different figures enough times that now, if you hand any one of us an income statement and leave out a few numbers, we can fill them in."

Each week the company shuts down the machines for half an hour while its employees break into small groups to study the latest financial statements. The workers have more than a passing curiosity in the numbers: Last year SRC distributed $1.4 million in bonuses pegged to how each division performed against line items like profit before taxes.

Open-book management has paid off for Stack. . . .

–Fortune

discipline of always thinking out your problems and talking about them *in hard numbers*. Ideally, your MIS should be 95 percent numbers and only 5 percent written notes. The numbers must speak for themselves.

This is especially important to people starting out in small business. Many are used to thinking "qualitatively." That's fine, up to a point, but not when your business's ultimate survival and long-term success depends entirely on the bottom line in your P&L being a positive dollar amount–not a word but a number. If your company's "raison d'être" is a dollar figure (with a plus sign in front of it), then you'd better think numbers and talk numbers.

Numbers are the language of profitability.

The trouble with "business talk" is that everyone interprets words the way that makes them feel most comfortable. "How're sales?" "Oh, they're down a bit," or "Great, just great." Words are easily used to avoid facing up to harsh realities. If your business has a hard time making a small net profit and 5 percent up or down in sales can mean the difference between a bottom line profit or loss, mushy phrases like "down a bit" or "great" can be dangerously misleading.

Doctors don't want to hear from nurses that the patient's "got a little temperature." Traffic cops don't give tickets just for "driving very fast." If your temperature's high, what's that in degrees Fahrenheit? If you were speeding, what's that in m.p.h.? If your sales are down, what's that in dollars and cents, and by what percentage?

Numbers are the language of business.

By planning, setting up and regularly studying your business's MIS reports, you will automatically force upon yourself and upon everyone else in your business the discipline of *thinking numbers and talking numbers*.

"MIS"–It's Only a Label

I've tried to avoid getting you bogged down in MIS detail, to concentrate instead on showing you *why management information is so essential yet too often ignored.* If you've convinced yourself of the need, you'll automatically make sure that the basic MIS mechanisms are set up for your own business, and the details will be taken care of as a natural part of your internal work.

Don't allow yourself to get frightened off by the sophisticated label: *Management Information System.* It can conjure up images of mainframe computers and crazed computer scientists. All it really is, is a handy way of describing a mixed bag of internal administrative duties and routines that, when completed and pulled together in a folder or binder, gives you an invaluable management aid kit, containing all the key informational goodies you should regularly be checking out to keep your business healthy.

The reason to think of and talk of this package as your "MIS" is only so that it acquires a face and an identity of its own. What are you going to call it otherwise . . . That Bunch of Notes in the Manila Folder over There on the Desk? If it has a name and a label, you can't forget it, ignore it or run away from it. If MIS sounds too intimidating, how about Jill's Business Info Kit or Joe's Management Hygiene System. Whatever pleases you.

But, call it what you will, *think MIS–and make it happen.*

12

YOUR PC SHALL
SET YOU FREE:

*Management Weaponry
for Entrepreneurs*

PC Proficiency Is the Price of Admission

There's no kind, gentle, nonjudgmental, uncritical, politically correct way to say this. So let's stick with old-fashioned brutality:

If you don't know how to operate a personal computer (a.k.a. PC) with reasonable proficiency, and you can't or won't learn, for whatever reason, justifiable or not, stay away from small business. Write poetry instead . . . by hand, with a quill pen. You'll be trotting along in your horse and buggy, while your competitors and the world in general will be whipping by you on the business freeway at a mile a minute. The competitors and the world will eat you alive.

You will not survive. Period.

Clear 'nuff? This is *not* about surfing the Internet, logging on to AOL, designing a Web page, having your own Net address, cyberchatting with entrepreneurial geeks, establishing a cybercult, downloading porno pictures, E-mailing Grandma, playing Mortal Kombat, or designing your new patio onscreen. That's all about playtime, spare time. That's your choice.

This is about small business time. Here you don't have a choice.

This is about using your PC daily, naturally and routinely, like you use your phone or fax, as the greatest management weapon ever invented, to help you and your small business beat the odds on surviving and succeeding.

It's that important.

Even if it requires a little time and effort to bring yourself up to speed in handling a PC, it's remarkably easy these days. What's the investment in a little personal time and some brain strain, compared to the risk of losing your entire money investment in your new small business? Just count yourself incredibly lucky that you didn't have to master business computers ten or twenty years ago, when they were *really* complicated. Now it's a snap.

In large companies, it's still possible for some corporate bozos to work in basic ignorance of PCs, although they'll never admit it. They think of themselves as "computer literate" because they know how to turn on the computer terminal in their office, view someone else's information on the monitor, plug some numbers into a ready-made spreadsheet, type a memo into a prepared format and print it out, or send an E-mail message. That's just using the machine as a communications tool and glorified calculator.

In contrast, operating a PC is a dynamic, creative process where you use the machine and its software as a management tool, to construct just about anything your managerial mind can dream up, to help you operate your own business better, faster and safer.

No owner-operator of their own small business can give themselves the luxury of thinking like a corporate bozo, where PCs are concerned. You actually have to know how to *work* the damn thing . . . and enjoy it.

The PC is to small businesses today what the telegraph, telephone, typewriter and electronic calculator were to business when they were first introduced. Except possibly more important.

And it's the perfect tool for Small Business, rather than Big Business.

The Right Tool, at the Right Time

The PC revolution came along at just the right moment for small business owner-operators.

Perfect, felicitous timing.

HIGH-POWERED HOME OFFICE
Retired CEO Launches New Business with Help of a Few Computers and Off-the-Shelf Networking Package

An interview with Jim Burns, 65 . . .

Do you think it is unusual for someone your age to use computers this much?

"I do find many of my peers to be intimidated by computers, even executives. Eventually, though, you realize that if you make a mistake it won't be the end of the world, and the computer is a great tool to help you do the things you need to do."

—Alison L. Sprout, *Fortune*

Today's business world is a jungle: more competition, faster competitive moves, constant change, narrowing profit margins, increasing costs, tightening cash flow and so on.

The consequence is that all owners of small businesses, whatever their size and whatever they do, must stay wide awake, constantly alert to developing problems and quick to take management decisions when needed. The option of finding some cozy, slow, sleepy little business tucked away in some forgotten corner of America doesn't exist anymore. Wal-Mart has infiltrated every Sleepy Hollow there once was and carpet-bombed it into submission.

Like it or not, you're on a business freeway; you don't have the option of driving at slow speeds.

This accelerated business world means that owner-operators of small businesses need good, reliable information, both external and internal, to guide their business decisions and their management actions. They need it right there on their desk, they need it correct, they need it fast and they don't have "gofers" to go fetch for them.

External information is not usually the problem. The communications revolution is zooming along and you can follow developments that concern you and your business in newspapers, television, magazines, newssheets, trade magazines, on-line services and so on. Whatever your type of business, you should be able to keep yourself pretty well informed about news of what's going on in the outside world, which may affect your business activities–markets, competitors, new products, trade developments, economic fluctuations, whatever.

Internal information is usually the big problem. You need faster, more accurate and more complete information, on each and every key facet of your business, than small businesses ever needed only ten or twenty odd years ago. If you had tried to generate this information in those days, you would have been looking at tens of thousands of dollars invested in clunky computer hardware, thousands more in your own software programming and development, plus high payroll costs for qualified data-processing employees, just to keep your internal system up and running. Such investments and expenses would have turned most modern small businesses into economic disasters if you'd tried to operate them in those days with that kind of computer equipment.

So you're very lucky. You're starting up in better times, in a new computer age. At exactly the right moment. The PCs now available in any store or mail order system have turned that costly old equation upside down, in your favor. Today, with a single powerful PC, with

> **MOM AND POP, UNPLUGGED**
> **The Smallest Companies Still Shun Computers**
>
> Despite falling prices and ubiquity, personal computers are used by only a third of the country's so-called mom-and-pop shops, according to [a survey]. And only about 17% of those small concerns have plans to buy PCs.
>
> Of course, not all small outfits are PC laggards. Some 57% of the companies with up to 100 employees use computers. . . .
>
> But mom-and-pop operations–typically retailers and service companies with a dozen or fewer workers–continue to resist technology, complaining of expense, lack of training and plain old-fashionedness.
>
> *–The Wall Street Journal*

off-the-shelf business software, plus a few hours of self-training (provided by the PC and the software itself, in its own tuition software) and no one but yourself to do the work, your total cost will be no more than $2,000, maybe $3,000. And the quality, quantity and speed of the information you will be able to generate for your own use is truly mind-boggling, compared to that prehistoric age.

It's as close to a business miracle as you'll ever see. It's marvelous. It's magnificent. It can bring tears to the eyes of even hard-bitten, cantankerous old bean-counting controllers.

Yet some entrepreneurs, both newcomers and those already in business, simply don't and won't "get it." They don't think any of this is a big deal, they pay minimal attention to this area, and they use their PCs for maybe 10 percent of what they could and should actually be doing with the hardware and software sitting on their desks.

By not "getting it," they miss out on this extraordinary opportunity to protect themselves with this amazing business weapon, and thus to improve their odds of surviving and succeeding in their small business activities.

Why this neglect of something so potentially valuable?

Kids' Stuff No Longer

Problem #1 in not "getting it": underestimating and underutilizing the latest PCs.

There's a younger generation that has grown up using the earlier PCs for assorted schoolwork, college studies and playing computer games. There's an older generation that has watched that younger generation, doing those same things.

Thus, some members of *both these generations* have difficulty in thinking of PCs as anything other than homework word processors and/or game machines.

They have difficulty switching mental gears, when they start operating their own small businesses. They don't "get it" that they now need to look at their business's PC in a whole new light–as one deadly, high-tech, killer business weapon, to be held in the highest regard for its muscle, memory, speed and firepower, and to be used to the limits of its extraordinary capabilities.

It's no longer a toy or a homework tool. It's pure business. If Arnold Schwarzenegger's Terminator ran a small demolition business, this would be his weapon of choice.

It's like having a Ferrari in your garage and only using it to drive to the corner supermarket once a week. It's like having the perfect mine detector but still strolling out in the minefields without it.

It's one helluva machine.

Treat it with respect.

Old-Fashioned Thinking

Problem #2 in not "getting it": sticking with ingrained habits and old-fashioned thinking.

For decades, managers, controllers and accountants dreamed of the ultimate Management Information System–that perfect control panel that would, at the touch of a button, show you everything that you could possibly want to know about the different facets of your business, instantaneously and accurately. But to businesses with limited financial resources, that was so much science fiction, an impossible dream. It would have cost far more to create such a system than the improved information could ever have been worth to the business.

So everyone lowered their sights, their standards and their expectations. They "made do" with information systems that were, at best, merely adequate. And were often very inferior, with chunks of key information missing and others poorly organized. At that time, there was no alternative . . . a so-so MIS was better than no MIS at all.

This was as true in large corporations as in small businesses. *And in many cases, it continues today.* So if you are a recent refugee from the Big Business world, don't take the information systems you have seen in your old job as any standard of perfection. Very often, you can do better by yourself, in your own small business. Bigger is not necessarily better.

Thus, some entrepreneurs, now that they are starting their own small businesses, can still find themselves sticking to those old, unimaginative habits and that restricted thinking, even though they own their own powerful, modern PCs. They could be using their PCs more creatively, to generate information that was never possible before and would be invaluable to them today. Yet they don't. They're at least driving that Ferrari every day, but at 30 m.p.h. instead of 70 m.p.h.

This, by the way, is not a weakness restricted to business owners. You can also find it in your trusty (rusty?) accountant and bookkeeper. They can easily get stuck in those old habits and outdated routines, rather than hassle with new ideas and improvements to the systems they recommend to their clients. Often they could easily help their clients greatly improve their MIS and internal controls, just by taking advantage of the resources offered by the latest generations of PCs. Yet they'd rather not fix what they think ain't broke–what's to change, it's worked fine for the last ten years, hasn't it?

Try kicking them around a little, in a friendly sort of way, to get their attention and start their creative juices flowing again.

That is, really, what we're talking about, isn't it?

Creativity.

The creativity to think through every piece of essential information and every control mechanism that should exist, for you to manage your small business as efficiently as possible, and then to puzzle out how to create the different bits and pieces on your PC.

Who said business has to be dull? Get creative.

PCs for Management or for Production?

PCs can be used in a business for two entirely different purposes: as part of the management process or as part of the production process. Sometimes a single PC can serve both purposes; sometimes you should keep matters entirely separate, on two machines.

THE WAY IT WORKS
With the Right Venture, the Right Equipment and the Right Temperament, Jill Shtulman Is a Home-Business Success Story

Working at home brings out the best in Jill Shtulman.

The 44-year-old copywriter runs her own creative-services agency from her 18th-floor apartment in Chicago. . . . She starts composing at her computer at 8 a.m., when her imagination surges. . . .

She makes out better than most home-business owners. She expects her five-year-old company to take in revenue of $150,000 this year. . . . She says she earned about $76,000 before taxes last year. . . .

The reasons behind her success? Her home business suits her skills, experience and business contacts. . . . She also offers her customers a good price. With no employees and minimal overhead, she charges $1,200 to $1,500 for an average project. That's about half the rate charged by large advertising agencies.

Just as important, she is mastering the challenges of working at home.

She marshals the latest technology to keep her business running smoothly. She owns two personal computers, a laptop for trips, a cordless telephone, a cellular phone, a fax machine, an answering machine and a device for identifying callers. She respects her customers' demands for constant communication. When she's out, she checks her answering machine every hour. . . .

She finds the freedom of working at home so enjoyable that she no longer harbors thoughts of taking commercial space someday.

–Barbara Marsh, *The Wall Street Journal*

In this chapter, there is only one focus: the use of your PC, printer and other accessories, for *managing and controlling your business as efficiently as possible*. Whatever that business does, however small or large, and whatever its products or services.

Here, we are *not* talking about a PC's use for "production"–the tens of thousands of different ways in which you can nowadays use computers to help create your business's actual products or services. That area for application of the PC's capabilities is fascinating, amazing, mind-boggling and bursting at the seams with small business opportunities. Specialized software and hardware now exist for everything and anything imaginable: interior decorating, construction, landscaping, store layouts, real estate listings, architectural design, clothing design, publishing, printing, graphic design, sign making, manufacturing flow systems, warehouse layouts, computer-controlled heavy machinery, automatic telephone and fax dialing, livestock breeding, crop control, hookers' engagements scheduling . . . you name it, it exists.

That is not something that can be covered in this book; you have to do your own detailed research, to discover what is available, for the specific type of business activity you are contemplating. Whatever type of small business you are in or are entering, you should always try to find and use the latest specialized PC software and hardware that probably already exist for your particular type of business activity. This is your other major PC weapon, to give you an essential competitive edge within your field. The offerings are constantly improving and prices keep dropping, as the result of the steady overall advances in PC technology. Small businesses have a major advantage over larger businesses, in their speed of evaluation and flexibility for adoption of new advances. Large companies get "locked in" to using specific hardware and software. For them, it can be too expensive and traumatic to switch to better stuff, if they already have a major investment in hardware, software and employee training. Whereas a small business can switch, discard the old stuff, upgrade and stay ahead in the technological game.

The key warning in this area, if you have this type of "dual use" for your PC, is to be aware of the danger of conflict between the two fundamentally different uses of your PC. If yours is one of those business activities that also uses PCs (or even more powerful "workstations") as a key tool in producing your business's products or services, *if possible try to keep all such equipment entirely separate from the PC you use for basic management control purposes*. There is always the temptation to rationalize: "Well, I can save a couple of thousand dollars by using the same computer for everything." Almost always, this will mean that your management controls and administrative routines will start getting the short end of the computer stick. That single, precious PC will always find itself monopolized by your more important technical and client work. Conflict is inevitable.

Of course, if your business is a one-person show or very small, it may be unavoidable that you only use a single PC for everything, especially at the start. This will demand considerable self-discipline in your personal work habits, so that you don't start neglecting your (boring) day-to-day management tasks and duties, because you are always busy (having fun) designing fashion wear on-screen, or whatever it is that your business does.

It will be a constant temptation that can lead to unpleasant consequences. Resist it, until you can buy that second PC.

Management Controls on Your PC

Here's an illustrative checklist of some of the more basic kinds of *management controls* you might be handling on your PC:

- **Sales Control.** Daily sales, by type or category. Cash sales versus credit sales. Month-to-date (accumulated) versus last month or last year.
- **Bank Control.** Daily deposits. Checks written. Balances. Statement reconciliation.
- **Purchases Control.** Daily purchase orders and deliveries. By type, by supplier. Month-to-date, year-to-date. Average cost per item.
- **Stock Control.** Daily stock levels. In/out/balance. Reorder points, reorder red flags.
- **Accounts Receivable Control.** Balances, by client, by due date, by overdue. Paid/receivable.
- **Accounts Payable Control.** Balances, by supplier, by due date, by overdue. Paid/due.
- **Payroll Control.** Salaries paid, by employee. Calculations, gross, withholdings, taxes, net, payroll checks.
- **Materials Cost Analyses.** Analyses of all incoming invoices, to determine costs by category and subcategory.
- **Production (or Job) Cost Analyses.** Allocation of labor costs, materials costs and other costs, to each product or job, to determine its true cost and profitability.
- **Expense Analyses (and Coding).** Analyses of all expense payments and bills, by category and subcategory. Coding (by the chart of accounts) for accounting processing.

- **Operational Statistics.** Routine calculation of important statistics (sales by time of day, by salesperson, hours of production time).
- **And so on . . .**

The possible variations are many, due to the different characteristics of each type of business activity. The listing above is only an illustration, to start you thinking in the right direction. Never blindly follow our list or anyone else's list. Develop *your own list* of those controls that you feel are of key importance to understanding and controlling *your own business's vital signs.*

It is your personal responsibility as owner-manager to: (1) decide what information you need to control on your PC; (2) discuss with your accountant what details should be covered and how to find them; (3) decide if you are going to use an off-the-shelf business software package for the purpose; or (4) use a spreadsheet program instead, on which you will build the control sheets your own way.

Whatever you decide, get the basic software organized and *get started.* Your controls on your PC will *never* be complete or perfect the first time around. The only way you'll be able to improve and fine-tune them is by first setting them up and starting to use them.

Any start, however clumsy, is better than no start at all. If you talk yourself into "let's wait until the business is more advanced," the odds are that you will never do things right and never build your system into a brushing-your-teeth-daily office routine. And you'll be flying blind every day that goes by, without decent informational feedback on your business's vital signs.

That'd be dangerous, that'd be negligent.

Data-Entry and Close-Out Disciplines

Depending on the size and nature of your business, you might make your PC entries daily or twice a week or once a week or once a month. There's no best way; that decision will be an exercise in common sense and caution. But whatever routine you choose, *never break it.* It's just too easy to start letting things slide, with this kind of work.

Remember, it's always possible to set aside an hour or two to do all your PC data entry from a small stack of invoices, check stubs, notes, etc., and get them off your desk. But if you allow them to accumulate for a couple of months, it'll take days to process the pile of backed-up paperwork. You may never find the time to bring the work up to date. So never let your data-entry routines slide, in the first place.

PC data entry is like dental hygiene. Think daily toothbrushing.

And who makes the data entries?

You make the data entries. Unless your business is medium-sized or larger, and you can treat yourself to the luxury of an office manager or personal assistant. But even if someone else is making the entries, you must still check on their work progress very closely, at least until your system has been totally "debugged." There will always be problems to resolve and improvements to make. That won't happen unless you take a close, personal interest in the work.

No employee will ever love your PC like you love your PC.

Too often, some people will get the data entry done, but then will rush on to the next month's work, without properly closing the month and wrapping up the results, thus losing much of the value of the management information they just finished creating.

Carefully close out the controls at the end of every month, so that you have separate performance figures for each month. Wrap it all up by producing final summaries and reports for the month, showing each of the different pieces of information that you (and your accountant) need. They will all become part of your final MIS report package.

Ultimately, of course, your MIS package will be nothing more than the combined results of all the bits and pieces of control work described above. However, you (and your staff, if you have any) must be able to study it carefully and refer to it quickly and easily. So, ideally, the final figures produced by each type of control should be summarized and presented readably, on some kind of spreadsheet or report form, printed out from the PC.

Add all those pieces of paper together, stuff them in a binder and, bingo, you just produced and published your first Management Information report for your own business. Do it the first month and it's only a report. *Do it every month and it's a system . . .* a Management Information System.

Deciding on Hardware

If you are already comfortable working with a certain type of PC, stick with whatever hardware (operating) system you know best, whether it be Apple's Macintosh or Microsoft's Windows. As you probably know, there are fanatical adherents to both camps and you will hear every imaginable argument as to why one is the greatest and the other the worst. The truth is that, for all the basic tasks involved in managing a business, the two competing hardware systems are equally good, and their prices are pretty much even these days. What will make all the difference to you is not choosing one or the other, but the technical configuration of the specific machine you buy–speed, power, memory, that sort of thing. Which is what will decide the price you pay.

If you're already competent and fast in working with one of the two systems, it'll be frustrating and irritating to have to slow to a crawl and stumble through the process of learning a different one. Why waste your time? Your time and efforts should instead be concentrated on becoming familiar with the new software you will be using and on how to adjust it to your business's specific needs. Not with learning new PC tricks. It won't make any difference to the software, either; the basic, off-the-shelf business software you will need is equally available in both Mac and Windows formats.

I must confess to being a Mac freak from way back. If you are a beginner at the PC game and are not yet "computer literate," my friendly advice would be to choose a Mac. Strictly because of its "user friendliness," in which–in my humble opinion–Mac is still ahead of Windows, in spite of Microsoft's many recent improvements. You will need all the user friendliness you can get, as you struggle to get started, with both your business and your PC. With a Mac, you will probably learn quicker, faster and easier, and enjoy the process more (with all due apologies to Bill Gates.)

As for technical specs, go as high in price as you can afford, in exchange for: (1) greater speed (when you are doing dreary stuff, late at night, you'll understand how irritating slow speed can be); (2) more RAM, i.e., "brainpower" (so your software programs work as smoothly and efficiently as possible); (3) greater hard drive storage capacity (so you don't need to be constantly messing around with your files, to economize storage space); (4) a good automatic backup system (you *will* forget to back up your files, sooner or later, and that *will* be the day before your hard drive crashes) and (5) a nice, large, easy-on-the-eyes monitor (back to those late nights).

The rest of the bells and whistles? Fuggeddabouddit, you don't need them for small business basics. If you get off on that kind of stuff, go ahead and get

PROGRAMMER? WHO NEEDS A PROGRAMMER?
Nowadays, the Best Way to Get the Business Software You Need May Be to Roll Your Own

A growing number of small-business owners are finding that the best way to get the software they need is to roll up their sleeves–and roll their own.

What's making this possible are the twin trends in PC software: the emergence of office "suites" that include all the basic business packages–spreadsheet, database, and word processing programs–and relatively simple programming features for tailoring suites to the particular needs.

Starting with the spreadsheet, which has a variety of sophisticated math capabilities, a company might create a custom sales reporting and forecasting system–without ever hiring a professional programmer. . . .

The resulting semi-custom programs hold the greatest promise for small companies since the PC made computing affordable.

—Enterprise/Business Week

yourself some PC toys, but never let them distract you from the business basics we're talking about here.

Small business is about basics. So your PC can be pretty basic, too.

Keep playtime out of this discussion.

Deciding On Software

Think word processing, always.

Think spreadsheets, always.

Think databases, maybe.

And don't think about anything else, until you've got these licked.

The rest is up to you. Buy all the fancy gizmos and fun software you want but don't touch them until you become a word-processing and spreadsheet wizard. Databases also, if your type of business makes it necessary.

Those "bundled" office management software packages ("suites") are the most practical choice for most small businesses. They all include programs for word processing, spreadsheets, and databases, among other programs. Microsoft Office is one of the best, but there are other good options.

These "suite" programs will not do your work for you. You will still have to become proficient at word processing and using spreadsheets. That means working at it, either training yourself (not too hard to do) or taking a quickie course, of which there are many.

It is distressing that so many businesspeople are not particularly good at word processing or spreadsheets, even though they will happily play around for hours with E-mail, Internet and other nonproductive bells and whistles.

So first things first . . .

Word Processing: A Priority

Well-worded, well-presented, well-laid-out written communications (letters, memos, faxes, proposals, quotes, etc.) are some of the most important marketing and management weapons of a small business. Far more so than in Big Business, where nowadays you will find some of the lousiest writing habits imaginable. Because it doesn't really make much difference in the larger corporations.

In a small business, often your entire business and personal image, along with your one and only client, may be riding on the impressions left by a one-page letter you just sent.

You're sitting in the cramped kitchen of your small restaurant, your hands smelling of garlic, your PC balanced on an empty packing crate, your printer on the greasy floor, beside the spilled ketchup, writing a fax to a major supplier. That supplier will form an opinion about you and your restaurant, only from the appearance and content of that fax . . . they don't need to know about the kitchen, the ketchup, the garlic and the grease.

We've all heard those musty gems of management advice for efficient communication in the corporate world: about handling problems verbally, not wasting time writing, if it can't be said on one page it's not worth saying, and so on. That stuff is out of warmed-over "advice" books from the distant past, before the age of the computer. Much of the advice originated in the days when only a typist or secretary could prepare typed documents, and it took a whole day and five draft revisions before you had your final document. No wonder they wanted you to cut back on written stuff.

You don't find typists or secretaries in small businesses anymore, and one exceptional benefit of the PC is that you can fire off all kinds of written communications, very quickly, very easily, very impressively . . . and all by yourself. Well used, this is one of the most powerful weapons for the entrepreneur.

In this modern business world of unreturned voice mail messages and ephemeral E-mail notes, it's the well-written document that stands out. Those dumb old rules no longer apply (if they ever did).

One especially useful trick with word processing software and PCs is that you can perfect any number of standard "template" letters, memos, faxes and forms, fine-tuned for your specific busines, and file them on your hard disk. Then, when you need to bang something out in a hurry, you pull up that template, change a word here, a sentence there and print it out. It takes all of five minutes, looks damned professional and *you put it in writing.*

The more you read about problems with lawyers, employees and outsiders, the more you will realize how much better off you will be, if you always "put it in writing." People are much more respectful of written documents than of verbal communication. Lawyers won't want to mess with you, if you leave clear "paper trails" to substantiate your actions and confirm your decisions.

So your English is lousy, your spelling awful or your grammar atrocious? *No hay problema, amigo.* Get someone to help you prepare some of those standard templates in good English, for future use. There are even cheap little software programs with hundreds of model "most used" letter formats. Find what's nearest to your need, pull it up, amend it and, zap, you're in the quality letter-writing business.

There are hundreds of situations and problems that will arise in your small business as time goes by, where your ability to sit down at your PC and knock out a quick, effective letter, fax or memo will give you a tremendous edge. But to do that you must not only learn how to use the word processing program but also spend some time learning the simple tricks of margins, fonts, type sizes, formats and so on. It's easy, it's no big deal and it will enable you to produce *documents that communicate and documents that impress.*

This is a superficial modern world.

"Looks" matter, especially on paper.

The smaller your business, the bigger and better and more competent you can make yourself look on paper. Word processing on your PC is your "image" weapon for doing this.

Learn to use it and use it well.

Spreadsheets: Another Priority

Personal computers only started making sense for business purposes when the first spreadsheet software program came on the market. That was Visicalc, dead now but never forgotten . . . that was where it all began. Then came Lotus 1-2-3, then Excel, then a variety of others. To some business users, their PC is their spreadsheet program. That's all they ever use . . . that's all they ever need to use. It's that good. Only people who use their spreadsheet program daily, like they use their phone or fax, know just how miraculous those little on-screen boxes are for handling every task that pops up, big or little.

If you don't understand, and don't want to learn to use the spreadsheet program on your PC, you might as well just use the PC to play games. Come to think of it, why not take the PC home and close down your small business, before it closes you down? With that kinda attitude about spreadsheets, you're not going anywhere, anyway.

That's how important the spreadsheet program is, to you and your small business. It's a far more important tool in a small business than in a large corporation. In a small business, the spreadsheet can do what assistants, analysts, gofers and entire departments do in big business.

So what is a spreadsheet program?

It's so versatile, it's a little hard to summarize its full potential. The essence of any spreadsheet program is very simple. It's just like the old printed spreadsheet pads, with columns and rows, creating boxes ("cells") where they intersect. Thousands and thousands of cells. These cells can store numbers or text, just like you used to write stuff into the boxes on the old printed forms.

Now comes the magical part. In the printed forms, you had to make all the calculations yourself, with your calculator. On the PC, you can instruct these cells to do everything imaginable with each other, whether mathematics or storage of data. The flexibility is truly amazing and the possibilities become endless. Flick through any manual on Excel or Lotus 1-2-3, or review onscreen the sample templates they give you with the program, and you will begin to get an idea of how far it can go.

Spreadsheets will go as far as your creativity can take you.

Business is basically about numbers and words. So are spreadsheets. So there isn't a business problem that can't be laid out in a spreadsheet format and solved on your PC. You "construct" within a spreadsheet whatever type of control system, calculation method or data storage you need.

Now for the practical part.

You remember all those "management controls" previously discussed? Well, one obvious choice for handling them would be a business (e.g., Microsoft Office) or accounting (e.g., Quicken) software package that you can use for this purpose, after making a variety of adjustments, to tailor it to your specific needs. But you can also do everything we listed, *everything*, on a spreadsheet program. It'll take you more time to "construct" the specific spreadsheet, it won't look as fancy when you print it out . . . but *it will do the job,* and may well be better suited to your needs than a prepackaged program. And when you need quickie, informal stuff, the spreadsheet is much faster and more flexible.

That's why God created spreadsheet programs for start-up small businesses.

For example: The day you start *thinking* about opening a business is the day you also open a blank spreadsheet format on-screen, entitle it, say, "Initial Notes on My Business Project" and get rolling, listing all your ideas, with estimated dollar investments. Only as an illustration, here's how it might go in your first months, with a series of spreadsheets containing, let us say:

- List of stores available for rent, with rental conditions
- Breakdown of estimated business capital requirements
- Specifications for store remodeling
- Detailed list of projected costs of store remodeling
- Estimates of future sales and profits
- List of all key suppliers, with names, addresses, etc.
- "To Do" checklist, before business opens
- List of planned merchandise, with estimated unit costs

- Running sales control, from day of opening
- Running expense control, from day of opening
- Preopening expense list
- Running petty cash control, from day of opening
- Invoices prepared and printed from spreadsheet
- And all other sorts of odds and ends of controls
- And all other sorts of bits and pieces of calculations
- And on and on . . . into the distant future.

Franchise System PCs–Gift Horses?

A word of caution for small businesses that operate franchises.

The bigger, better franchise systems will usually supply you with (and charge you for) their standardized PC systems, with their own special software. This, of course, can be wonderful when you know little or nothing about such matters. The franchise operator hands the whole system to you on a plate, ready to roll. Just plug and play. You have all your controls and information needs, fully functioning from Day One. No sweat, no hassle. Another free lunch.

But don't forget the less-than-complimentary comments in the chapter on franchising and franchisers. These folks are not in the Good Samaritan business. The franchise PC system you receive will certainly cover everything that interests the franchise operator, most of which will also interest you, the franchisee. Also, it will permit them to gather useful data on your operations, for their own systemwide analyses. But . . . there may well be some controls and key information that could be of major importance to you, but not to them. Stuff to do with royalties, franchise fees, advertising contributions, purchases from the franchise operator, costs of special promotions, etc. Without your own independent system, you may have difficulty generating additional information that might tell you more than they feel is healthy for you.

It makes business sense to look gift horses in their mouths. Check out these franchise PC gift horses with that same healthy, cynical attitude we recommended for franchise offers in general. You may find the horse is missing a few teeth. Maybe it doesn't matter . . . maybe the advantages outweigh the disadvantages. But it's sure worth thinking about, and asking prickly questions about, before you finally sign off on that franchise agreement.

Who knows, you might consider having your own humble PC in a back room, to keep an independent view of what's going on in your franchise business.

Cash Registers: Oft Neglected PCs

Many small businesses are retail operations. Almost all retail businesses need to use a cash register. However, new business operators often view their cash register as just that–a simple cash drawer, providing only a customer receipt and a day's end sales tally. And thus fail to take advantage of their most valuable business machine, after their PC.

A modern cash register is a smart and versatile machine that helps you catch employee mistakes and theft, and supplies you with invaluable information about every aspect of your sales. Modern cash registers are basically specialized PCs, and the best ones are impressive in their capabilities.

The register supplier can (and will) program them individually, to register your sales just about any way you can imagine or desire. This allows you to ring up each sale, by a particular type or category, have your sales prices already in the register's memory, plus make any number of other individual adjustments to the specific needs and characteristics of your store, restaurant or outlet.

Carefully programmed in advance, your cash register will prove amazing in its versatility and management value. It will provide you with daily figures that make it far easier to control cash movements, detect employee theft or mistakes and track sales trends. At the end of the week or month, it can tell you exactly how much you sold, of each type and category, the average price you charged, discounts given, sales by time of day and so on.

Yet most small business owner-operators think of their cash register only as part of their store equipment, not as part of their information and control system. They're overlooking a major hidden management asset, which would not cost them one cent more to help them run their business better. Take full advantage of what your cash register system can offer you and you'll have far more complete and reliable sales information, as part of your MIS.

- Pay a bit more and buy a new model cash register that uses advanced PC technology (NCR, Panasonic, etc.). Resist the temptation of buying used registers; they're cheap and there are a lot around (would you buy a ten-year-old PC?). Use a reputable, established, factory-authorized local supplier, who will also provide start-up programming, follow-up programming and emergency repair service. Don't buy cheap, off-the-shelf registers. You need the more sophisticated models that can be individually programmed, and you won't find them in office supply stores.

- Well in advance of opening your retail business, think through exactly how you want to organize and break out your sales, by type, by category, by whatever. Think through your pricing, item by item. Make sure your register is fully programmed and functioning, with all this information inputted, long before you open, so you will still have time to make last-minute adjustments, if needed. Most new retailers forget this until it's too late.

- Before you close the purchase, negotiate as many hours of free future programming changes as you can get. The hourly costs will quickly add up, if you haven't nailed this one in advance. Also negotiate one free, follow-up reprogramming visit, say, three months later. By then, there will always be things you'll have decided to change and improve.

- Take the monthly final, analytical paper tape, with all its summary statistics, and reenter the information in a spreadsheet on your PC. Make it part of your MIS. If you want to pay more, you can even get the information on a diskette or fed directly into your PC from your cash register.

In short, cash register systems are absolutely invaluable and the new ones are highly versatile. They must be taken seriously, if yours is a retail business. Too often, the purchase and programming of the cash register system is a last-minute afterthought. Just think of your register as an extension of your PC and pay equal attention to both.

Accessories

Then there are all the other optional bits and pieces of business equipment and services to consider, such as:

- PC Laptop
- Color Printer
- CD-ROM Drive
- Telephone Line
- Voice Mail
- PC Notepad
- Scanner
- Fax Machine
- Fax Line
- Mobile Phone
- Printer
- Modem
- Fax/PC
- Copier
- Pager

> Most stuff sold for use with personal computers will mess up your system and waste your time.
> —Stratford Sherman, *Fortune*

And so on. Each business is different, each owner is different and there is no way of saying which choices are best, for whom, and how much you should spend. What does need saying is that, if you're a sucker for gadgets, gizmos and the latest toys, you can end up spending an unhealthy hunk of your small business's limited initial capital on stuff that may make you feel glowingly entrepreneurial but is totally irrelevant to your business's basic needs in its first years. Wouldn't it be better to spend the money on stuff that directly improves your business's immediate performance?

This point may seem obvious but it needs to be emphasized, because you are fighting a lone battle against major marketing muscle on a national scale. Small businesses and new entrepreneurs are the top marketing targets for all these kinds of products. The hype and the hustle are overpowering. The message that gets hammered into your skull, via TV, radio and print ads is: *No small business can succeed with having our (whatever) in their office, car or briefcase.* Their advertising combines fear *(without our laptop, you're doomed)*, snobbery *(all the cool entrepreneurial dudes use our warp-speed laptops)* and plain lies *(our laptop will improve your sex life and grow your hair back).*

All this stuff can be bought and installed easily, any time that suits you. It won't go away, there will constantly be new and better products on the market and prices will keep falling. So buy *only* those things that are of obvious, immediate, productive benefit to your business and your work, not to your ego. When you have to buy, buy only basic models in the low price range (so if you made a bad choice, you can afford to trash whatever it was and get something better, six months later). Keep adding things as you go along and acquire more knowledge and self-confidence. But only buy when it is transparently obvious that the new stuff will be of immediate, measurable benefit to the business.

In other words, use your common sense. Your business's needs to improve performance and profits are the only consideration, not your ego or your personal preferences. Keep them separate and you will avoid squandering precious money and limited personal time.

And What About Cyberstuff?

What about it? Wanna go Net surfing? Shouldn't you be concentrating on basic business instead? Have you forgotten about survival?

The Internet, the World Wide Web, intranets and E-mail have nothing to do with what this chapter has been about. Zero, zilch . . . their only connection is that they both share the same piece of hardware: your PC.

There's a memo in the Odds 'n' Ends appendix that gives you the author's opinion on the role of the Internet in small business. Check it out if you're one of those Internet fans who believe that the Internet will help your small business make money. Don't keep your hopes up.

Your PC, Your Small Business Partner

In a nutshell:

- One of the keys to survival in the tough first years of a small business is knowing all the key details about your business and how it's performing . . . not flying blind, without an instrument panel.

- Another key is keeping tight control of those details and making adjustments and changes, as soon as you see both problems and oppportunities . . . flying it correctly and reaching the destination.

- So we're talking, first, information and, second, control. *Information and control.* And it's the creation of your own Management Information System that will give you both that information and that control.

- But there's no point in knowing you need information and knowing you must exercise control, if you don't have the machinery and the means of generating the contents of the MIS and keeping it up-to-date.

- PC hardware is that magic machine and PC software is the means. Together, they give you the tools for handling information and control, and for producing and maintaining your MIS.

- The PC is the pickup truck of your small business. Learn to drive it well and maintain it in good condition. However much money and time you invest in your business, your best investment will have been in your PC.

- Love your PC and it will love you back.

13

STEALING CANDY FROM BABIES:

*Lawyers Feed Off
Small Businesses*

Justifiable Lawyer Bashing

For the superstitious small business reader, Chapter 13 was reserved for lawyers and attorneys. A chapter for those who still believe in witches, gremlins and creepy-crawlies that go bump in the night. With these professionals on your side, your worst small business nightmares can easily come true.

For a profession that touts itself as counselors to the helpless and defenders of the weak, business lawyers take the all-time cake for bald-faced hypocrisy and unrestrained greed, in their dealing with neophyte entrepreneurs. For them, it's stealing candy from babies. Corporate clients and experienced businesspeople have enough knowledge of lawyer antics to be able to stand up to them reasonably well; fearful, inexperienced newcomers are sitting ducks for exploitation.

Lawyers are "service providers." Yet of all the many different services small businesses pay for in their first years, the legal advisers they use are the most likely to sell them expensive services they do not need immediately (if at all), and to cost them the most. By a "value-for-money" criterion, these service providers will provide you with the least benefit for the highest cost.

With counselors like these, who needs counsel?

Never trust them unconditionally. The worst abuses always happen because businesspeople have this good-natured tendency to place more trust in an attorney than in the plumber they call in to fix the toilet.

That's poor judgment. Plumbers are more ethical professionals than most lawyers you will have the misfortune to deal with. Plumbers will diagnose your problem more precisely, will fix only what needs to be fixed, will get the job done better, will do it as quickly as they can, will get out of your house as soon as they're done, will be more honest in charging for the work they actually did do, and will be less likely to charge you for work they did not do. Lawyers who meet these demanding plumber standards are few and far between.

Maybe you feel these comments are unfair and mean-spirited. Maybe everyone in your family is a lawyer (so why are you reading this book about small business?). Well, then, just think economics . . . *your own economics.* We've already discussed the precarious financial balance of most small businesses in their first year or so, right? Often the biggest service cost in that start-up period will be legal fees. A major cost of this nature can spell the difference between survival or failure. So what kind of descriptive label do you suggest we reserve for those people who, by charging you too much for services you usually do not need or could postpone, are in effect putting your new business in financial jeopardy?

Your best defense will always be in keeping a healthily suspicious attitude in all your dealings with any lawyer. Never place your trust in your trusty counselor. Adopt the same mindset as when you walk city streets, with a watchful eye out for muggers and pickpockets. Better clothes; same ethics.

> **RULE OF LAW**
> **by Warren E. Burger, Former Chief Justice of the Supreme Court:**
>
> The reputation of the legal profession is at its lowest ebb since I started practicing law more than 60 years ago. With ever increasing frequency, the public is questioning the competence, integrity and honesty of lawyers. Indeed, over just the past few years, a number of judges and all too many lawyers have been guilty of self-dealing and other forms of professional misconduct in and out of the court-room. These transgressions not only diminish the public's confidence in the profession, but they also subtly undermine the public's respect for the rule of law. . . .
>
> All of the profession's current problems—the eroding public respect for lawyers, the lack of professional dignity and civility on the part of many lawyers, and lawyers' insensitivity to the litigation explosion—are clear indications that the profession-alism of the bar has been in sharp decline.
>
> —*The Wall Street Journal*

Attitude, Ignorance and Arrogance

So your best friends are lawyers and these hardball comments hurt?

So you indignantly jump to their defense: "Okay, Okay. Maybe there are one or two bad apples, but it's just not possible or believable that the majority of business lawyers are unprincipled crooks."

That's *exactly* the problem.

Crooks know they are crooks. But most lawyers are regular folks like you or me. They *aren't* crooks. They don't *see* themselves as crooks. They sincerely *believe* they have principles. They genuinely *think* of themselves as ethical and professional. They have been thoroughly brainwashed by their law school education to believe sincerely that all their services are vital and essential to the survival of a business, any business. They are convinced, after so many years "invested" in law school, that their professional expertise is automatically "worth," say, $250 per hour, regardless of what that time is spent doing–even if it's only operating the copier or sending out faxes. It's their rightful "return" on their law school investment . . . they're owed it. By someone. Probably you.

They are often astoundingly ignorant about the simplest, most basic economics and operations of a small business . . . the kind of stuff discussed in this book. That's understandable. The less they know about their client's economic pain and financial suffering, the better; the less problem they will have in justifying, to their own consciences, their often needless services and their often excessive fees.

It's all a very peculiar form of business arrogance. They're providing services that very often the client may not need, or can't afford, or could at least do without for a few years. Yet they price their service not based on any criterion of "economic worth" to the customer or on competitive prices, but on a totally arbitrary formula like: "Well, we worked ten hours on this job, our hours cost $250 each, so the bill's $2,500." And they make it stick.

Now that's the damnedest thing you've ever seen. It doesn't exist anywhere else in the real world of business, where businesspeople fight tooth and nail over every penny of the cost of services, products, materials, whatever.

It's surreal.

How in the world can they get away with it?

Here's how:

CONTRACTS

Institutions once felt a sacred obligation to stand by their contracts. Today, lawyers have rendered any such sense of moral obligation as obsolete as modern politicians have made the commitment to stand by a handshake. For pricey lawyers, breaking a contract is a function of whether the client can get away with it. Does the other party have the resources to sue? If the suit is lost, what will it cost? Is it more expensive to keep your word than break it? If so, break it and save the money. It's an economic decision, not a legal one–and certainly not a moral one.

–Joseph A. Califano Jr., former Secretary of Health, Education and Welfare, quoted in *The Miami Herald*

Author Fran Lebowitz Tells Mirabella:

Maybe I wouldn't be the best president, but I would be an excellent dictator. . . . I would make some amendment to the Constitution about the number of lawyers that would be allowed at any one time in the country.

Perhaps it should be tied to the number of plumbers. The ratio should be about a million to one. For every million plumbers, we'll take a lawyer.

–Quoted in "People," *The Miami Herald*

Scaring-Your-Pants-Off Marketing

Lawyers exploit the "fear of future catastrophe" and the lack of experience of their clients, especially their small business clients, in being able to judge the real probabilities of such catastrophes *actually* happening. You might call it the Sky-Is-Falling School of Marketing Legal Services.

Some typical pitches:

- *Sure, you could draft this memo yourself but you'll be running the risk of losing millions, if you're ever sued for (fill in the blank).*
- *Sure, this looks like a straightforward rental agreement but what if the landlord ever decides to (fill in the blank).*
- *Sure, you desperately want to sign this long-term supply contract with your best customer and pick up the first check, but what if next year he decides to (fill in the blank).*
- *Sure, you don't know if your business will make it through the next six months, but without this twenty-page stockholders' agreement, what if five years from now your partner decides to (fill in the blank).*
- And so on, with all the variations and permutations on these scare tactics that you can imagine.

It happens all the time.

So the inexperienced entrepreneur becomes paralyzed with fear of all the many impending catastrophes that loom in the distant future, and won't even go to the toilet without calling, consulting and meeting with his attorney.

Until the invoices start coming in.

Fees that may exceed a month or two or three of the business's total revenues. Amounts that, even if they don't break the small business, will still represent a huge financial burden. Way in excess of any real, immediate benefit to the struggling new business.

Cost-benefit analysis is not a concept lawyers care to understand.

Naturally, with the invoices in hand, the client hits the roof and complains to his attorney: "Hey, I had no idea you were clocking me at $250 per hour when we chatted on the phone, had lunch together, played tennis, discussed the Cowboys game, and then reviewed that one-page

The verdict is in: By a majority vote, *Nolo News* readers have condemned the legal profession, declaring it to be infested with inept and unethical sharks.

On questions of competence, communication and fees, the overwhelming majority found lawyers to be sorely lacking. . . .

The vast majority of respondents would not recommend their lawyers to family or friends.

—*Nolo News*

memo. You never even gave me a quote or an estimate, f'crissakes. I'm only going to pay you half and even then you're being grossly overpaid."

Whereupon the final fear exploitation technique snaps into action:

- *I'm an attorney and I'll sue your amateur ass off, if you don't pay what you've been billed.*

And it works. Because *that they will do*–they will sue your amateur ass off–*and they will win.* They did the work, didn't they? You didn't ask for a written estimate, did you? You didn't insist on a fee agreement, did you?

You trusted them, didn't you?

You owe them their return on that law school investment, don't you?

The defense against these kinds of tactics is simple. Lose your fear of distant future catastrophes . . . what can happen *worse* than your business failing in its first year? And thus lose your fear of lawyers. There's only one big, legitimate fear in small business. It's the fear of going bust *tomorrow morning,* because you're losing money and you can't pay your suppliers, employees or yourself. That you should truly fear. And that's *far more likely to happen* if you've gotten into the bad habit of using lawyers for anything other than critical, essential and immediate problems. Otherwise their bills will eat you alive.

Never fear lawyers themselves. Live in terror of their bills.

Lawyers, for Advice and Consultation

Entrepreneurs starting up their new small businesses and learning to operate them naturally encounter situations and problems where they are not sure of what they are doing and are afraid of making the wrong decision.

So they turn to a lawyer for advice and help.

With a little more time, experience and self-confidence in managing your small business, you will discover that most such situations and problems are simply no big deal. They can be handled by you alone or with some over-the-phone advice from your bookkeeper, accountant, friends or business acquaintances. The matter may not be resolved as perfectly as your lawyer might manage to do it, but that is irrelevant. Perfection at what cost?

None of this would become a problem, if you were dealing with a true

A Raleigh, N.C., federal grand jury indicted an attorney who officials say billed the Resolution Trust Corp. and other clients for more than 1,000 hours a month; a 31-day month has 744 hours.
—Albert R. Karr,
The Wall Street Journal

professional with the integrity and honesty to say to you: "Listen, pal, don't waste my time and your money. You can do all this minor stuff on your own, one way or another. You can't go too seriously wrong and anyway, your small business just can't afford to pay me what I would have to charge you for my time. Call me when you are in a truly horrendous jam. Then I'll save your miserable ass and you can pay my bill in twenty-four monthly installments. See ya when that happens."

Such lawyers *do* exist . . . they can be found. But your odds of finding one with these unusual character traits are no better than one in ten. The other nine will say: "Hey, that's dangerous stuff. Don't touch it, don't talk, don't write, don't sign, don't pay, don't so much as take a breath without me. Rush on over here with your files. We'll examine it all with great care, then maybe have lunch together . . ." and so forth.

Did you hear the fee meter just start ticking?

Do you know when it will stop?

Lawyers, When You Want to Sue

Sooner or later something unpleasant happens in your small business. You feel you have been screwed, robbed, fooled, hoodwinked, slandered, injured, abused, discriminated against or otherwise mistreated. You're steamed up, you're fighting mad. You've read about those incredible indemnities and huge damages other businesspeople have been awarded in similar situations. You pick up the phone, call your lawyer and yell: "I wanna sue those *≠∞*¡!*#@!s."

Here again, that one-in-ten lawyer will say: "Hold on a second, pal. Even if your case is watertight (and very few are), by the time it's over you'll have devoted most of your working time and personal energy to this fight. You'll be checking old files, gathering evidence, doing legwork, having meetings, giving depositions, going to court. . . . It'll go on interminably, far longer than you can even begin to imagine. Your legal fees will be monstrous and that's not even counting all the other costs associated with the case. And in the end, even if you win, you probably won't be indemnified for your legal costs. At best you may break even. Whereas I and your opponent's lawyer will both walk away smiling, pocketing our fees . . . we'll both have won. Instead, you should invest the time and the money in your small business, concentrate on running it well and forget this dumb fight. I'll write a couple of threatening letters and make some nasty phone calls and let's see if we can't shake down those *≠∞*¡!*#@!s for a quick, small settlement or some business concessions

. . . and I won't charge you more than a couple of hundred bucks. Go sleep on it, cool down, think about it and then call me back. See ya."

And the guy's right, of course. Entrepreneurs and small businesses, when they initiate legal battles, almost always end up deeply regretting their decision, regardless of whether they won or lost. The worst is that once you've started, you're probably being countersued, the lawyers on both sides have a financial and professional stake in carrying on, and it takes more guts than most businesspeople possess to decide coldly for themselves: "This is plain stupid. I'm going to throw in the towel."

You can guess what kind of advice the other nine lawyers will give you, when they receive your steamed-up call: "Right on. Let's sue the bastards for millions. Come see me first thing in the morning and we'll file suit right away."

And a long, miserable chapter in your small business life will have just begun, to which there will never be an end in sight.

None of which means that there cannot be legitimate situations where you can and should take legal action for damages to your business. But it requires cold-blooded, objective thinking and analysis before such a serious decision is made. Most lawyers have far too much to gain by convincing you to proceed with the fight, for you to be able to trust their impartiality.

They have their own agenda. It's called fee income.

Lawyers, When You're Being Sued

When your business is sued, you will have to defend yourself, like it or not, and you will need a competent attorney, like it or not.

Other people or other businesses may feel they have some legitimate complaint against you. Far more often, however, it is likely to be an outrageous claim for imagined damages or an entirely frivolous lawsuit. Here, it's the other party's lawyer who is instigating and goading them to go for your throat, telling them they can't lose. Again, what's on the agenda is fees, not justice.

Another incentive for third parties to initiate lawsuits, frivolous or not, is the

DON'T LET A SUIT CATCH YOU COLD

It's a moment every employer dreads. The envelope bears the return address of an unfamiliar law firm, and the document inside says you're being sued.

What's an honest business to do? You can't panic, but you can't dismiss it either.

Sometimes a quick settlement is the best alternative. Whether or not you believe the accusations are valid, the cost of a legal battle goes beyond lawyers' fees.

"It's distracting," says [a CEO]. "You lose sight of your real goal—which is to build your business—and can wind up losing it."

There are plenty of ways to get sued. A customer who slips could sue the restaurant. A vendor could sue a contractor for not paying bills. Employees could allege discrimination based on age, sex, race, religion or national origin.

Find a lawyer you can turn to when there's any question or threat of legal action.

—Susana Barciela, *The Miami Herald*

contingency fee system, where the attorney gets a percentage, usually from 30 percent on up, of the award. It's a major incentive to generating meritless litigation, gambling on jackpot awards.

The problem remains, however: What to do? There's no alternative. You must have a competent lawyer to defend you and your business, even if the case against you is groundless, unfair and frivolous. You're going to have to spend precious time and scarce money defending yourself, however unfair that may seem.

That perfect, one-in-ten lawyer will work every legal and business angle, to end the case at the lowest cost to you, as quickly as possible. That's all that matters from a business perspective . . . not the rights or wrongs of it. Businesspeople can get so upset at such perversions of the legal system, of which their business has become the innocent victim, that they *want* to fight back, no matter what the cost. They're being mugged by the legal system and their outrage is more than understandable.

But if you do that in a small business, you're often betting your family home and your business on the outcome. You can drain all your resources in defending yourself and in counterattacking. You have better things to do with your precious time and scarce money. Your business is more important.

It may seem like giving in to legal blackmail–let's face it, that's what it is–but often a quick low-ball settlement offer will be accepted, because the opposing lawyer calculates that cash in hand is better than the uncertainties of a trial. Greed is a great motivator.

Being poor is also a great defense. If you have no spare cash and your business's funds are tied up in assets that have little resale value (ever tried to sell restaurant tables and chairs, old computers, used cash registers?) and you couldn't afford the liability insurance premiums (so there are no insurance company deep pockets to hit up on), your (good) lawyer will put together some solid notes displaying the obvious and talk to the opposing lawyer: "Listen up, esteemed colleague (or however they talk to each other when no one else is listening). There's no gold in these here hills. Look at the facts. Even if you win, my client won't have a dime to pay you and will have to declare bankruptcy. Here's $1,000 in nuisance money, for you and your gold-digging client to both take a hike and go piss in someone else's pond. Take it or leave it, last offer."

Done with conviction and smarts, this approach will often work, unappealing as it is to give in to blackmail. Again, the real problem is those other nine lawyers. They'd rather go to trial, defend you with ardor, dedication and many billable hours, rather than dedicate the few hours it might take to pay off the blackmail intelligently . . . and maybe crawl a little to get it done.

The Pendulum Swings

Lawyers will usually defend their profession with the pat explanation so often given for the outrageous, generalized abuse of the legal system: *America is a litigious nation.* Somehow implying that ordinary people and hardworking businesspeople actually enjoy suing each other, gambling precious time and considerable money on a roll of the judicial dice. It's got nothing to do with the lawyers, you understand. No way. It's their greedy clients who want it that way.

Right, and pigs fly too.

How many people or businesses, of their own volition, would embark on protracted legal battles and judicial skirmishes, with all the risks, problems, time, costs and uncertainties involved, if they were not actively provoked and instigated to do so, by those who have the most to gain and the least to lose–the lawyers?

It's a litigious nation because the litigating attorneys make money out of litigation . . . and the more litigation there is, the more they benefit.

So don't let's lay the blame on the clients.

SCARED OF LAWSUITS, SMALL BUSINESSES APPLAUD REFORMS

As Congress moves to reduce the soaring number of civil lawsuits, few are watching with as much interest as small-business owners. Many feel beleaguered by lawsuits and live in dread of them.

Landoll Corp., a Marysville, Kan., maker of farm machinery and specialty trailers, says it gets sued about five times a year. "Nine out of 10 are frivolous, but you have to defend each of these," says [an executive]. "We are burdened by litigation."

Suits aren't always as frivolous as defendants think, but there's no doubt that undergoing a lawsuit can be especially wrenching for small firms. Unlike many large companies, most small concerns–which usually lack legal staffs–don't have sufficient funds to fight suits, much less settle them or pay judgments.

And then there's the time and emotional energy for a small-company owner. Bruce Hoegger, president of Remanco Hydraulics Inc., tells of a product-liability suit filed last year against his company. His insurer picked up the legal costs, but during one three-month period, [he] spent 50 grueling hours in depositions and meetings with lawyers. Throughout the case, he also lived with the prospect that a big punitive-damage award–which insurers usually don't cover–could bankrupt him personally. He eventually settled the case for $25,000, which the insurer picked up.

He says the pressure strained his 15-year marriage. . . . His wife is [company] treasurer. "We were worried we were going to lose our livelihoods," he says.

Indeed, while under the cloud of a suit, a small company may find it impossible to get financing. And all the while, the owner may worry that his company won't survive. "One punitive-damage award can put a small company out of business," says [a spokesman] for a tort reform group. "I've heard from countless small-business owners whose very livelihoods are in jeopardy because of the mere threat of lawsuits," [a congressman] told a House hearing.

–Michael Selz and Jeffrey A. Tannenbaum, *The Wall Street Journal*

The good news is that the pendulum has started to swing against lawyers and their excesses. The inexorable laws of the economic jungle (those laws all small businesses have to live by, daily) are now savaging the legal profession itself. There has been so much well-publicized abuse that the general public and the business public have entirely lost their respect for and awe of lawyers. The food supply for lawyers (i.e., clients and fees) is diminishing, as businesses and individuals question and challenge the fees, the hours, the billing practices and the need for certain legal services. While in parallel there is now a massive oversupply of lawyers, all fighting each other for a steadily diminishing supply of food. It's becoming an interesting feeding frenzy to watch.

As a result, competition among lawyers is becoming fierce and low-cost alternative legal services are becoming widely available. The client, once the patsy in the system, is starting to have stronger bargaining power and better alternatives. The balance of power has shifted somewhat, in the client's favor. It's not ideal yet but at least you can now take better, cheaper care of your small business's legal needs, if you use your head and lose your fear and awe of lawyers. They don't warrant it and certainly don't deserve it.

Again, think plumbers.

Plumbers deserve respect for their technical competence and working ability. But fear? Awe? C'mon, get serious. Same goes for the boys and the girls in the game of law. They've blown their credibility.

So the playing field is now at least a little more even, in your favor.

Protecting Yourself Against Your Protectors

You should use a lawyer for your small business's problems, about as much and as often as you would visit your dentist, and for needs just as specific . . . when you *know* you have a serious dental problem and you *know* that only a visit to the dentist will fix it. When there's absolutely no alternative. How often is that? Once a year? Once every two years?

Otherwise, brush, floss and gargle once a day, constantly reminding yourself of all the time, money and aggravation you are saving, by taking care of your legal hygiene yourself.

Some practical suggestions:

- Resist asking your lawyer for general business advice. They know little about the realities of day-to-day business life and their advice will be irremediably skewed by the distortions inherent in the legal system. It won't be good advice and it will cost you more than it's worth.

• Get your basic business advice from your friendly accountant or bookkeeper. From their experience with many small clients such as yourself, they will be able to tell you of the few situations where you are going to *have* to get legal help.

• Find a decent, competent lawyer, only through recommendations of your accountant or bookkeeper, or through business friends or family. If you use the yellow pages or answer advertisements, you deserve to suffer the consequences. Contact the lawyer, check him/her out, ask questions. Never pay for this introductory meeting. If satisfied, make it clear that you plan to use his/her services, only if and when needed, on a "standby" basis, not as a regular client. Thus you'll have your dentist's name and address, for when that filling actually does drop out.

• Use to the fullest extent possible: self-help legal books; legal kits from office supply stores; standarized preprinted agreements and contracts; storefront legal services, offering fixed prices for specific jobs (much like haircuts). These are all great innovative services of the '90s and ideal for small businesses. Many of them are first-rate. Law firms detest these innovations and will give you major scare talk on their supposed dangers. Consider their motives: it's competition. You have to live with competition, why shouldn't they?

• Get in the habit of writing quickie confirmation letters, memos and faxes, for every business matter that is the slightest bit important or potentially troublesome. Put things in writing. In the plainest no-frills English, write documents that start

---

William Raspberry
(quoting the late Arthur Miller):
A legal education is a form of brain damage.
—The Miami Herald

BAR REJECTS CALL FOR WIDER USE OF NON-LAWYERS

Can Florida lawyers bolt the door and keep paralegals out? Maybe not, but they can sure try.

The Florida Bar Board of Governors voted overwhelmingly to reject a committee report . . . urging the bar to set up a standing committee of lawyers, nonlawyers and paralegals to pioneer ways to deliver legal services to the public. . . .

The vice chairman of the committee says he doesn't think the board can turn back the clock, even if it wants to.

"People want to be able to have access to the legal system without spending $200 an hour. If lawyers aren't going to get back into the marketplace and provide affordable legal services, the public is going to find a way around it, and I don't think the Florida Supreme Court is going to stop them."

Meanwhile, Sherrie Marcus, the South Miami lawyer whose lawyer-owned paralegal clinic was one of the models the board rejected, says the board's decision certainly isn't going to stop her. Marcus says she's going ahead with plans to franchise her operation nationwide . . . modeling herself after H&R Block.

—Rosalind Resnick, The Miami Herald

with phrases like: "In confirmation of yesterday's meeting, I understand that our agreement is as follows . . ." and lay it out, clearly. The grammar can be lousy, the spelling atrocious, but only one thing matters: that you put in writing what you think was agreed. No "she said, he said" disputes later. It's the best defensive habit you can develop to prevent future legal hassles, and it's also a good basic business discipline, to avoid misunderstandings.

- Your PC is your perfect paralegal assistant. Either by copying standard formats from those self-help books or getting a software package with "templates," you can load up a file on your hard disk with ready-to-use models of all the types of formal agreements, letters and faxes you may need to send out. When needed, you pull up the specific model you want, make a few quick changes and, zap, it's ready in ten minutes . . . and there's no charge for legal fees.

- Very few normal day-to-day business deals require a formal, long-winded, clause-riddled contract or agreement (prepared by you-know-who at you-know-what-cost). A clearly written letter covering what has been agreed, point by point, detail by detail, and signed by both parties, is usually equally effective legally. Often better, since it is written by those who are making the deal. A lawyer's main input is often the "what ifs" and the penalty clauses. You and the other party can and should discuss frankly what should happen if things fall apart, agree on it and spell it out in plain English: "If so-and-so does this, such-and-such must happen." Common sense and clarity are the key ingredients. It doesn't need to be written in legalese to be legally valid.

- Conversely, *never* put it in writing if you don't feel it's wise to do so. Your business conduct is your own business; maybe there are some matters about which you'd rather not leave paper trails, for opponents' lawyers to one day maybe use against you. You cannot follow our first rule, "put it in writing," if you know it shouldn't *be* in writing. If you think you may live to regret that piece of paper . . .

- When you receive drafts of proposed contracts and agreements from third parties, read them through yourself, slowly and carefully, two or three times over. Businesspeople who sign important documents without both reading and thinking first deserve the consequences. You'll discover the tricky bits, sure enough. Negotiate those changes you can negotiate. Often you won't have much bargaining power–ever tried to change a rental agreement with a major shopping mall?–and will either have to swallow what you don't like or walk away from the deal. At least you did your detective work. For any changes you can agree on, either write them in by hand and initial each one, or add a covering letter. Always get the other party to sign off, too.

- When you feel you *must* get legal help, spell out to the lawyer the specific problems and exact questions you want resolved. Never hand over, say, a sixty-page lease agreement with the open-ended question: "What do you think of this?" If you do, you'll get an opinion on each one of those sixty pages and you can blame yourself for the high invoice you will receive.

- When it comes to fees and expenses, treat lawyers just like any other service provider . . . remember plumbers, think toilets. Never let them pull their "esquire" stunts on you, so that you become embarrassed to talk about grubby, yucky, embarassing money matters. You have to pay your rent just like they do. Ask them to spell out the cost details, ask them for clear estimates, negotiate fixed fees if possible, get it in writing, make sure it is clear. If they won't do that, don't work with them . . . you'll regret it if you do.

LEGAL AID ON A DISK

A new [software] package for Windows . . . is based on the principle that most paperwork produced by lawyers is fill-in-the-blanks boilerplate. The $99 program provides the boilerplate, offers advice on how to fill in the blanks and turns out professional-looking documents. . . .

It lets you do your own paralegal work and save fees because "the time you normally spend explaining what you want to a lawyer, plus the time it takes for a lawyer to draft the document" won't be billed.

[It has] a menu of 70 mostly business-oriented forms, ranging from a bill-of-sale to an employment contract to a partnership agreement. . . .

For most needs of a smaller business, this software can ease the pain and the cost of legal affairs.

–Stephen H. Wildstrom, *Business Week*

HIRING A PRO? SHOP AROUND

There's an art to maximizing both your peace of mind and your dollar when dealing with service providers. . . .

Diane Huth, president of Skinny Snacks, who has built a business that has $5 million in annual revenues, offers an example: her company's contract with manufacturers of snack chips.

She's not a lawyer, but she knows her business and its needs better than anyone else. So Huth wrote the 25-page contract herself, detailing everything from technical specifications to pricing. Then she gave it to her lawyer to review, to make sure all the legal bases were covered.

Asking a lawyer to write such a contract from scratch could cost as much as $5,000, she says. "If I do the contract, I only pay one-tenth of that. . . . The point is to do what you can do well, and only hire outside for the skills you don't have."

–Susana Barciela, *The Miami Herald*

Hide the Candy

Apply to lawyers, both individually and as a breed, even greater caution and skepticism as to their monetary motives, ethical standards and professional conduct than you would to competitors, suppliers, bankers and the other coinhabitants of your corner of the business jungle. Lawyers believe they are in a class by themselves, and that they do not have to conform to the normal rules of normal business. Nowadays, they prize cleverness over ethics, opportunism over trust. If yours is a baby business, the greater is the temptation for them to steal your candy . . . legally. Yes, there are honorable exceptions, but experience demonstrates that most stories about lawyers' work for entrepreneurs and small businesses are tales of grief, woe, exploitation, deception and disappointment.

Forewarned is forearmed. Take the obvious precautions.

John Grisham's books are more fact than fiction.

The "Red, White and Blue Mess" below reads like fiction. But it's fact.

A RED, WHITE AND BLUE MESS
by Pete Van de Putte, President of Dixie Flag Manufacturing Co.

What does it feel like as the owner of a small business to discover you have been hit with a frivolous lawsuit? Imagine that your doctor tells you: "I've got some bad news for you." Because, to get sued these days is a lot like contracting a terrible illness. At the very best, after a long, costly struggle, you just manage to survive. At the very worst, you [meaning your company] die. Either way, you keep asking yourself in outrage: "Why me?"

Let me share my personal lawsuit horror story—one that shows why legal reform is vital, and why it is only fair to expand it to include protections for small businesses. . . .

My company . . . grew out of a family decorating business my mom and dad started in 1958. In 1974, my father sold the decorating business, but continued the part he loved most—the flag business. In 1980, I joined Dixie Flag and now serve as president. We employ 63 people.

In 1991, my firm and eight other businesses were named as defendants in a lawsuit over an incident that allegedly occurred in 1987. According to the plaintiff, he had been driving when he noticed a large flag being lowered in the parking lot of a local business. The plaintiff, claiming concern that a corner of this large flag would touch the ground, parked his car, got out and offered to help the employees of this business lower the flag. He then claimed that, as he was feeding the bottom corner of the flag into a container, a powerful gust of wind billowed the massive banner and yanked it into the air. According to the suit, the plaintiff was then thrown 70 feet into the air and, of course, injured.

Four years later, he sued for unspecified damages claiming that the American flag was an "unreasonably dangerous product" that should have been required to carry instructions and warning labels.

At first I was mystified. Although my company makes large flags, my best guess was that we didn't make that flag. We immediately had to stop everything we were doing–stop taking orders, checking inventory, working with the factory–just to get to the bottom of this story.

After devoting a week of several employees' time combing through ancient invoices, we confirmed that our company did not make or sell the flag cited in this incident–or the flagpole. In fact, we had no connection whatsoever with this bizarre flag injury except that, coincidentally, we happen to be a flag company. Relieved, I called my liability insurance agent to give him the good news.

His answer floored me. He told me that none of this mattered. I would have to settle in order to stay out of court. I was livid with anger, not just for the way I was being treated by an unfair system, but for my employees who joined me in wasting a week of our lives on our knees, sifting through mountains of paper.

The company that actually sold the flag and the flagpole to the business was not even included in the suit. It was a one-man business operating out of the back of a pickup truck and had no insurance and little money. But Dixie Flag had insurance and money [a "deep pocket," in other words]. So under something called the doctrine of "joint and several responsibility," we were a perfect target. There was no possibility of being dismissed from the case. I would have to prove in court that I had no connection to this incident.

Against my instructions, my insurance company settled for $6,000. Later the attorney called to tell me how "lucky" I was. He said it would have cost $10,000 in attorney fees to get the case thrown out in court. As he saw it, we saved $4,000.

Two other flag makers were sued–neither of which sold the flag or the pole–and settled for $14,000 and $1,500, respectively. That means the plaintiff in this case was able to extract at least $21,500 from three small businesses, none of which were involved in any way in the incident, without ever having to prove his claim in court–all because of the doctrine of joint and several liability.

Ending abusive lawsuits is a critical issue to small business. But it is also an issue of basic fairness for all Americans.

My experience proves that our legal system is seriously broken. It has to be fixed, but there is no sense in fixing it just for manufacturers like me.

–The Wall Street Journal

14

OUTSIDE HELP . . . ESSENTIAL OR NOT?

Accountants, Bookkeepers, Consultants: A Mixed Bag of Helpers

The Need to Go Outside

Start-up small businesses have less operating experience, less business knowledge and fewer internal management resources than older and bigger businesses. So, as a small business owner-operator, you will probably want the support of some trustworthy outsider for certain business services, advice and help. Because some business tasks are better or cheaper done outside . . . because you'll sometimes need to bounce your problems off someone whose opinion you trust . . . and because it can get damn lonely out in the cold.

The four outsider groups are: lawyers, accountants, bookkeepers and consultants. Enough said about lawyers. That leaves three to discuss. Happily, accountants, bookkeepers and consultants are a better bunch, on average. All three *can* give you decent "value for money," *can* talk your language and *can* relate to your small business problems. *Can* . . . but not necessarily *will*.

Caution is still essential. Too often, newcomers can be vulnerable: (1) to contracting for the wrong types of service, because they don't properly understand the exact nature of their problem; (2) to "overkill," where the advice may be of the right kind, but there's no way they'll have the money or the management resources to follow through and implement the recommendations; (3) to overpaying, where the work takes more time, effort and money than the problem justifies; or (4) to simple, old-fashioned rip-offs.

> An expert is one who knows more and more about less and less.
>
> –Nicholas M. Butler, former president, Columbia University, quoted by James Russell, *The Miami Herald*

Accountants Speak Your Language

There's something about the accounting profession that keeps most of its independent practitioners honest, reliable and down-to-earth, and well tuned to the problems, anxieties, struggles and realities of small businesses and entrepreneurs.

Maybe it's because most independent accountants are themselves small firms and most of their clients are small businesses; they talk the talk and walk the walk.

Maybe it's because there are millions of them, all over the country, each operating within a small geographic area, and within a small segment of the local business community. They're usually totally dependent on "word-of-mouth" recommendations by satisfied clients. Like your local dentist, it's their satisfied customers who bring in new clients. They can't afford to run the risk of taking unfair advantage of their existing clients . . . they might lose the ones they have, and new referrals would dry up.

Maybe it's because the stability and profitability of their small firms comes from charging low fees, every month or every year, to the same regular business clients. The work for each client becomes routine, repetitive and reasonably easy to perform. All in all, it provides a good, comfortable living, even if they don't get rich. So there's little incentive to take their clients for a ride; it would simply jeopardize their nice, well-balanced little businesses.

Maybe it's in their nature. Accountants have to be meticulous, methodical and honest, with large quantities of numbers and calculations, if they are to work fast and efficiently. It keeps their noses to the grindstone and generates a work ethic, which makes it a little harder to transform themselves into the con artists and opportunistic vultures that often hover over small businesses.

Maybe it's because the older hands among them have seen close up almost all the mistakes and misfortunes that can hurt their small business clients. They've seen them get taken to the cleaners, make fatal mistakes, get stupidly lazy . . . and get needlessly destroyed. When that happens, that's one more nice, stable little year-to-year client just went down the tubes. Now they're going to have to scramble to replace them with a new client. If they can give some helpful advice that could prevent the worst from happening, they'll do it–if only out of self-interest, to keep a client alive.

And maybe it's because there are very few "get-rich-quick" stories in the accounting world. Unlike their contemporaries graduating from law school, newly qualified CPAs don't start their careers already thinking of their clients as so many fat cows waiting to be milked.

In a nutshell, accountants have a personal and professional self-interest in seeing that your small business stays alive, and that some predator doesn't come along and stomp you into the ground. Not necessarily because they love you. They'd just like to see you stay alive and continue as their client, long-term. From professional experience, accountants know the predators and their tricks, and can often give you sound advice on staying alive. Often for free.

Remember family doctors, before they went the way of the dinosaur? Well, your accountant is your small business's family doctor. Find a good one and stick with him or her, long-term.

Accounting Services

Your accountant is a CPA (Certified Public Accountant), who has passed tough professional examinations and is technically qualified: (1) to advise you in organizing the structure of your accounting system; (2) to make the correct decisions as to what goes where within your system (your chart of accounts); (3) to prepare your business's annual balance sheet and profit and loss statements, and (4) to use them as a basis for preparing your federal, state and other tax returns.

The accountant has to know a great amount of technical detail about two fundamentally distinct areas: (1) how different types of businesses should best organize and prepare their accounts, so that the final figures accurately and honestly show the precise status of what the business possesses and owes (its assets and liabilities) and what the business makes (its revenues, costs and thus final profit or loss), as well as (2) the hundreds of thousands of rules and regulations, at federal, state, county and city levels, that relate to your business taxes and other obligations, and knowing how to juggle those financial figures so that your final tax bills are as low as possible, within the limits of those rules and regulations . . . and the law, of course.

Bookkeeping Services

Your "bookkeeping" is simply the underlying system of daily and monthly office and paperwork routines necessary to ensure that everything (sales records, bank records, purchase invoices, bills, payroll, etc.) is properly organized, added up, reconciled, checked, summarized and then filed.

The bookkeeping system is what feeds the correct numbers into the accounting system. The bookkeeping details can be retrieved and shown to auditors or IRS inspectors, if they ever come knocking at your door, even years later. If you ever "go public," your bookkeeping records will be of vital importance in confirming past financial performance to auditors.

Some small businesses do all their own bookkeeping, and only see their accountant once a year, at tax time. If you are an organized, disciplined and methodical individual, such an arrangement can work fine. There are various excellent, inexpensive software packages for use on any kind of PC, which make the task easy and manageable.

However, many businesspeople are either not that well organized, or would prefer to concentrate their time on the business. Often, they and their few employees are too busy with the pressures of managing the business to do the bookkeeping as it should be done. *As it must be done.*

Most accounting firms also provide bookkeeping services or are associated with bookkeeping services. There are different ways of handling the work. A typical routine for a small business would be:

- Daily, weekly and monthly, you do your own basic internal paperwork and organize it (following the system you have agreed with your accountant), relating to sales, receipts, check stubs, bank statements, payroll and so on.

- You hand over the "package" of documents at the close of the month to the bookkeeping service.

- They do the final work of entering everything into the accounting system and checking that there are no errors, omissions or discrepancies.

- They wrap it up for the month, making sure there are no loose ends or errors in your work. Usually they will print out monthly statements and reports, summarizing everything they have processed for you.

If you follow this procedure, every month's operational and financial transactions get "closed" promptly and efficiently. You can be confident that everything is correct and in its right place. You get all the key information that you (and your MIS) need, for tracking your business's performance. When tax time rolls around, all the heavy work has already been done. The accountant can wrap up your returns quickly, correctly . . . and inexpensively, since it will not be necessary to waste many frantic hours, puzzling over errors and omissions from each of the past twelve months.

Bookkeepers to Crack the Whip

One major justification for this system is that your external bookkeeping service becomes your *internal policing agent . . . your heavy.* They will (or at least should) crack the whip unmercifully, to pressure you or your employees into delivering the month's "package," a few days after each month has ended. This counterbalances that terrible temptation all small businesses face, to keep delaying the tedious, boring paperwork of closing each month's accounts, because there are always more important business problems to worry about.

There's no way to tell you that's fun work. It isn't. It's a pain in the butt. So businesspeople tend to keep putting it off. *We'll get it done next week.*

Once you start down that tempting slippery slope, letting the paperwork go to hell, you may be headed down a one-way road of no return. Once your routine monthly bookkeeping starts getting delayed, it usually gets worse and worse, and harder and harder to bring back up to date. Your MIS becomes a joke, since its main source of key data is the bookkeeping and accounting records. Once the MIS ceases to operate, you and your employees are back to flying blind.

And you know what can happen to small businesses that fly blind.

So, even if you are one of those exceptionally well-organized people who are good with numbers and can "wrap up" the entire month's accounting paperwork on a software program on your PC, you should still consider working with an external bookkeeping service–if possible, one that works closely with your accountant. It should not cost you more than $100 or so per month (especially if you have already done most of the paperwork for them) and can be well worth the cost, if only in terms of peace of mind.

Your Local Cop, Doctor and Priest

In addition to the obvious benefits of these administrative services, you will have bought yourself a form of "insurance" for your business.

Whatever business distractions arise, these friendly "cops" will bully you and pressure you, to keep your business's financial records up-to-date and in order, and to hand them over for final processing at the end of the month.

Also, you will have acquired a business ally (and possibly a friend) in both your accountant and bookkeeper, to whom you will be able to turn, for informal opinions and off-the-cuff advice on a wide range of problems. A form of business family doctor . . . or local priest, for that occasional visit to the confessional booth, when you did something you shouldn't have done.

Even if you don't want to hear it, if they suspect you're about to do something *really* dumb, they're probably going to tell you, if only to stop you from destroying yourself . . . and them from losing a client. Obviously, you can't keep bugging them for advice every day or they will want to start charging you, but a lunch here and a phone call there can work wonders. Remember, you're not using them as experts in whatever is bothering you. Just as fellow businesspeople who have seen most of the bad stuff (and the good stuff) that can happen, and who know their way around your part of the jungle.

Try to find an accountant/bookkeeper who has a good few years of experience in working with small businesses, and who has been in your geographic area a long time. They'll know the ropes and they'll know the neighborhood. Try to find them through personal references. You'll always find someone in a local business who can give a recommendation. Anyone who has a good, reliable accountant or bookkeeper, loves 'em and will recommend them enthusiastically.

You will discover that people in *other* small businesses–*those who are not your direct competitors*–are often more than happy to give you advice and recommendations. They know how hard it can be and it makes them feel good if they can be of help.

Businesspeople can have hearts of gold, so long as it's not their business you're messing with.

Consultants: a Luxury

A word of advice to newcomers in small business planning on using outside consulting services: *resist the temptation.* You'll almost never be able to put their recommendations to immediate, practical use and to immediate, profitable advantage. It will almost always cost you far more than the financial resources of your small business can justify.

The "cost-benefit" equation will seldom work in your favor, when you pay for outside consulting help.

That's not a criticism of consultants. There are good ones, there are bad ones. It's just a statement of fact, reflecting the limited financial and managerial ability of small new businesses to put consultants' advice to profitable use.

The term *consulting* covers such a wide range of types, shapes, colors and sizes, that there can always be valid exceptions to these hard-nosed comments. There are very competent, well-qualified and highly motivated consultants out there, in any number of different technical fields and management specialties. Unfortunately, however, the fact remains that, on average, small businesses are never well enough organized to be able to put the advice they receive to effective, immediate advantage. Too often, all it produces is indigestion.

In most cases, it ends as a frustrating waste of time and money. It's not difficult to understand why. The small business owner-operator is usually at a beginner's level and needs to move slowly and cautiously; the consultant is at an advanced level and is paid to produce fast results.

So there's a huge "expectations gap" and "execution gap," between the client and the consultant. And when it doesn't work out, they invariably blame each other for the failure of the consulting project.

Ground Rules for Consulting

Consultants can be tricky. That's why they're consultants. There's a hoary old definition: consultants are those guys contracted to find out what time it is in your business, who borrow your watch, tell you the time, charge you their fee . . . and keep your watch.

They prefer to avoid overly specific language and too precise targets for their projects. That gives them greater leeway to cover the fact that they're not too sure of what they can (and can't) deliver, plus giving themselves a comfortable cushion for stretching out the time, fees and expenses.

They have to be nailed to the wall, if you want results.

So if you are *convinced* that you *must have* a consultant's help for your business, your attitude should be that you will sign up for consulting services only if the following kinds of rules can be made to apply:

- The end product of the consulting work should be absolutely clear in everyone's mind *(we will have the stock control system up, running and fully operational, on our existing PC)*, instead of some mushy, nebulous objective *(your employees will learn to relate customer volume demands to anticipated inventory availability and thus optimize the stock carrying cost equation).*

- The potential benefit to your business should be clear and specific *(we will be able to fill 90 percent of our orders in thirty minutes, while reducing our investment in stock by 50 percent)* instead of more mush *(the cost-benefit equation of enhanced order filling versus minimalized working capital investment will maximize your long-term payoff).*

- The execution time of the project must be defined *(we will start next Monday and finish in three weeks)* instead of open-ended *(we will commence after preliminary diagnostic evaluation and aim for completion when all operating parameters are in place).*

- The support requirements must be spelled out *(this project will require you to provide us with all purchase, stock and sales records for the past twelve months, your PC will be inaccessible for three days, and your office manager will need to work with us for three hours, every day)* instead of left dangling *(we are counting on the whole-hearted cooperation and enthusiastic support of your entire organization).*

- The cost must be defined and fixed *(we will charge $3,000 for our services, plus the cost of any hardware alterations to the PC, which cannot exceed $500)* instead of vaguely upwardly mobile *(consultants' time is billed at the standard hourly rate, for the total number of hours that prove necessary for satisfactory completion, plus any additional hardware, travel and other costs, to be determined later).*

Just the process of preliminary friendly discussion of these "rules" will force both you and the proposed consultant to compare the reality of your business's situation, with the feasibility of achieving anything worthwhile.

This "reality check" may well prevent both of you from embarking on an exercise that may be doomed to failure from the start, through no fault of either party. You and the consultant may just be too far apart to ever produce worthwhile results for your business. Better to know before you start and to abort the project, rather than endure the disruption, cost and ultimate disappointment, followed by the inevitable catfight at the end.

Refugee Consultants from Downsizing Mania

Another word of caution, both to refugee consultants and to their prospective small business clients.

As a consequence of restructuring (downsizing, reengineering, consolidating, whatever buzzword pleases you) fervor, very large numbers of competent managers have been "outplaced" (fired, in English) from large corporations all over the country, in recent years. Many of these displaced refugees from corporate life are now being actively encouraged, by seminars, books and business articles, to set themselves up as "consultants," working out of their homes. Yet their technical knowledge and business experience, good as they may be, almost never relate to the harsh and humdrum realities of small business life. They're used to the working environments of large corporations, and often do not understand how difficult it is to put their ideas and suggestions to fast, effective use in a small business with very limited resources (financial, managerial and staff).

If you are one of those many well-trained, qualified and experienced middle and top managers who have been summarily guillotined by corporate America's restructuring lynch mob, you have this author's sympathy. However, pal, there's no point in following one wrenching, agonizing professional experience with another equally distasteful episode.

You should only offer your services as an independent consultant if you have technical knowledge in specific fields, where your help can be of clear and immediate advantage to the new client. For that to happen, you will usually find that your new clients should be of the same kinds, types and sizes as the company where you previously worked . . . that is, where you already know the territory and you can be fairly confident you will produce results. The prime examples of this are the frequent cases of former employees who return to their ex-employers, as consultants.

But if your working experience has been in general management, however competent you may be, you may have little of concrete benefit to offer small businesses, as a consultant.

That's neither your fault nor their fault.

The small business client will always expect the impossible from you: concrete results and financial benefits from your work, almost immediately, with you alone doing all the brainwork, the legwork and the grunt work, for low fees. And will become your worst enemy, when you can't deliver. And you probably *won't* be able to deliver. You'll find that it's much harder to implement any recommendations you may have, in a small, inexperienced business, with none of the internal resources of a larger company and where you are an outsider, not someone with the managerial authority to give orders.

It seldom works out.

Hmmm . . . lemme see now . . . where's the calculator? . . . hmmm . . . got it! . . . I'll recover the entire cost in my first 15 minutes of consulting . . . only another 200 hours and I can buy the BMW . . . whatta deal !

It could totally demoralize you, because you'll feel it's your fault that it hasn't worked out. It isn't . . . they've got to learn to ride the bicycle by themselves and you holding the handlebars will just drive both of you crazy. You don't need one more lousy professional experience of this nature, to depress you even further.

Managers manage, they don't consult.

Go start up a small business, any small business, anywhere, anyhow, and manage the hell out of it yourself. You're a manager, aren't you? You'll have a considerable edge over less experienced competitors, you'll quickly learn to adapt to the tougher world of small business and your chances of survival will be far greater than as a consultant. Your ego may get hammered (running a small business never sounds as prestigious as saying you are a consultant) but who cares? By now you should have learned that you're on a survival trip, not an ego trip.

Consultants Are Habit-Forming

Starting your own business and getting the hang of operating it is like learning to swim. You can read up on it, you can study it, but when the time comes to take the plunge, a management consultant holding your hand will not only be pretty useless, it will prevent you from instinctively learning to swim.

If you have so little self-confidence that you feel you need a consultant to help you manage your small business, you are probably not cut out for entrepreneurial life. The essence of being an entrepreneur is learning to live with risk; hiring consultants is an attempt (a vain one) to avoid risk.

Consultants, even if they perform well, must ultimately finish their work and go on their way. When they do go, you may discover that you've only been using them as a crutch. They did most of the actual work and you learned very little from it. All you got was a bad dependency habit. The first minor problem that arises in future, you may find yourself calling them back in again.

It's better to save the fees, bust your butt learning to do whatever it is you must do, on your own, even if it takes you longer and causes you short-term grief. No small business can survive economically, if it comes to depend on the constant use of consulting services and the constant payment of their fees.

Outside Advisers versus Outside Services

The underlying message in our discussion of the four outside groups most used by small businesses (lawyers, accountants, bookkeepers and consultants) is: *Approach them all with great caution and use them only when the cost-benefit equation is very clearly in your favor.*

Some are much better, some are much worse, but even if they were all wonderful (and they're not), small businesses simply don't have the resources to become hooked on outside management help. It's a habit they can't afford. The more they depend on outsiders to help run their businesses, the less they learn and develop their own management capabilities.

There is a key distinction to be made between outside management help and routine external services. Low-cost, fixed-price, specialized external services, such as those provided monthly by an accountant or bookkeeper, can be entirely justified. Outside management advice and consulting assistance is more often where the dangers lie.

Successful small entrepreneurs are always the ones who try to do all the critical management stuff themselves, or at least make sure they fully understand it. Later, as they grow bigger and more profitable, they can afford to hand over some responsibilities to managers, employees and even outsiders.

Whoever or whatever you use for outside advice or assistance, it must always be you calling the final shots and making the important decisions.

Outside management advice can become a habit.

Just learn to say no.

NO ACCOUNTING FOR SUCCESS
Your Problems with Accountants Begin the First Time You Ask One of Them Whether Your Projections Make Sense

I have nothing against accountants. I was trained as one myself, and I know they serve an important function. But you should never rely on an accountant for business advice, especially when launching your first venture.

Why not? Because accountants are basically historians. That's how they've been educated, and that's how they think. They can do a great job of explaining what has happened in the past. But making things happen in the future? Forget it. . . .

If you want business advice, you need to go to someone who has run a company over an extended period of time, and by "company," I don't mean an accounting firm or law practice. You want a person who has had a real operating business. It doesn't have to be in the same industry as yours, or even a related one, but it should have been around for 10 years or more. Why? Because you mainly learn about business from failures, especially your own. Anyone who has run a company for 10 years has had plenty of failures—with luck, not terminal ones. . . .

The person who has already made the mistake is the one who can warn you about it, before you do the same thing.

—Norm Brodsky, "Street Smarts," *Inc.*

15

PERSONNEL . . .
IT'S PERSONAL:

Employees Make or Break
Your Small Business

Headaches and Heartaches

Being an employer is the least palatable of all the responsibilities facing a new entrepreneur in a small business. Nothing beats it for headaches and heartaches. It ain't fun, it's just gotta be done.

Employees are a key survival factor in small businesses. Far more so than in Big Business. A few good 'uns or bad 'uns aren't going to make or break IBM. But if you have only a handful of employees, it can take just one good 'un or one bad 'un to either make your business a success, or bring it to its knees.

Small business failures can result *solely* from employee problems. And when there are such problems, it's your survival at stake, not the employees'. They can always tell you to take your job and shove it, walk out the door and go find another job. You can't go set up a new business, as soon as the old one fails; you'll be in too big of a mess.

Yet many new entrepreneurs will do their damnedest to run away from confronting the problems of handling employee relations and personnel management. It's unfamiliar territory to many. It's painful, stressful, confusing, nebulous and very personal . . . even if you're only halfway human, you can't help but hate the responsibilities.

They're employees. Like it or not, that makes you an employer. With all the headaches and heartaches that go with it.

On the positive side, good employees can keep your customers happy and loyal; ensure the quality of your product or service; keep all your administrative routines and business operations working smoothly and efficiently; protect your business's best interests, as if they were their own; be part of a well motivated, enthusiastic team, all working together with you to create a successful, profitable business.

On the negative side, bad employees can alienate and drive away your customers; damage or destroy the quality of your product or service; turn your administrative routines and business operations into chaos and confusion; rob you blind; permeate your team with politicking, hatred and hostility; cause your business to lose money and ultimately to fail.

It's tougher than ever dealing with employees. The job has become more difficult, complicated and unpleasant in recent years because of:

- The many dramatic changes in social habits and personal lifestyles, which make it much harder to reconcile the business's needs with the demands of employees' private lives.
- The suffocating number of government rules, regulations and taxes that relate to jobs, employees and employment.
- The constant threat of legal pressures and harassment related to employees and their possible complaints of mistreatment or discrimination (remember lawyers?).
- The massive restructuring/reengineering of corporate America, with its resultant layoffs of millions of people, which has generated an embittered and distrustful attitude toward *employers in general,* by many who still hold a job and most who are looking for a new one.

Who ever told you being an entrepreneur was all fun? *Being an entrepreneur also means being an employer.* Unless you're a one-person business, which you won't be for long if you want your business to start growing.

Get Trendy or Get Real?

These days, you can go one of two ways in dealing with employee relations and personnel problems: get trendy or get real. Trendy is a Big Business luxury. Real is for small businesses who want to survive.

Get cozy with the sensitive gurus of touchy-feely employer-employee theories . . . or get realistic about human nature and employer-employee conflicts, and apply basic common sense, sound psychology and equal doses of human kindness and business toughness.

Trendy means being politically correct. Addressing employees as associates, team members, colleagues, partners in progress, whatever. Treating them as intimate, equal members of your business family. Paying for sensitivity training sessions. Calling in cultural diversity counselors. Sending employees to three-day motivational seminars in the Rockies. Giving them little plastic-coated cards with your inspirational mission statement, to carry in their wallets and close to their hearts.

Or you can concentrate on doing business, which means being tough and realistic with everyone, including your employees. Simply because business itself is tough, because it's a hard world out there and because there's little margin for idiotic behavior in managing your employees. There's bad tough and good tough; tough doesn't have to mean being unfair, exploitative or acting like an SOB. You can be both tough and decent.

The trendy stuff is Big Business BS. It exists mainly because much of corporate America has so alienated its employees with its disgraceful binges of restructuring and reengineering that it now has to pay some kind of highly visible lip service to the notion that "employees matter."

For large corporations, the trendy stuff doesn't do much good but doesn't do much harm either. It's only games human relations departments play, to justify their existence. It costs a lot of money and wastes a lot of time, but they can well afford it. It's still far cheaper than keeping more people on the payroll or raising wage levels.

You, in your small business, can afford neither the money nor the time, nor can you afford to appear a softheaded, softhearted wuss with your harder-hearted employees. It might lead them to think you're a pushover, which might not be good for your business's financial health.

One path probably leads to failure of your business. The other probably leads to survival. You can guess which.

If you want to know more, just follow Scott Adams's Dilbert cartoon strip regularly. Dogbert and Catbert (the evil human resources director) know all about being trendy.

Your Monkey, Your Back

It's in the very nature of small businesses, where the boss has to decide on everything that's really important, that the boss also has to be the personnel manager. You can't afford to hire a qualified personnel manager. Even if you have a competent office manager, he/she will only be handling personnel administrative matters. The hard decisions will still all have to be yours, since you cannot risk the consequences of bad personnel decisions by an office manager.

The risks are too great. The stakes are too high.

Many new business owner-operators have never had direct, full responsibility for hiring, firing, pay levels, work scheduling and similar decisions relating to employees. Maybe in a previous job they held hierarchical responsibilities over other employees. That's not the same thing–that's simply supervision. They could usually off-load the sensitive problems on a personnel manager, or blame the chief executive for the decisions when they had to serve as messengers of bad news to their subordinates.

All that changes in your own business. You're responsible for all the decisions, minor or major, good or bad, and all the employees know it. There's nowhere to run, nowhere to hide. There's no way of making excuses or shifting the responsibility or the blame.

The monkey's firmly and publicly sitting on your back.

You're the boss, the owner, aren't you?

When someone has to be fired, or a new employee has to be hired, or changes in work schedules interfere with employees' home lives, or an employee has child care problems, or employees start quarreling among themselves, or scheduled hours need to be cut, or female employees say you are favoring male employees (or vice versa), or minority employees say they are being unfairly treated, or some workers' salaries are raised and others not, or an employee has to be reprimanded, or is injured on the job, or stays home sick, or is suspected of theft, or mistreats a customer, or starts waving a gun around the shop floor, or, or, or . . . *it's always your problem.*

Yours and yours alone.

Since there are *never* perfect solutions when dealing with human problems and human beings, and you are unlikely to possess the wisdom of King Solomon (and even he would have made one royal mess out of palace personnel problems if he'd been around in the '90s), whatever you do, there will be some bad feelings, from someone, for some reason, somehow. And it will be personal, directed at you, the owner, the boss.

It will always be your fault.

In large corporations, the top executives and managers can often conveniently distance themselves from the unpleasantness and human pain of employee problems. They can make broad "policy" decisions that may devastate many employees' lives, circulate them in a dry, unemotional memo, pat themselves on the back for a difficult job well done, and still get home in time for a couple of drinks, a nice dinner and maybe catch the latest movie.

In small business, analyzing a personnel problem and deciding what to do . . . that's *the easy part.* Any corporate bozo can do that.

The hard part is being the messenger, executioner, hatchet-man, jailer, schoolmarm and family priest, all rolled into one giant "boss person," and having to live with the human consequences of your decisions. If you have an ounce of humanity in you, and a conscience that drives you to attempt to behave fairly, you'll never get to feel entirely comfortable with this part of an owner-operator's responsibilities . . . nor come to enjoy it.

However, there's a positive side to this unpleasant coin. By not running away from these personnel problems and responsibilities, and by taking a close, personal interest in everything that relates to your small business's employees, you will be able to form a friendly, cohesive team of well-motivated employees, far more productive and far more dedicated than any large corporation could ever hope to have . . . which will be a major competitive asset to your business.

Said in cold-blooded business-speak, being a halfway decent human being and genuinely caring about your employees and their well-being, can also turn out to be good for your bottom line.

So there *is* an upside to carrying that monkey on your back.

The upside is improved profitability.

> **WORKER SATISFACTION FOUND TO BE HIGHER AT SMALL COMPANIES**
> **People at Smaller Businesses Are Happier with the Pay and Their Jobs, Poll Finds**
>
> Small companies are often known for skimpy pay and benefits, but a poll [by *Inc.* magazine] showed their workers are more satisfied with their jobs than employees at big companies. . . .
>
> According to *Inc.*, small-business workers are more likely to feel that they have "the opportunity to do every day what they do best." Compared with big-company workers, small-company employees more often feel they can learn and grow on the job, and can express opinions that count.
>
> —Jeffrey A. Tannenbaum, *The Wall Street Journal*

Downsizing Has Changed Attitudes

Not too many years ago, this chapter on personnel could have been short and sweet. A few words about employees, motivation, payroll administration, cheerleading, this and that, and we'd have been done for the day.

But things have changed dramatically, in everything that relates to jobs and employee attitudes, and they're going to change even more in the coming years. For the worse. These changes are of major consequence to anyone owning and running a business, especially a small business that depends on satisfied, well-motivated employees for its success.

The massive "downsizing" of American corporations, in recent years, has led to: (1) millions of qualified people being fired from good jobs in which they had been led to believe they were secure; (2) permanent reductions in take-home pay, from middle management level on down; (3) virtual elimination of

So the Reengineering, Restructuring and Downsizing Trends Are Corporate America's Latest Wonder Drugs? Not Everyone Agrees

I don't know when I've read such depressing mail . . . the responses blew me out of the water. Keep reading if you want to know what is really happening in Corporate America:

"During the last layoff, my entire department was eliminated, and I was downsized out the door. I found myself competing with several hundred others for practically nonexistent jobs. . . . I found a job in another field making 50% of my former salary, but I consider myself lucky."

"My husband's company went from 11,000 workers to 4,000. The cream of the crop is being let go while corporate profits are soaring. Those who have jobs are doing whatever it takes to hang on."

"My husband and I . . . come home every night totally wiped out. There is no time or energy to work on our home. It's not just us. Everyone we know is overworked, overstressed, overextended and undercompensated."

—Ann Landers, *The Miami Herald*

The conventional wisdom that layoffs are inevitable is nuts. It's corporate insanity. And it's wrong. . . .

I have no patience with CEOs who make excuses for layoffs, who say they're cutting jobs only to make the company more competitive in the future, to protect the interests of shareholders, to avoid bigger layoffs down the road, or whatever. The implication is that, by downsizing, the CEOs are just doing their job and earning their salaries.

Bullshit.

Layoffs are a sign of management failure. You lay people off when you've screwed up, when you've guessed wrong about the market, when you haven't anticipated some critical development or created adequate contingency plans. . . . The people who get hurt are invariably those who had nothing to do with creating the problems in the first place. That is a tragedy. It is a terrible injustice.

—Jack Stack, *Inc.*

Of all the cockamamie rationalizations uttered in defense of large-scale layoffs, the most ridiculous is that they strengthen a company's foundation for the future. The truth is precisely the opposite. Every employee marched before the firing squad signals the death of a possible innovation, the evaporation of another revenue stream or the abandonment of a new opportunity to serve customers. Downsizing encumbers tomorrow's growth for a quick fix today.

—Thomas Petzinger Jr., *The Wall Street Journal*

On the human side, reengineering is a complete catastrophe. All you got was wage and benefit reduction, so what you have is a completely unmotivated work force that says, "Tell me what you want me to do and I'll do it, but that's all I'm going to do."

—James P. Womak, *Fortune*

To Charles Handy, reengineering has become "a polite word for downsizing, which is very unfortunate. It wasn't meant to mean that. [It] has got itself a bad name. For example, I reengineer you. It's not nice. Blowing organizations apart is not conducive to a state of commitment and euphoria. The trouble with reengineering when it is done badly—which it mostly is—is that it leaves people shattered, even the people left behind. They begin to realize that they could be reengineered next and begin thinking about looking for a better place to work. So, in sum, good concept, bad practice. By now, it's probably damaged beyond repair. I say to hell with reengineering. . . . In the end there will be no results, if there is no investment in people."

—Charles Handy, quoted in *Fortune*

new management-level openings offering attractive salaries; (4) virtual elimination of good "entry-level" jobs, paying anything better than the minimum wage; (5) raising of top executive salaries to sports celebrity levels, in the millions of dollars, in recognition of these dubious achievements.

So corporate profits have gone through the roof, which has certainly pleased shareholders, the folks on Wall Street and those CEOs with the stock options. But you don't see too many others cheering this Brave New World:

- If you're reading this book and are considering small business, the statistical odds are that you've either been fired or "early retired," or are finding it difficult to find and hold on to an attractive job;

- Even if that's not your case, you almost certainly know close friends or family members who are in that situation;

- If you're still holding a good, comfortable job, you're well aware of what has happened to the less fortunate and, in the dead of night, may wonder when your turn will come to face the chopping block;

- All this has created one huge pool of disgruntled, distrustful and deep-down-angry people, scattered all around the country.

You had nothing to do with creating this depressing situation. It was the employers in corporate America who did it to the employees of corporate America. You're not corporate America. Yet you are or will soon become an owner of a small business. Owner means boss. Boss means employer. *Employer* can be a dirty word to many employees. Maybe some of yours.

So you will find yourself selecting employees for your business, many of them out of this pool of unhappy people. The attitudes and motivation you encounter will not be what you would have found only a few years ago. Some will be fine; other less than fine.

"Less than fine" can have consequences, ranging from surliness with customers . . . to murder and mayhem with assault rifles.

There's little you can do to change these attitudes, if they exist among your employees. You're running a small business, not a psychiatric ward. But you must be aware that such attitudes exist.

You may not be able to change the attitudes, but you can at least be cautious in protecting your business against the damage that poorly motivated employees can cause.

It Can't Happen? Sure It Can

MURDER IN WORKPLACE IS A MAJOR PART OF THE LATEST DEATH-ON-THE-JOB STATISTICS

If you work in an office, restaurant or store, you have a greater chance of dying on the job than if you are a construction worker . . . and, unless you are a truck driver, you have as good a chance of being murdered on the job as of dying any other way there . . . according to statistics released by the Labor Department.   —Asra Q. Nomani, *The Wall Street Journal*

LAID-OFF MAN KILLS MANAGER AT WAREHOUSE

Miami, Florida.: Angry after being laid off, a warehouse worker shot down his boss, police said. The manager died of multiple gunshot wounds. . . . The worker was charged with first degree murder. . . . "Apparently he was told to work to the end of the day and then he was laid off," said [a detective]. "He confronted the branch manager and shot him."   —*The Miami Herald*

FIRED WORKER COMES BACK SHOOTING, KILLS 3 AT N. CAROLINA COMPANY

Asheville, North Carolina: A man fired from a machine-tool company for fighting with co-workers walked back in and started shooting, killing three people, authorities said. Four others were hurt. . . . He was charged with three counts of murder.   —*The Miami Herald*

5 GUNNED DOWN AT TEXAS COMPANY

Corpus Christi, Texas: A man believed to be a former employee opened fire in a refinery inspection company, killing the owner, his wife and three workers before fatally shooting himself, police said.   —*The Miami Herald*

And if you're still tempted by the trendy, touchy-feely approach to employee relations, try it with these "less than fine" employees. You'll soon change your mind . . . if you're still in business.

Distinguishing Sheep from Goats

You'll find yourself between a rock and a hard place, in selecting and managing your small business's employees.

You can't and mustn't automatically trust your employees, especially the new ones, much as you may want to. Some could be simmering with that deep-rooted anger that can become a self-justification for any kind of "what-the-hell" behavior on the job. Some could be the product of home, school or college environments that no longer place any value on ethics, honesty, courtesy, hard work or other socially acceptable behavior. Some could have such desperate personal problems (finances, spouses, children, drugs, alcohol) that those problems will override any other considerations toward their employer.

Yet many others will be good people, decent people, even wonderful people, with excellent qualifications, positive attitudes and great potential.

There is almost no way you'll be able to identify the sheep from the goats–the potentially good ones from the potentially dangerous ones–at the time of hiring. Especially in a small business, where you have neither the time nor the money to engage in any kind of professional or psychological testing. Let's face it, your hiring decisions will be made largely on gut feel.

Even if your gut is fine-tuned and you get it right 80 percent of the time, what are you going to do about the 20 percent of undesirables who slipped through your net?

If you give everyone the benefit of the doubt and base your management style on blind trust and unfettered confidence in all your employees, you can be certain that those 20 percent of undesirables will see the opportunity you're so generously handing them and will not hesitate to take full advantage.

Your business may not be able to survive the consequences of what they might cook up for you.

Yet if you treat all your employees as a bunch of no-good thieves, liars, psychopaths and sociopaths, that's exactly what you'll be left with, since all the really good people will tell you, in the words of the song, to *take your job and shove it.*

Controls and Discipline Come First

There's no perfect solution to managing employees in this modern world. Anyone who tells you they have one is either a liar, a dreamer or a con artist.

THE HEAVY BURDEN OF LIGHT FINGERS
Trust Doesn't Keep Employees from Stealing; Prevention Does

Chris Daniel used to treat employees like family. That is, until his bookkeeper allegedly swiped $122,000 from his company's coffers which, he says, nearly put him out of business. To cover the loss, Daniel had to cut his salary by 25%, lay off five employees, and take out a second mortgage on his home. . . .

In need of an easy fix–or just some way to get back at the boss–a growing number of workers are ripping off their employers these days. . . . Smaller companies are more vulnerable to its effects . . . they generally don't screen employees very thoroughly . . . nor do small businesses have sophisticated accounting controls in place.

What puts small companies especially at risk, however, is the level of trust that exists between owners and employees. . . . Small-business owners delegate a lot of responsibility to a chosen few. . . .

"No matter how much you trust your employees, you have to monitor their activities–or at least make employees think that you are," says [an accountant].

–Barbara Hetzer, *Business Week/Enterprise*

However, by following a policy that balances tight controls, tough disciplines and clear orders on one hand, with personal trust and close involvement with employees on the other hand, you can end up with a better than average team of dedicated and well-motivated employees.

First start with the tough stuff:

- **Tight Controls:**

  Good employees will not become upset or offended if a business exercises tough and rigid controls . . . as long as they see them applied fairly and evenhandedly to *everyone*, and understand the obvious business necessity for each control. Owners should identify every possible weak link, where employee dishonesty or disinterest could hurt the business, and set up tight controls to prevent it or detect it. Put yourself in the opponent's mind: *"If I were crooked or malicious, how would I go about stealing from or hurting the business?"* Here again, a savvy accountant has often seen the worst and can advise you in setting up the necessary controls on your PC. You can do most or all of it yourself. These would include controls designed to detect signs of weird and suspicious activity in your:

- Petty cash	- Cash register transactions
- Customer invoices	- Daily "take" and bank deposits
- Issuance of checks	- Payments of accounts receivable
- Vendor deliveries	- Supplier invoices
- Inventories	- Employee hours
- Commission calculations	- Payroll calculations

  And so on, depending on the key vulnerabilities of your specific type of business. Each business is different in its potential weak points, just like each home is different in possible break-in points for burglars.

- **Tough Discipline:**

  Establish a disciplined work environment, where there are clear rules of conduct and behavior, and anyone who does not follow them is reprimanded and if necessary fired. The best employees will always prefer tight discipline, applied with fairness and evenhandedness. When there is a lack of discipline, standards automatically drop, always to the benefit of the worst employees and the detriment of the best. Such discipline must be constant and consistent, not capricious, varying from day to day, depending on the boss's mood. Such things as:

- Controls that follow an inflexible, predetermined routine, instead of sometimes on, sometimes off
- Personal appearance, uniforms or dress code, if those are key to your business's image
- Conduct and language toward customers, vendors and outsiders in general
- Working procedures and operational methods
- Workplace cleanliness and safety procedures

From "THE POOR? I HIRE THEM" by Richard L. Barclay

For unskilled and semiskilled work, it's not trained people that businesses need; it's dependable, hard workers. Of course, I'd prefer a dependable worker who's already trained if you've got one, but if necessary, just give me an unskilled but dependable person of character, and I'll take care of the rest.

Before I go any further, let me tell you a little about our company. We're a small family-owned and managed business. We remanufacture telephone equipment for customers all around the country at our plant in Riverside, Calif. Our technicians are formally trained in electronics, but our refurbishers come from the unskilled, so-called disadvantaged segment of the labor pool. We train our refurbishers to do their jobs, and we start them just above the minimum wage.

One of my responsibilities is human resources, which I have slowly but firmly come to conclude is the most important function in a company. . . . For me, this has been a learn-as-you-go process.

The Unemployable

After five years of interviewing a jillion applicants, checking up on references, getting results from drug labs, and employee counselings and firings, I've come to two very simple conclusions about people and their employability. . . .

First, there are some people who are simply unemployable. They are physically and mentally competent, but they literally cannot work. They look normal, they sound normal, they are trainable, and they may even say they want to get a job. But they confuse "wanting money" with "wanting to work," which for some weird reason they just can't do. They simply can't be on time. They simply can't work fast. They simply can't follow instructions. It's just the way they're built.

Charitable persons would use the word "misguided" or "disadvantaged" and would prescribe job training or vocational development. The less charitable person would use the word "lazy" or "undisciplined" and would recommend a good kick in the pants. But I have come to the conclusion that there are people out there who simply cannot change their aversion to work any more than they can change their preference for their favorite ice cream flavor. And I've seen it in every color, ethnic group and sex.

This observation has led to a second conclusion. . . . For the lower-echelon, unskilled positions, companies don't need "trained" applicants nearly as much as they need people of character. I can train a person to disassemble a phone; I can't train her not to get a bad attitude when she discovers that she's expected to come to work every day when the rest of us are there. I can train a worker to properly handle a PC board; I can't train him to show up to work sober or to respect authority.

—The Wall Street Journal

- **Clear Internal Communication:**
  Small businesses cannot waste effort and money on bureaucratic, time-consuming "employee communications" policies, typical of large corporations. However, at least make sure that all the key rules are communicated to all employees, clearly and simply spelled out in brief memos, and repeated verbally. All rules, disciplines and policies must be so clearly communicated that no one can ever say, "Oh, I didn't know about that, nobody told me."

Trust and Motivation Come a Close Second

With tough and inflexible ground rules clearly spelled out and even-handedly applied, only then does it become possible for you to loosen up, on the human side. You can now delegate important responsibilities to specific employees, you can show them that you trust them to do a professional job, and you can motivate them by your personal involvement. You can tolerate genuine mistakes, so that they can learn by their mistakes, only because you now have your controls to stop such mistakes from degenerating into something worse.

Your advantage in small business is that you can become personally involved with each employee.

It's a balancing act. You counterbalance the obvious rigor of the controls and the disciplines, against the fact that you, the boss, are personally involved with each employee and are openly demonstrating your confidence in their professional abilities.

It may appear to be a manipulative double standard, but it isn't.

At one level, you are making it clear to everyone, indiscriminately, that *the business* (not you personally) has certain rules (a kind of security safety net) that *everyone must follow,* to ensure the business against being badly hurt or even destroyed, by the unpredictable actions of a dishonest or irresponsible employee. Who could be any flawed member of the group.

At another level, you are demonstrating personally to each individual employee that you are sincerely interested in them and their work, that you care about their well-being and that you trust them to perform well.

In a small business you are vitally dependent on your few employees. They can make all the difference between success and failure. By making it your personal responsibility to handle all key personnel matters (at least until the business is bigger) you can achieve a balance between: (1) having everyone accept willingly the business's tight controls and tough disciplines, yet (2) getting the best possible performance from each individual employee.

The Boss Sets the Example

Employees aren't happy campers . . . neither are you. To them it's only a job. To you it's a business and probably your life.

You naturally care far more about the business than any employee ever can or will. You're the owner, the boss. You have far more at stake, so you set the example.

A strong, personable boss, who acts, walks, talks and thinks like a boss is far more effective than a wimp boss who just wants to be one of the boys and girls, and is afraid to throw his/her weight around, for fear of offending them. Business is not a social club and you'll never be accepted by your employees as one of the boys and girls . . . they'll just see you as insecure, weak and ineffectual if you try desperately to be loved. And as manipulatable, by those who would like to take advantage.

Never be ashamed or embarrassed about being the boss and acting the boss. It goes with the territory.

Small businesses always assume some of the style and personality of the owner-operator. That is all to the good. A business with character will always operate better than a faceless one. Especially in regard to the employees. They feel more comfortable in a business that reflects the personality and presence of its owner.

It may sound hackneyed, but there is still validity to the notion that a small business can operate as a kind of family. A traditional, disciplined, severe family, with rigid rules and punishments for bad behavior, maybe . . . but a family nevertheless. Of which you are the "head of the household," whether Mom or Pop.

This family nature of the business is up to you to build; it doesn't happen naturally. It requires human characteristics that have little to do with your business abilities. It can be most frustrating, when your working time is taken up by employees' problems. It can be most irritating, when you have to become involved in petty employee disputes.

Yet it pays off, if you're willing to make the effort.

The end result of making this personal effort is a clear and quantifiable business benefit. An insurance policy, if you will. By creating a "family environment," you can protect your small business against some of the bad stuff and the bad attitudes that the outside world sends you along with the job applicants–the anger, dishonesty, rudeness, drugs, you name it.

But it's a very personal thing and it depends entirely on how much of a "people person" you are. If you aren't, so you aren't and you shouldn't even try to act it; it would look phony and forced. However, most entrepreneurs have a natural bent that way; they tend to be outgoing and able to relate to other people.

On the other hand, if you're one mean-spirited SOB or simply a first-class horse's ass, that does not necessarily mean you will fail in small business. There are major SOBs and certifiable horse's asses out there who have been most successful in business. But if you are, you should forget everything we've just covered, operate a tight and unpleasant police-state style of management and expect the worst from your employees. Because they'll be sure to meet your expectations. Your small business may still be a success, done your own nasty way . . . different strokes for different folks.

Hey, even the mob runs successful businesses, and just look at their methods for settling employee disputes.

"No" Men, Not "Yes" Men

Most people starting off in their own businesses have come from positions as employees. Now, even if they have only a couple of employees, they're transformed into "boss people."

They may suddenly discover how smart and brilliant they are, since the employees may agree with anything and everything they say and do. All their ideas and suggestions and actions are inspired.

It's human nature.

It goes by the age-old label "brown-nosing."

And it's particularly dangerous for the inexperienced, lonely, scared newcomer, who will often eagerly discuss problems and ideas with the employees in the genuine, democratic belief that their comments will be sincere and well-intentioned.

They may be . . . they may also be cynical and manipulative.

Keep a skeptical eye on employees who agree with you too often. A little disagreement is good for the health. You don't need "yes-men" . . . you need "no-men."

Seminars and Training

The hype and the hustle goes on.

It proliferates in the fertile ground of employee training and human relations. Since there is no business where employer-employee relations are perfectly smooth, and there are always problems in dealing with employee issues, so also there will always be "experts" out there, pitching "solutions."

You will be exposed to a constant stream of sales pitches and marketing messages, attempting to convince you that both your business and your employees will be magically transformed, if you and they attend seminars or training sessions on any one of thousands of techniques or disciplines or "business religions."

Some of these have merit. Many don't. Either way, it's most unlikely, at this incipient stage in your business life, that you, your employees and your small business could derive enough benefit, even from the better ones, which would justify the dollar cost and the wastage of precious time.

Even the better training courses or seminars for employees are usually aimed at trying to solve those intractable employee problems that large corporations often face, in dealing with that unmotivated, resentful, scared and deep-down-angry workforce we've already discussed. That's why so many of them include that magical word, "motivational." If they need motivation, it's only because they're decidedly unmotivated right now. Back to Dilbert!

First piece of advice: instead, rely on that personal touch and involvement to help your employees and keep them well motivated and enthusiastic. It'll work far better and cost much less than any seminar. It'll take up some of your time, but it's time well invested. It's a huge personal advantage you have over any large corporation. You can do, with good intentions, dedication and a little time, what the biggest human resources department in the largest corporations can never achieve.

Second piece of advice: if you do decide to invest in training and seminars, either for yourself or your employees, make it educational and/or technical, never motivational . . . on critical software programs, specific computer hardware, marketing techniques, advertising methods, production systems and so on. Such training can give you an immediate business "payback."

The rest is only "payout," with little or no return.

DISGRUNTLED EMPLOYEES

Percentage of companies hit with lawsuits after terminating employees:

1990: 10%
1991: 44%
1992: 52%
1993: 53%
1994: 57%

[From a survey of larger companies]
—*The Wall Street Journal*

Laws, Rules and Regulations

The more your small business grows and the more employees you have, the more you will feel the weight of an overpowering number of government rules and regulations, related to who you hire, how you hire, who you fire, how you fire, how they work, when they work, where they work, how you pay them, when they go to the toilet, what kind of toilet, which quality of toilet paper and on and on, endlessly. It can make you nervous. Or insane, if you try to be perfect. In this area, perfection is impossible, so just do your best, within reason, and leave it at that.

Approach rules and regulations on employment matters with a large dose of plain common sense:

- There's no way any small business can ever comply with each and every rule and regulation regarding employees. Since it's impossible, relax and stop getting nervous. While you're small and new, you're not a target and no one's going to bother you much.
- Talk to your accountant. Based on his/her real-world experience, learn about the major stuff you should seriously worry about and when. The minor stuff you can forget about, at least for the moment. Catch up with it when you can . . . if ever.
- Don't start worrying before it's time. You'll go crazy trying to plan for the sky falling in, you'll neglect the business and run the risk of going bust. Be pragmatic, instead of losing your mind.
- Keep up your regular press reading on news items that relate to laws and regulations on employees and employment. It'll keep you up to date and on your toes.
- Never forget about the lawyer virus. Suing employers for every imaginable offense against downtrodden, defenseless employees, under these many laws and regulations, keeps many of them fat and wealthy.

Your Personnel Manager's Checklist

So now you're also the personnel manager, among your many other duties. You'd probably rather not be congratulated, but you've gotta do what you've gotta do. Growth and success inevitably mean hiring employees, and having employees inevitably means that someone has to supervise the personnel area. It's far too important to be neglected. So, until you're bigger, that job has to be yours.

Personnel management and everything that relates to employees is all detail, none of it very exciting and much of it pretty boring. But some of the detail can be vitally important and some downright dangerous. Here's a brief checklist of reminders, pointers and suggestions, all from the small business owner-operator's perspective:

- **Wage Levels:**

  Check around. Pay the locally prevailing hourly rate for your type of business. No higher, until you know what you're doing. Otherwise you may dig yourself into a permanent cost hole. If you're having trouble hiring, you might consider offering a "starting bonus" for those who make it through their first thirty or ninety days.

- **Salaried versus Hourly:**

  This depends on your type of business. Usually it will be hourly wages, but remember that sometimes a fixed salary can be better all around, in terms of motivation and productivity.

- **Hours Worked:**

  A good time clock is essential if you pay by the hour. Employees may not like clocking in and out, but if you leave it to signing in and out on a control sheet, some cheating will always happen. By the end of the month, this can represent a fair piece of change, in the form of inflated payroll costs.

- **Overtime:**

  You can go bankrupt allowing employees to run up overtime hours at "time and a half," uncontrolled. Only permit overtime work if authorized and under tight control. It's a big temptation for an employee to "hang out" for an extra hour or two, and let the clock run up.

NOW BUTCHERS, ENGINEERS GET SIGNING BONUSES

Gone are the days when only the top dog got a signing bonus. These days, everyone from butchers to burger flippers is getting one. [A] 19-year-old college student will collect an extra $150 Friday, after making hamburgers for three months for $5.50 an hour at a Burger King. . . .

Signing bonuses now pop up at almost every job level. . . . Companies say one-time cash payments help them fill vacancies and reduce turnover in shortage-plagued regions and occupations, without inflating their pay levels; individuals typically reap the rewards within the first six months. The recruiting tool works the best when you're the first to offer it in a certain locale.

—Joann S. Lublin, *The Wall Street Journal*

WORKERS GET "A FRACTION OF THE ACTION"
Motorola Sharing $15M in Profits

Motorola's two manufacturing plants in S. Florida raked in record profits last year. Now their 5,500 employees are raking in $15 million for their part in it. Employees are ecstatic.

"Our people have been working extremely hard and turning in a lot of overtime," says [a manager]. "Things like this make them feel pretty good." A consultant calls profit-sharing a "fraction of the action."

"They earned it and they deserved it," he said. "I wish more companies would share profits with their employees all the way down the line, because morale at most companies these days is very bad. We know how to fire people, but we don't know how to reward them."

—James McNair, *The Miami Herald*

- **Bonuses and Incentives:**

  If carefully thought out, well structured and clearly understood by each employee, these can work beautifully in motivating employees to do their best. They share in both the low points and the high points of your business. But if poorly designed or unfair, incentive systems will create more resentment than no incentives at all.

- **Health Insurance, Other Benefits:**

  One of the biggest personnel problems in a small business is deciding how far you can go, economically, in paying for health insurance and other employee benefits . . . or whether you can afford to provide them at all. There are no easy answers. Check competitive conditions in the local employment market, find out what similar businesses are doing and make careful calculations of what it might cost you. Preferably, provide no benefits until you are up and running and know how far you can realistically go, without ruining your business.

- **Scheduling Working Hours:**

  If yours is a nine-to-five, five-days-a-week business, scheduling is easy. However, many small businesses work longer and more variable hours and days, making scheduling of employee time one of the toughest, most complex pieces of detail work you will find. It's never finished,

FINDING INSURANCE, STAYING PROFITABLE IS OFTEN A DILEMMA

For a small company, it's a conflict—how to offer health insurance to your workers without going broke. For startup firms, it's a benefit that's often out of financial reach. Even larger companies say figuring out how to pay for costly employee health benefits is a major concern.

Companies that do offer health benefits to their workers are shopping around . . . for better deals. Many employ part-time workers to avoid having to offer benefits. Others are requiring employees to pay part of the cost. All are unsure what the future will bring.

—The Miami Herald

WORK & FAMILY
Parents Go to Bat for a Little Time Off to Back Kids' Teams

Many, if not most, jobs can be managed more flexibly than they are, permitting not only parents but all employees to attend to important personal needs—doctors' appointments, friends' or relatives' crises, or personal business. The potential benefit: more productive, committed workers. . . .

Dan Logan, president of Trinity Communications in Boston . . . lets his 45 employees control their hours and encourages community involvement. Though he would fire anyone who abused the freedom, he hasn't had to.

"If you give people flexibility, they give back to you a lot more by coming in early, working late or even coming in on the weekend," he says. "If you want the best people, you have to give them a lot of room."

—Sue Shellenbarger, The Wall Street Journal

never perfect, always keeps changing. It's so important, you must control it yourself. For better or worse, work scheduling dramatically affects productivity, efficiency, motivation, customer service, total payroll costs, etc.

- **Displaying Work Schedules:**
  Put it in writing, display it clearly. There are preprinted forms that are available. But doing it on PC spreadsheets is fast and easy, since you can prepare updated versions whenever there are minor changes . . . and there are always minor changes.

- **Flexible Hours:**
  Many home-pressured employees value a flexible work schedule more than a higher wage. It can have advantages to both sides. The major disadvantage is that it requires constant control and supervision, as schedules keep changing.

- **Recruiting:**
  The usual route is classified ads, but interviewing many candidates can be a chore. Employment agencies can save time and may be worth the expense. Word of mouth and personal recommendations, through current employees, often produce the best results.

BALANCING BOSSES AND BABIES

Parents know it's one of the hardest things they've done. Working and having a baby. Having a baby and working.

Yet more and more, it's the scenario for women. "It's not a choice for most women," says [an author]. "Women have to work. We need two incomes to support families."

That's one major reason that child care . . . [is] among the top concerns of American women. It's one reason behind the corporate flight of professional women who stay home—when they can afford it—or start their own firms, rather than continue to work for rigid organizations. "It's difficult for employers because the workplace is designed for getting jobs done," she notes.

[But] quietly, without much fanfare, creative companies and employees are finding ways to take care of both business and children.

—Susana Barciela, *The Miami Herald*

SURVEY: NIGHT SHIFT LACKS ACCESS TO CHILD CARE

When graveyard shift workers at a food processing plant began leaving their sleeping children in parked cars because they couldn't find child care after normal business hours, authorities knew they were looking at a problem that would become endemic to modern American society. A report addresses the dilemma shift workers face when they can't find off-hours child care.

The U.S. economy is becoming a 24-hour operation as employers move toward more flexible scheduling.

—*The Miami Herald*

- **Hiring:**

  Treat all job applicants equally and fairly. Make sure that each completes a standard application form. Read these carefully. Interview thoroughly. Ask tough questions. Check references. Check Social Security cards and other ID. Keep all paperwork on file, especially rejections, in case you are later accused of discriminatory hiring.

- **Records:**

  Keep complete, well-organized files for each employee. More information is better than less. Too often, small businesses throw everything together in one fat file, and cannot retrieve key information about an employee when they most need it. Keep files of all departed employees; you may need them one day.

- **Temps:**

  There is a major trend toward the use of temporary workers, through "temp" agencies. This can make economic sense for large corporations but can be counterproductive in small businesses, where you need a much closer relationship with your few employees.

- **Probationary Period:**

  Give all new hires written advice that theirs is a ninety-day probationary hiring, even if you feel confident they will work out. Check if you are still satisfied before the ninety days is up. Only retain the employee if satisfactory. This will also help lower your unemployment insurance premiums.

- **Immigrants:**

  The INS (Immigration & Naturalization Service) can get you into serious trouble if they catch you hiring illegal immigrants, even unknowingly. Your best protection is those file records, to prove you checked out what you could. In spite of current anti-immigrant sentiment, remember that immigrants are often some of the hardest-working, most honest and best-motivated employees you will find.

> **71 ALIEN WORKERS ARRESTED**
> Federal officers at a New Jersey perfume factory last week arrested 71 undocumented immigrants. . . . Officials are still investigating whether the factory or a temporary agency . . . should be penalized for hiring illegal immigrants.
> —Melody Petersen, *The New York Times*

- **Firing:**

  Firing is never a pleasant task, unless you're a sadist. Learn to fire politely, fairly and considerately. If you have clear justification for the firing, hand over (or mail) a "for cause" letter. Make it factual, not offensive. This will help reduce your unemployment insurance rates.

- **Quitting:**

  Discuss their reasons (you may learn something you didn't know). Ask the departing employee to sign a standard form, confirming it is their decision to quit. If they don't, mail them a letter confirming that they left voluntarily. This can prevent future allegations to the contrary.

- **Working Conditions:**

  Use common sense. Don't expect employees to work under conditions you would not accept yourself. Check the conditions personally (lighting, seating, heating, cooling, ventilation, restrooms, etc.). Make improvements, in part to avoid legal problems but above all to boost employee morale.

- **Safety Conditions:**

  Think carefully about accident prevention and do what you can to create a safe workplace. Your worker's compensation insurer will give you free help. Take full advantage, it's mutually beneficial.

- **Worker's Compensation Insurance:**

  You must carry this (state-regulated) insurance, if you have employees. The premiums can be costly, if your business activity has a high risk of workplace accidents. But actual premiums will be higher or lower, based on the number of work accidents you have or don't have. So serious attention to injury prevention can save you money.

- **Employee Appearance:**

  If your employees deal directly with the public and your business requires uniforms, caps, clean appearance, whatever, make it stick. Make no exceptions, treat everyone equally, be fair, be considerate. But don't make exceptions. If you are in the same workplace, set the example yourself.

- **Workplace Security:**

  Take all possible commonsense precautions against crime, to protect your employees, your customers, your business and yourself. Apart from the direct cost of a crime, there can be the indirect cost of lawsuits by victims of crime on your premises.

- **Employee Handbook:**

  Larger businesses will often have a "handbook," given to all employees, spelling out all employment details. In theory, all employees read this with loving care. In practice, few ever look at it, and it's strictly a defensive measure against potential complaints or lawsuits. If you feel you need one, standard formats are available in office supply stores or from employment consultants.

- **Payroll Processing and Taxes:**
  Either have your bookkeeper do your payroll processing and payroll taxes or use one of the various good (and cheap) payroll processing services. Don't try to do this yourself. You will not save money, you will waste time, you may make mistakes in payroll checks, you may make mistakes in tax calculations. You may get into trouble. This way, you will at least keep your nose clean with your payroll taxes and withholding taxes.

Who Says Personnel Is Fun?

Yes, you're right.

Personnel management doesn't sound like much fun.

It isn't. It's full of headaches and heartaches, especially for the owner of a small business. It's messy, fuzzy, detailed, time-consuming, emotionally charged, unpleasant, psychologically draining, bureaucratic, confrontational and more.

It's definitely not fun entrepreneur stuff.

But that's no excuse for neglect. It's still one of the most critical areas of small business management. It can make you or break you.

So just do it. No whining.

Be your own personnel manager and a good one.

With time, you'll find out what a wise decision that was.

16

THE GOVERNMENT, YOUR BUSINESS PARTNER:

*Gotta Learn
to Get Along*

So You Know a Better Place?

Everyone complains, whines, moans and groans.

About taxes, bureaucracy, paperwork, rules, regulations, interference, excesses and plain dumb-headedness. On the part of the government, in all its different forms, shapes and sizes, whether federal, state, county or city.

You'll be sorely tempted to join the chorus, when you discover that you just got yourself an uninvited guest . . . a bumbling, irritating and demanding partner, who will eat up your money, waste your time and drive you up the wall with dumb demands. The government, your partner . . . forever!

Try looking at it from a different angle. In America, the government, its many services and the prices you pay for them (i.e., taxes) are the best deal you're going to find anywhere in the world. No other country comes close.

So you know a better place? You'd rather operate a business in, say, Mexico? Brazil? Italy? India? Russia? Indonesia? Uganda? You'd go out of your mind, in the first month. Believe me . . . been there, done it.

Now hear this: The U.S.A. is a small businessperson's paradise, compared with the government interference, political pressures, bureaucracy, corruption and extortionate taxes you would face in those countries or any other. Just try being an entrepreneur anywhere else–*anywhere*–and you'll come winging back to the good ol' U.S.A. and passionately kiss the airport apron on your return. Still think that you know a better place? So go there, and *hasta la vista, baby!*

So be fair. Be appreciative of what you've got, which is the opportunity to pursue a small capitalist's entrepreneurial dream, in the best business

65-year-old Ruth Dusenbury of Holyoke, Colo., owner of Speer Cushion Co., a 20-employee operation, said her daughter, who will inherit the business, now spends more time making sure the business is in compliance with federal regulations than she does on management issues.
—Stephanie N. Mehta, *The Wall Street Journal*

Many small businesses find they must buy computers or hire accountants just to comply with IRS record-keeping requirements for inventory. . . . Glenn Silverman, 36, owner of Glenn's Custom Photo in Chicago, as a small-business owner, spends three hours a week handling records and forms for federal, state, local and payroll taxes. " I'd love to see the elimination of the IRS," he says.
—*Time*

Payroll-tax rules top the list of regulations branded as "the most significant burdens to small and midsize businesses," says a survey of owners of these businesses by Arthur Andersen. Next came OSHA regulations, followed by environmental rules.
—*The Wall Street Journal*

environment in the world, bar none, for taking a crack at it. The price you pay is that you have a partner in your business: the government . . . the much-maligned gummint. A dull, lumpish partner, with no graces or table manners, which can often be one royal pain in the butt; which you are unlikely ever to love, or even to like; which needs regular tax feedings to stay docile; which may sometimes make unbelievably stupid demands on your business.

But your partner, none the less.

Y'know, that's not such a bad deal, by a long shot. The taxes and the irritating demands are a pretty fair trade for the opportunity to do business in the world's most prosperous, stable and law-abiding country.

So why not cooperate with your unwelcome partner, and do what you can to keep relations cordial? You've just got to learn to get along amicably with your lumbering, bumbling Big Brother government partner. Fighting won't get you anywhere and cooperation will keep you sane and in business. Or go enlist in some wacko, nontax-paying, hillbilly militia group, and forget about ever having a successful business. You can't have it both ways.

The rabble-rousers would have you believe the government is some kind of Evil Empire. In fact, in general it's remarkably fair, evenhanded, reasonable and surprisingly logical, when it takes some action against some business for infractions, evasions, noncompliance or whatever. Dumb maybe, inefficient certainly, but seldom malicious or avaricious.

You don't have to like the government, but it's in your best interest to learn to live with it.

No Hiding Behind Your Accountant

On the one hand, there's no way you, a small business owner-operator, can or should be aware of every major and minor detail there is to know about federal, state, county, city, borough and neighborhood taxes, fees, laws, rules, regulations, restrictions, licenses, permits, papers and so forth. There's just too much of it.

On the other hand, you can't just shrug your shoulders, sigh "too much stuff" and leave everything to your accountant, while you go play with the fun stuff in your small business. The accountant can't pay every tax obligation for you, check that all your paperwork is properly done and anticipate every problem before it happens. The accountant can't be aware of everything you're up to, in your daily business activities, some of which might get you into trouble.

You can't hide behind your accountant. You see it happen in small business, because the owner-operator doesn't want to be bothered by those tedious, boring, bureacratic matters. Which they definitely are.

Then, when everything finally hits the fan and taxes aren't paid, heavy penalties are levied, tax inspectors come knocking, you'll hear: "Oh, it's all that damn accountant's fault."

Bull. It isn't. It's the owner's fault.

Anyway, if you start trying to shift the routine office work in this area over to your bookkeeper or accountant, be prepared for a hefty monthly bill for services. They will charge you for doing routine nonaccounting work that you or your office manager can and should be doing. It's an option, but it's an expensive one.

So take the middle ground. At least learn about the important, dangerous stuff. Become aware of your business's key responsibilities and obligations. It's not difficult, just tedious and boring. The big advantage is that, once you've gone to the trouble of learning about it, everything stays very much the same, month after month, year after year. The second time around, it's a snap.

You don't want to become an expert, but you can at least train yourself to become aware of all the key obligations and bureaucratic routines that relate to your specific type of business, and then control them yourself, intelligently, efficiently and on time. Such as:

- **Local Stuff:**
  Discuss with your accountant all the odds and ends of routine obligations, for your particular type of business, in your neighborhood, city and county. Things like operating licenses, building permits, local taxes, restrictions on specific business activities, etc.
- **State Stuff:**
  Again, check with your accountant on everything needed to keep your nose clean in your own state, such as state tax ID number, annual

corporation fee, collection and control of sales taxes, payment of sales taxes, payroll taxes, other taxes and licenses, periodic reports to file, etc.

- **Federal Stuff:**
  Likewise, at the federal level: federal tax ID number, self-employed income tax, corporate taxes, payroll taxes, withholding taxes, periodic reports to file, etc.

- **Trade Stuff:**
  Certain businesses have specific obligations and duties that relate to their type of trade or activity, like health inspections for restaurants, certification for certain workers, safety inspections for factories, disposal of dangerous waste, operating regulations for specific activities, dangerous products, construction activities and so on. These can be checked out easily with your local trade association. Join the main trade association for your type of business. Subscribe to the principal trade magazines. You will be able to read about key trade problems that are of concern to similar businesses.

- **And the Hairy Stuff:**
  You can't protect your business, in this modern, socially sensitive world, without reasonable awareness of what can only be labeled the Hairy Stuff: workplace safety, working conditions, workplace injuries, minority rights, handicapped rights, age discrimination, sexual harassment, environmental safety, wetlands legislation, endangered species, emission restrictions and all the rest of it. Welcome to the Age of the Spotted Owl. Maybe none of the Hairy Stuff will ever touch your business and you'll cruise along, happily unaffected. Or maybe the Hairy Stuff'll jump you with something totally bizarre, unpredictable and uncontrollable, and your business will be blown to smithereens, just because you happened to be standing in the wrong place at the wrong moment. Read the papers and business sections regularly, and you will be able to follow the evolution of the kinds of Hairy Stuff that might affect your type of business. Your awareness of the risks and dangers may help you avoid needless pain.

Dates and Deadlines

There's always a date and a deadline, by which something's got to be paid, some form filled in, some document mailed. That's how bureaucracies operate. And usually it's up to you to know what and when and how. Bureaucracies don't often mail you polite little reminder notes of what your obligations are for the coming month. They assume you know, and they punish you with fines and penalties, when you miss your deadline.

So don't miss your deadlines.

Once you've checked out what your principal obligations will be, sit down and block out for the year, month by month, what has to be done and by what date . . . tax payments to mail out, license renewal fees to pay, reports to complete, inspections to schedule, whatever.

Control all these dates on a highly visible wall calendar, agenda book, PC tickler or something similar. Do each task well before the deadline, never on the last day. You can count on it: if you leave it until that last day, inevitably that'll be the day that something more important comes up and you'll miss that deadline.

You'll be pleasantly surprised. Doing it this way, you'll find that it really isn't that much work, at least while you're still reasonably small (when you're bigger, you'll also have the staff to handle it). You have your files neatly organized in each area, you have all the information handy and the work gets done. It's a nonevent. And each following month or year will be an almost automatic repeat. So get it right the first time, and the rest is a breeze.

Government obligations turn into a nightmare for small businesses only when owners do none of these things. When they don't do their homework, don't check with their accountant, expect to receive advices and notices in advance, assume someone else will be doing what they should be doing, and don't follow up on who has done what. Finally, when a major crisis develops, it can be shattering: heavy back taxes, interest due, severe penalties levied, rushed documents, no cash to cover the obligations and turmoil all around, hurting the entire business.

None of this needs to happen. All you need to do is manage your government obligations, just like you do the rest of your business obligations.

There are no excuses.

Paying Taxes on Time . . . or Late

Following these suggestions, you'll know what taxes your business owes and when. Work closely with your accountant on all tax matters. That's one of their specialties. Calculate your taxes correctly and pay what you owe, when you owe.

But what if you just don't have the money?

With rents, supplier invoices and other business payments, you can always finagle a little more time, with a few phone calls and a good sob story.

But Big Brother doesn't operate that way. The rules are inflexible. Your accountant will tell you how you can pay taxes late and how much it will cost you in penalties, but paying taxes late is a dangerous game. It can be the beginning of digging yourself into a deeper and deeper hole, out of which you may not emerge.

As an exceptional measure, in a cash crunch emergency, paying taxes late can *occasionally* make business sense . . . gain some time, pay the penalty and get out of the hole quickly.

But *never* make it a habit; it's the same as getting locked into loan sharks. There's often no way back out. The cost of the money you are "borrowing" from the government, with interest and penalties, is very expensive. You tend to keep running later and later, and the total tax debt keeps building up.

Owing overdue taxes to the government is a possible game for large corporations with tame tax lawyers in tow . . . but never for small businesses. You are dealing with a huge bureaucracy and with government employees. Once you owe too much, just the process of trying to explain, negotiate and work out settlement plans can be immensely time-consuming. It can paralyze you and your business while you're doing it. It's not as simple as running late on the rent, calling the landlord, gaining ten days and that's that.

So even if it appears financially tempting, it's just not worth it, if only because of the later disruption to your management work.

In states with sales taxes, there's an even greater temptation to delay in paying the sales taxes you just collected from your customers. The monthly

MESSING WITH THE IRS

A wrong turn that is almost invariably fatal in my experience is when people who are in a bad cash bind turn to the tax accounts—their withholding accounts—for sources of working capital. The IRS is very specific about withholding taxes from employees: That's the employees' money, and it now belongs to the IRS. It was never your money as a business owner.

If the cash sits in the bank and you commingle it, the temptation is there to use those dollars because they're there and you really need them. The truth is they're not there. It's not your money and it never was. And if you use that cash to operate the business instead of paying it to the IRS, they're not only going to be upset, they're going to come in and close you down and they're going to make it stick. And once you get into that game, it is almost always fatal.

—Interview with Wendell E. Dunn, Professor, Wharton Business School,
The Wall Street Journal

SNITCHING ON TAX CHEATS MAY LEAD TO BIG REWARDS FROM THE IRS

Do you have evidence that someone is cheating on taxes? Hand over the information to the IRS and you may be eligible for a reward of up to $100,000.

—"Tax Report," *The Wall Street Journal*

payments can be large amounts of money, especially in retail businesses, and there can be a serious temptation to run late.

Don't do it.

First, because the penalties are very high, much higher than with your own taxes. Second, because this is a more serious matter than not paying your own business's taxes. *It's not your money and never was to begin with.* The sales tax was paid by your customers; you're only a collection agent for the state. You're meant to receive it and hand it over. If you don't pay it, you're talking larceny. Make a habit of it, and the state will not only close down your business, but might show you the inside of a jail cell as well.

Don't screw around with sales tax payments. It can be bad for your health.

Skimming? Never Heard of It!

Now for some *really* sensitive stuff. Ever heard of "skimming"? Nooooo, you say, not me. Never heard of it. What in the world's *that*? Skimming the cream off the milk?

Precisely. That's *exactly* what it is.

Trouble is, it's not your cream and it could land you in the slammer.

You'll never hear anyone recommend it openly, but it's no big secret that in some (many?) small businesses, where the owner is the sole manager and the

---

WHAT GOES ON UNDER THE TABLE
Restaurateurs Are Big Tax Cheats

As a restaurant owner, I often encounter evidence of widespread tax cheating. . . .

I have many part-time employees. I pay some $7 an hour; that costs me about $9.50 once Social Security, Medicaid, United States and Illinois taxes are included.

Suppose one employee also works part-time in another restaurant and gets paid $7 in cash. My competitor's costs are substantially less, in an industry in which a few percentage points can make a difference between profit and bankruptcy.

There are other advantages to skimming. You can hire illegals, and immigration authorities may never find out. If you pay cash, who will know that you don't pay overtime after 40 hours? And you can violate the child-labor laws with near-certain impunity. . . .

What's the solution?

Random surprise auditing. The IRS should maintain a stable of auditors who can drop into a restaurant at any time and demand to see the current books, invoices and employment records. . . .

Tax cheating is widespread nationally because businessmen know that the rewards greatly exceed the risk. . . .

As long as taxes remain uncollected, honest businesspeople will have to work harder to stay competitive in the restaurant industry, in which cheating is the norm.

—Hans W. Morsbach, who owns three restaurants and a pub in Chicago,
The New York Times

So You'd Like to Learn a Little More About Skimming, Would You Now? Read on:

OFF THE BOOKS
For Some Entrepreneurs, Skimming Cash Is Simply a Part of Compensation

Napoleon Barragan and Stew Leonard Sr. once were spectacular business successes. Mr. Barragan, an Ecuadorean immigrant honored by President Bush, founded Dial-a-Mattress Co., and built the Long Island City, N.Y., concern into the nation's third-biggest mattress retailer. Mr. Leonard won kudos for building a small dairy outlet into two of Connecticut's biggest food stores.

Each also admits he illegally skimmed large amounts of cash off his business's books for himself or employees. Mr. Barragan got caught in a routine state audit. He ended up paying New York $1 million to settle his tax fraud case last year and is now on a work-release program from jail. Mr. Leonard's undoing came when federal agents raided the offices of Stew Leonard's Dairy Stores. He paid $17.5 million to settle a federal charge of avoiding taxes and now is serving a 52-month prison term for tax evasion.

Strong Incentives

Messrs. Barragan and Leonard won't discuss why they did it. Accountants and consultants say it is increasingly common for small-business owners to skim cash from the books for themselves or employees. Intensified competition, along with a need to reduce taxes and attract certain workers, propels the practice. Also . . . entrepreneurs sometimes lose sight of legal strictures when the companies they nurture balloon in size.

A Dial-A-Mattress executive concedes that Mr. Barragan once ran the company "like a bodega, taking care of the bills that could shut him down tomorrow. The government came last." Mr. Leonard's son . . . says his father "is a marketing genius who never read financial statements and ran the company like a small business and didn't think about the consequences."

Small companies that sell directly to the public, such as Dial-A-Mattress and Stew Leonard's, are more likely to skim cash for their executives and employees because cash transactions account for a lot of their business, consultants say. The construction industry, too, does it a lot, according to accountants. By paying employees off the books with cash, a contractor can lower payroll, unemployment and disability taxes and win jobs by bidding at least 20% lower than law-abiding ones. . . .

Hot Tips in New York

The New York State Department of Taxation and Finance in Albany says it gets 2,000 tips a year about tax avoiders from business competitors, disgruntled former spouses and unhappy employees. "At least about 500 of these involve off the books payments in cash by companies to their employees," says [a department spokesman].

Three years ago, the Department was tipped by several Long Island house-cleaning services that some competitors lowered their fees by paying employees off the books. "Of the 40 we checked, half were offenders," says the spokesman. Some offenders paid their back taxes plus penalties and interest, "but some had to go out of business because they couldn't afford the extra payroll and disability taxes."

Consultants say outside investors, vendors and lenders can spot clues, and cite three "give-aways": moving from a computer to a manual or paper booking system; firing the current accountant and hiring a friend to do the job; and keeping separate books for "cash" and accounting purposes.

A consultant [gave this final advice to a "skimming" client]: "I told him that if he cleaned up his act, he wouldn't have the constant fear of jail hanging over his head."

–Lee Berton,
The Wall Street Journal

cash controls are rudimentary, some businesspeople will pocket, say, 10 or 20 percent or more of the "take," and only declare the remaining 90 or 80 percent or less. Thus evading (i.e., stealing) part of their federal and state taxes, and pocketing part of the state sales tax that they collected, too. While they're at it, why stop there? They'll also use some of the skimmed money to pay their employees in unrecorded cash, "off the books," which means they also evade Social Security taxes and other payroll costs. Some go even further, and use the money to buy lower-cost merchandise "off the books," usually fenced stolen goods. Members of the mob are experts in skimming techniques; they probably give weekend seminars on the subject, down at the Fulton Fish Market in Manhattan.

All that stuff is criminal activity, just in case you're wondering.

There are estimates that in some cities over 50 percent of owner-operated restaurants and other small retailers indulge in the joys of skimming.

Skimming is not too difficult for a smart government inspector to detect, if he/she wants to take the time to investigate, and it is an easy thing for a disgruntled employee to blow the whistle on. Which is how most convictions are obtained.

If you have a naturally criminal bent or get your kicks from running risks, feel free to make your own decisions . . . it's your business. But if you and/or your spouse don't much relish the prospect of both losing your business and doing extended jail time, think twice before you start skimming. It's easy money and a hard habit to kick.

Give Leona Helmsley, New York's tax evasion queen, a friendly call, if you'd like to know more about the thrills of life in the slammer. Remember, she could afford take-out porterhouse steak, delivered to her cell; you may have to get by on the house menu.

Leaving aside ethical or legal considerations, skimming also has one major disadvantage, from a strictly managerial viewpoint. A businessperson who skims can never operate the business with tight controls and an effective MIS, nor delegate any major responsibilities to employees. The existence of good management controls would easily confirm any illicit skimming activities, to tax auditors or disgruntled employees. So if you skim, you'll have to get by without a good control and accounting system.

If you're running one popcorn stand on your own, you might decide to run the risk. If you want to grow to ten popcorn stands and still keep skimming, you will have to sacrifice your controls and your MIS, which are more valuable to you in managing your business than any short-term gains from tax cheating.

It's a crime that doesn't pay, in more ways than one.

U.S. SAYS PIZZA HUT BROKE SAFETY RULES

Twenty-six Pizza Hut restaurants violated child labor laws, by letting youths operate dangerous equipment like razor-sharp slicing machines and dough rollers, the Federal Government said. The company was fined $194,400 in civil penalties by the Department of Labor. . . .

Federal law forbids people under 18 to operate [dangerous machines].

—*The New York Times*

BATHROOM BREAKS FOR WOMEN BECOME A FEDERAL CASE

More than 30 women workers at Nabisco have filed sex-discrimination complaints with the EEOC (Equal Employment Opportunity Commission), saying they don't have enough opportunities to go to the bathroom. Women who work on the company's chili-canning production line in Oxnard, Calif., have only three chances to visit a restroom each day. . . .

Some women have worn disposable diapers to prevent embarrassing incidents, [their lawyer] says, while others have developed urinary-tract infections. Nabisco denies the charges.

—*The Wall Street Journal*

LABOR DEPARTMENT CLARIFIES RULES FOR FAMILY LEAVE

Lingering confusion over when an employee is entitled to unpaid leave for family or medical reasons can now be cleared up.

The Labor Department issued final rules . . . to implement the Family and Medical Leave Act. The law says an employee may take up to 12 weeks of unpaid leave each year for the birth or adoption of a baby or the illness of a family member. . . . Any company that employs at least 50 people is required to comply with the law.

—*The Miami Herald*

DISABILITIES LAW TAKES HOLD
The Americans with Disabilities Act (ADA) Passed Five Years Ago, and the Grace Period for Compliance Is Now Over

Doors are opening for the disabled in America, but greasing the hinges takes years of work, millions of dollars and, increasingly, the threat of lawsuits.

Wheelchair-welcoming playgrounds. A fire alarm to wake deaf hotel guests. Door knobs that can be opened without hands. . . . The ADA says a disabled person should have equal access to public places, that a walker or blindness or a missing arm shouldn't keep someone from getting a job, enjoying a restaurant or riding a train. . . .

Nonetheless, change doesn't come cheaply: It can cost millions to retrofit a building. And it doesn't come without confusion. Indeed, the cost and confusion have left legions of violations five years after Congress passed the act.

But the grace period has ended.

—*The Miami Herald*

THRESHOLDS OF PAIN

Like a canary in a mine, an obscure, high-technology entrepreneur named E.O. Schonstedt may have been a warning signal to the U.S. economy. In the 1970s, he learned that a friend of his, in complying with civil-rights reporting, demanded of government contractors with 50 or more employees, had been required to submit *eight pounds of paperwork.*

Mr. Schonstedt, believing he could not afford to divert his attention or capital from the productive work of his business, decided to halt his firm's expansion. Until Mr. Schonstedt's death, Schonstedt Instruments never had more than 49 employees.

Since first appearing in the 1964 Civil Rights Act, *"thresholds"* have proliferated to more than a dozen federal laws, with most added in the past decade. More still are in state law. . . .

Thresholds reflect the recognition of legislators that, while big businesses may be able to carry the costs of most mandates and regulations, they could force many small businesses to lay off employees or go out of business. The answer has been to exempt businesses under a certain size, varying with the actual law. But as thresholds have accumulated, so too have stories of companies like Schonstedt Instruments that have stopped growing, rather than face the costs and uncertainties of becoming subject to added regulations.

No wonder, either.

The list of federal laws with thresholds reads like a Who's Who of regulatory horror shows.

AT 15 EMPLOYEES OR MORE. . . .

Federal laws that, however well-intentioned, impose burdensome compliance costs on businesses whose numbers of employees goes beyond a certain "threshold":

• **Civil Rights Act of 1964 (Title VII):** banned race discrimination in employment . . . but became the legal basis of quotas . . . applies to companies of 15 or more employees.

• **Age Discrimination Employment Act of 1967:** banned forced retirement before 70 years old . . . 20 or more employees.

• **Employee Retirement Income Security Act of 1974 (ERISA):** . . . rules for pension and welfare benefit plans . . . 100 or more employees.

• **Occupational Safety & Health Act of 1970 (OSHA):** a regulatory monster . . . 11 employees or more.

• **Omnibus Reconciliation Act of 1986:** bans terminating . . . pension accrual because of age . . . 20 or more employees.

• **Immigration Reform & Control Act of 1986:** . . . bans hiring illegal immigrants . . . but makes it an offense to refuse to hire suspected (but not proven) illegal immigrants . . . 4 or more employees.

• **Worker Adjustment & Retraining Notification Act of 1988 (WARN):** . . . requires 60 days notice of layoffs and plant closings . . . 50 or more employees.

• **Emergency Planning & Community Right to Know Act of 1986:** reporting of toxic chemicals . . . 10 or more employees.

• **Americans with Disabilities Act of 1990 (ADA):** accommodation to needs of disabled . . . 15 or more employees.

• **Civil Rights Act Amendments of 1991:** . . . increases exposure to discrimination suits . . . 15 or more employees.

• **Older Workers Benefit Protection Act of 1990:** . . . extended age discrimination benefits and coverage . . . 20 or more employees.

• **Family Medical Leave Act of 1993:** . . . unpaid leave for birth, adoption, medical reasons . . . 50 or more employees.

• **Clean Air Act Amendments of 1990:** . . . forces increased occupancy of employee's commuting vehicles . . . 100 or more employees.

—Clark S. Judge, *The Wall Street Journal*

Employment and Employees

There are laws, rules, regulations and legal precedents covering everything under the sun, relating to employment and employees. Not something to attempt to cover in this book. There are entire books on the subject, if you're interested.

It's all about such things as: working hours, overtime hours, minimum wages, pay scales, overtime wages, unfair hiring, unfair firing, union organizing, minimum ages, legal immigrants, illegal immigrants, hazardous occupations, job discrimination by race, gender, nationality, age, religion or whatever, working conditions, workplace safety, handicapped accommodation, sexual harrassment and more, much more.

Instead, here are two pieces of general advice:

First, keep yourself informed on employment issues. Keep regularly abreast of business news in the area. Without having to study the details, you'll get a pretty good notion of trends and be able to watch yourself in business, to prevent dumb things happening, which could lead to lawsuits or fines.

Second, treat your employees decently and fairly. Most of the laws and regulations (however poorly some of them are written or applied) have the fundamental objective of getting employers to act fairly and humanely toward their employees. Your own common sense and standards of basic decency will go a long way toward avoiding potential problems in this area.

NOT WELCOME
City Zoning Laws Seek to Balance Economic Growth and Residential Peace
It Isn't Easy

For nearly two decades, Judy Corbett, the self-described "old widow lady," has made a living sewing costumes for movies and television. She and her four employees—her "costume techies"—ply their trade out of her North Hollywood, Calif., home.

They sewed in peace, until the City of Los Angeles sent Mrs. Corbett a letter ordering her to "cease and desist" business operations. Someone—possibly a neighbor—had turned her in for violating the ban on home-based businesses. "You're at the mercy of somebody who takes offense to the way your nose is planted on your face," Mrs. Corbett complains. . . .

Her frustration is echoed across the country, as the rise in the number of home-based businesses prompts scuffles over zoning laws. With no nationwide or even statewide model for how—or whether—to regulate businesses located in residential areas, cities of all sizes are struggling to define their own guidelines. . . .

Mrs. Corbett suspects it was a neighbor who reported her zoning violation; even so, many neighbors signed a petition in support of her. After wrangling with city officials for months and spending $3,500 in fees for permits and maps, she received a conditional use variance that allows her to continue operating out of her home. . . .

"In these difficult economic times, I do not see the value of denying people the right to support themselves," says Mrs. Corbett.   —Martha Irvine, *The Wall Street Journal*

Building, Remodeling, Setting Up

Many small businesses start up by building, rebuilding, remodeling or reorganizing, in an office, a store, a workshop, a real estate plot, a home office and so on. They can run into all sorts of maddening problems, unexpected expenses and time-consuming delays, because they are not aware of the myriad minor local rules and regulations, relating to what they are planning to do.

- **Permits:**
  Permitting can drive you insane, with hundreds of detailed requirements before you can even start remodeling or construction. The permitting process can be a bottomless pit of petty problems.

- **Zoning:**
  Zoning restrictions can bring major unpleasant surprises. Especially if you've bought or rented your premises before checking zoning restrictions. One problem much in evidence relates to home offices in residential zones; it varies from city to city, town to town.

- **Contractors:**
  These should be the people guiding you through the permitting and zoning problems, as well as getting the job done. There are good ones;

**YOU WORK AT HOME.
DOES THE TOWN BOARD CARE?**

When many government officials peek behind bedroom doors, institute "don't ask, don't tell" policies or ask people to "come out of the closet," they are not prying into residents' sex lives—they are trying to exercise some control over the booming growth of home offices.

With downsizing of American corporations coinciding with the advent of easy-to-use, relatively cheap telecommunications equipment, more and more professional workers are trying out entrepreneurial skills by setting up offices in spare bedrooms and basements.

As many as 40 million people work at least part time at home, with about 8,000 home-based businesses starting daily. . . .

For local officials, then, the question is whether to ignore all this or to enforce zoning or tax regulations that place home-based businesses in technical violation of the law.

Many communities see no threat in their residential nature, so long as home businesses stay out of sight; they are content with a "don't ask, don't tell" strategy that places a fig leaf of ignorance on a potential enforcement problem.

Others gently nudge those with home businesses to declare themselves and submit to regulation. Still others, though, are cracking down tightly, fearing that today's low-impact business could turn into tomorrow's neighborhood nuisance.

—Jon Nordheimer, *The New York Times*

there are poor ones; there are totally dishonest, terrible ones. Be most cautious. A bad contractor can destroy your new business, before it even gets off the ground. Your best bet is a locally established contractor with solid, verifiable, personal references. Your best defense is in having highly detailed, extremely specific plans, drawings and specifications; the more time you and the contractor spend initially, ironing these out, the more likely that you'll get what you want, at the price you agreed.

- **Disabilities:**
  Although well-intentioned, the Americans with Disabilities Act can be an introduction to insanity, as you try to adjust your hole-in-the-wall little T-shirt store to accommodate a hypothetical future flood of quadriplegics in wheelchairs, all clamoring to use a toilet even you don't fit into. It's good intentions gone bananas. It can screw up your remodeling plans, balloon your expenses and delay your permitting. Common sense often has little say in this matter.

- **Environmental Restrictions:**
  Here again, good intentions gone haywire can destroy existing businesses and hopelessly tie up valid new business projects. Stay away from any business project where your interests may come into conflict with environmental crusaders. Their cause is good; their pigheaded fanaticism is not. Small businesses take a disproportionate share of the heat, since they don't have the time and the money for lawyers' fees to defend themselves, unlike the large corporations.

- **Endangered Species Issues:**
  Same situation. With the best of intentions, some very surreal situations have developed, making it impossible for some property owners to go ahead with legitimate business projects, even those of benefit to the local community. If you see a spotted owl on your property, start your business elsewhere; the owl will win.

These kinds of problems can derail you and bankrupt you before you even start. Lumped together, they are one more excellent argument for doing the careful preplanning, investigation and detective work recommended earlier. At least you won't get sandbagged halfway into the project, when you've already committed too much money and can no longer back out.

Inventions, Patents and Trademarks

This is one area where a specialized attorney can be essential, depending on the complexity of your needs. They will usually work for a reasonable fixed fee, which means you can control the cost of their services. If your project is based on an invention, your entire business will depend on obtaining that patent and you will want to invest in competent, specialized legal help, in dealing with the government Patent and Trademark Office. Experienced inventors know how to file for their own patents, but it may not be worth your while to spend the time learning how to do this.

For less complicated needs, with trademarks, logos and such matters, there are some excellent legal "self-help" books available, which can show you how to handle the filing yourself. It's a simple, straightforward process.

However you do it, protecting your name and ideas is essential. Some small businesses develop valuable, creative ideas for their trademarks, trade names, service names, logos, ad slogans, etc., but cannot be bothered with the time and expense of having a search made (to check if someone else got there first) and of trying to register them. Years later, you can come to regret that negligence. If you ever face a successful challenge, the disruption and damage if you have to change your name, logo or whatever, can be very painful, if not disastrous.

Your business's name is worth nothing when you start. But it's worth everything to you once you are operating successfully. Why risk major problems in the future, if you can protect yourself properly at the beginning, for a modest investment in time and money?

Getting Cozy with Competitors

Don't forget that there are laws in this country that have been on the books for many years and that could get you into hot water if you start getting too cozy with your competitors.

Although these laws hardly ever can be or are applied to small businesses–where competitors are more interested in eating you alive than in getting cozy with you–one fine day you may find that the temptation arises to cut a friendly little deal.

So please remember that "price fixing" is still a no-no, by law, as are practices that can be lumped together under the label of "restraint of trade."

Just a short reminder.

Yes, It's Worth It

The government, in all the many ways it messes around with your small business's finances, operations and day-to-day administrative tasks, can be one royal pain in the butt.

But that's the price you pay for the opportunity of doing business in the United States.

It's a very fair deal.

So don't complain, pay the taxes, meet the obligations, do the paperwork, and get on with starting and running your new small business.

You, along with your barely tolerated, unloved partner, Big Brother.

17

PERSONAL ANGLES,
PARTING SHOTS:

*It Costs More
Than the Money*

If You Can't Take the Heat . . .

. . . don't even go near the kitchen.

Back to page one. The *S* word is not *Success*. The *S* word is *Survival*.
Along with one more *S* word: *Suffering*.

Entrepreneurs are a proud bunch, not much given to whining and crying.
They flash a tough exterior. No wimps here. They're Sigourney Weaver in
Alien, Bruce Willis in *Die Hard*. They'll tell you that the hotter the kitchen, the
more they relish the smell of boiling oil.

To hear the full story, take aside someone who has set up their own
business, survived and maybe even succeeded.

Sit them down in a dark corner in the local tavern. Ply them with their
favorite hooch (entrepreneurs are partial to the hard stuff). Ask what it cost
them, *apart from the money.*

By the third drink, they may start telling you what it truly cost.

Stories about running out of money, dipping into college funds,
canceled vacations, vicious family quarrels, screamin' and yellin', separations
and divorces, working nights and weekends, personal bankruptcies, evictions,
false starts and early disappointments, humiliations and embarrassments,
alienation of old friends, fear and loneliness, fights with partners . . . it will go
on and on.

The lesson? It ain't easy being small.

You have to want it real bad.

Question #1: Can I Do It?

The first question is easy to answer: *Yes, of course you can do it.*

It may look a little daunting right now, because all the essential (and sometimes heavy-duty) survival stuff has been compressed into this one book. Now that we're reaching the end, you're probably suffering from indigestion.

You don't have to know it all when you start. You'll have time to learn the essentials as you progress. When you're starting up in small business, things do not move at breakneck speed. There's always time to learn.

Newcomers do not fail because small business is technically complex or because it requires unusual intelligence or exceptional abilities. Some of the most successful entrepreneurs are truly remarkable in their ordinariness. Genius is not an entry requirement.

Character and personality are entry requirements. It's always a rocky road at the start. It requires persistence, stubbornness, self-discipline and large doses of self-confidence to keep yourself trucking, when you're going through those rough patches. Quitters will tend to quit, so they shouldn't even try.

And, as this book has repeatedly emphasized, the most important personal factor of all is the ability to focus, focus and focus. Focus on survival, always. Focus on just getting through that first week, first month, first year. Not looking to a point where your business is a wildly successful moneymaker, but to where it is at least stable and self-sustaining. A point when you wake up one bright morning, look in the mirror, smile and say in pleased surprise: *Hey, it's working!* And only then get to move ahead to the fun stage, when you start advancing toward true success and its many personal rewards.

Instead, if your initial focus is on the immediate easy success the glossy entrepreneurial magazines and guru motivational infomercials promise you, sorry, don't hold your breath. It's not going to happen. You'll have the wrong focus, you'll make the wrong decisions, you'll select the wrong priorities and you probably won't make it. You'll be so busy digging for that pot of gold at the foot of the rainbow that you won't prepare for the storm clouds ahead.

There's no such thing as instant gratification in small business. It's always hard work, it's always slow. But, with the right attitude, you can do it.

Question #2: But Is It Worth It?

That second question's harder. The answers vary from person to person.

Yes, of course it's worth it, is the rational answer for almost anyone looking strictly at their financial and employment alternatives in this modern business and economic environment. An emphatic: *Hell yes, it's worth it.*

> The entrepreneurial lifestyle is not for everyone. Specifically, it isn't for people who are unwilling to put their savings at risk, watch every penny they spend, give up creature comforts of a corporate life, and spend many hours a day by themselves.
>
> –Sara Olkon, *The Wall Street Journal*

But there are no easy answers to that question, when you measure it in terms of personal costs and family sacrifices. Some are cut out for the stresses and strains, some just aren't. That's no criticism of those who aren't. Some businesspeople who *are* cut out for it would never win any medals in a Most Decent Human Beings contest; they wouldn't even be allowed to register for the contest.

You may consider yourself one tough, hard-nosed, cold-blooded businessperson, but that's not the issue here. It's your human side we're talking about now . . . about personal and family prices that have to be paid by businesspeople embarking on a small business life.

Don't worry, this last chapter hasn't suddenly gone soft on you and switched to touchy-feely philosophizing. Your personal life's your own, handle it any way you wish. However, personal aspects are vitally important, only because they can become explosive; they can blow apart the best of business ventures. *That's* what has to be discussed.

The personal, human, friendship and family costs *are* high and they're *always* worse than you expect. So you have to think hard about the trade-offs between the personal pluses and the minuses. Only you will be able to make that final, very personal decision, as to whether it's worth it or not. You *and* your significant other, if you have one sharing your life . . . who should, by the way, read at least this chapter. Or maybe not?

Maybe it's worth it.

Maybe not.

Only you can make that evaluation. Too often, initial enthusiasm takes over and these personal questions are never asked, until it's too late. Don't make that mistake. Before you move ahead with your small business plans, try to decide for yourself whether it's going to be worth it or not, with all the family and personal pressures it will bring.

Being a Business SOB

As owner-operator of your own business, there will come a time when you have to be a hard-hearted SOB. Not maybe. For sure. It will happen. Quite often. You'll find yourself in a you-or-them situation, and there won't be any middle ground to choose.

Oh-ho, so you don't agree? You've been reading all that "win-win" stuff again, haven't you? Yep, that'll certainly give you a warm inner glow during your three-day, touchy-feely, corporate-sponsored sojourn in some guru retreat in the Rockies, hot tubs and all. But that's for the corporate bozos, pal. Let them play "win-win" in corporate America; it's innocuous enough stuff there, it can't do much harm. But play "win-win" in small business and it'll be "lose-lose" all the way to bankruptcy court.

Making business decisions when you are the owner of your own business often requires a singularly self-centered attitude. The competitive jungle environment of the modern business world leaves little or no margin for being generous and openhanded, trying to keep all sides happy and smiling. In many of the decision situations you will face in your business, it will often be a matter of black or white, win or lose, take it or leave it.

Either you fire a couple of employees or your payroll costs will stay too high and your business will become unprofitable; you believe that employees are stealing, you don't have the time or the money to investigate thoroughly, so you fire them anyway, using some other excuse; you see that you can steal customers from an already weak competitor, knowing that your action will force them to close down; you receive a temptingly lower price from a supplier who wants to "buy into" your purchasing, knowing that the faithful rep from the old supplier will be blamed and fired; and so on.

Since yours is a small business and you run it hands-on, in these cases (and hundreds of others) you'll know the people who'll be getting hurt, personally. You'll have worked closely with them. Had a beer or a sandwich together. You'll have met their husbands or wives, probably their children, at barbecues or parties. You'll know something of their financial situation, their medical problems, their family quarrels. You'll have been close enough to them to be unable to fool yourself as to what the painful consequences will be . . . you'll *know* what your business decision will do to their lives.

But you'll still have to face that hard decision. If your heart wins, you'll run away from it. Run away a few more times on similar decisions, and your small business may well be on its way to extinction. Or your brain wins, you make the rational decision which is in your business's best interests, and you'll be branded an SOB: "That self-centered bastard only cares about making money. Doesn't matter how many people get hurt."

That won't feel too good. Unless you really *are* an SOB, in which case you won't feel a thing.

Isn't this the same for any business, small or big?

Yes, similar hard decisions are made in large corporations, every day. But there it's far easier. It's impersonal. The bozos who give the final orders are far removed from the personal hurt and human devastation that are often the consequence.

In small business, when you make decisions that hurt people, there's nowhere to run, nowhere to hide. You're the boss, you did it. It's up close and personal. Whereas your counterparts in Big Business don't even break out a sweat on the human consequences of their decisions. Check out "Chainsaw" Al Dunlap, of Scott Paper and Sunbeam infamy, who proudly wrote a self-congratulatory book on his prized SOB qualifications.

> For many entrepreneurs, the biggest mistake is they should never have been entrepreneurs in the first place.
>
> The simple truth is this: Not everyone is cut out to be an entrepreneur. Some people have a need for a secure and structured environment, or an inability to think small. Others are unwilling to work long hours—many of them alone. And many don't have the patience that small business requires. . .
>
> For the would-be entrepreneur, then, it's important to do a lot of soul searching before moving forward. And perhaps the best place to start is at the beginning: Why are you even contemplating the move?
>
> —Sara Olkon, *The Wall Street Journal*

Some owner-managers of small businesses find it humanly impossible to worry only about the best interests of their business. In a competitive environment, where there's no margin for the cost of charity, they insist on being kind and charitable. Their hearts may feel good, but their minds aren't doing the arithmetic and they aren't calculating the economic consequences to their business. Which can be fatal.

It would be comforting if there were an easy out for the dilemma–to be an SOB or not to be an SOB–but there's none. Which means you have to decide before you start whether you'll be able to face such decisions when your time comes. If you are genuinely softhearted, and cannot make hard and sometimes brutal decisions, you should not go into your own small business. Seriously.

Either that, or convince yourself that the time has come to harden your heart and to run your small business strictly as a business, not as an extension of your personal or family life . . . no personal values to be applied, only business values. In other words, learn to live by a double standard, where you're one kind of person in your home and family life and quite another in your business life. Dr. Jekyll and Mr. Hyde, anyone?

Some people do that just fine; others can't live with the idea.

Don't look to this book for guidance on this dilemma; it's about business, is all.

What does this author know about the inner recesses of your soul?

Personal Sacrifices – For How Long?

The more seriously you take your small business, the greater your chances of success. Yet the more seriously you take it, the more it can absorb you and dominate your personal life, and the greater the stresses and strains this will place on family and friends.

Never underestimate the destructive power of your own business on your private life. It can be a major cause of family fights, domestic squabbles, separations, divorces, loss of friends and alienation of children. It becomes very hard for them to keep seeing it your way. At first, yes, they're your greatest supporters. But a year later? Two years later? How long, oh Lord, how long?

Even the family dog may end up hating you. It's:

- **Long Hours:**

  It's not just the hard work and the long hours. You have the same problem in many corporate jobs these days. Yet in a corporate job, at least you have the excuse that you only put in that extra effort because you must, to hold on to the job. In small business, to your family it can begin to look as if you love not them but the long hours and the weekends of work. They could be right. Often, in spite of everything, it can be stimulating and challenging. The long hours just don't feel like work, because you're doing it willingly, for yourself. Your family can end up feeling thoroughly neglected and left out of your new life.

- **Self-Absorption:**

  Same problem. The business takes you over. You go to sleep thinking about it. You wake up thinking about it. It's all you want to talk about, it's all you get excited about. Whether you work at home or not, the business invades your home life. You work on business problems at home, you talk business at home, you're on the phone with business calls at all hours. You become a "business bore." Your family starts losing its sympathy, after too many months of this kind of stuff: *Hey, what about us? Don't we exist? Don't we matter?*

- **Social Life:**

  There are always good business reasons not to take a break. Weekend outings become a thing of the past, you're too tired or busy to go out for a meal and a movie, you turn down friends' invitations, you stop inviting people over. Your family doesn't even get the occasional party break from your business absorptions, to check out if you're still human. Your friends are even less tolerant and may simply write you off.

- **Uncertainty:**
Risk and uncertainty are an integral part of starting any new small business venture. You've made your decision and you're able to live with the constant uncertainty. Will it succeed? Will it fail? You know everything you're doing and planning to do, down to the smallest detail, to overcome problems and make that dream of success a reality. You *believe*. You're confident, even in the face of bad news and serious setbacks. Your family members, however, hear mainly the bad news and see the problems. They have to live with the constant fear that their lives are about to be blown away by this wild venture that only you control and only you understand. *The fear is far greater for them than for you.* You can judge how things look; they can only pray. People can live with fear and uncertainty only so long . . . then they start cracking up.

- **Family Finances:**
Your small business always requires more money than you estimated, so naturally you tighten up at home–on the groceries, entertainment, fixing things, whatever. After all (you rationalize), it's only a short-term sacrifice and the whole family will be much better off very soon, when your ship comes in and your business takes off. You may see it that way and you may even be right, but your family may not have the patience and vision that you have. They may feel that you at least are having some weird kind of fun, while all they are doing is suffering hardship and paying the price for your apparent self-indulgence.

In the face of all that flak, what's to tell you? Stop work at 5 p.m.? Don't work weekends? Don't talk business at home? Stroke the kids? Kiss the dog? Or was that the other way round? Sorry, too busy to know the difference . . .

There's a very real and unavoidable conflict between the need to give your small business your undivided attention and wholehearted effort, until it's off and running, and the domestic demands of your private and family life. Somehow, if the bunch of you are to come through this hard experience together, you're all going to have to discuss the problems and the conflicts very openly, and show one helluva lot of mutual understanding and compassion. Communication's the only way out.

What more can one say?

The Fear Factor

It's not just your family who is fearful.

It's you, living with business fear all the time.

Fear it won't work, fear of things going wrong, fear of deals collapsing, fear of competitors. If you're a new entrepreneur, you'll be afraid. Later, when your business has stabilized and started to show good results, the fear will diminish, but it will never go away entirely.

You can try to pretend it doesn't exist, you can work at exhibiting a self-confident exterior, but it'll be there all the time. Your own little demon. You go to sleep with it, you wake up with it, and it follows you around all day.

Here's how you need to look at it.

Fear is normal, fear is natural, fear is good for your business health.

It keeps you on your toes, it keeps you looking over your shoulder, it makes you severely self-critical, it stops you from getting too cocky and making the idiotic mistakes that cocky entrepreneurs too often make.

The day you stop being fearful is the day you need to fear.

Learn to accept it, learn to live with it, learn to love your little demon.

> Fear is simply a part of everything else you are doing, and as my trapeze trainer often warned me, the greatest danger is when one stops being afraid.
> —Helen Wallenda, quoted by Rebecca Chace, *The New York Times Magazine*

The Ego Factor

Once you were somebody.

Now you're nobody. Maybe less than nobody.

Swallowing your pride becomes a survival necessity in small business.

All that matters now is your business, its survival, its success. Not your own pride, abilities, achievements, self-esteem. They're gone. Your personal success will be measured by the success of your business, now and in the future. Your business is you. Your business is all that matters. Everything else becomes secondary.

They keep you waiting on hold on the phone, and you don't complain. You leave phone messages that are never returned. You beg favors from people you don't know. You write letters that are never acknowledged. You crawl to get your invoices paid. You kick your heels for a couple of hours in a scuzzy waiting room, along with one hundred other reps and salespeople, waiting for a five-minute meeting with an imperious corporate buyer. When you finally get in to see the buyer, it's *Yes, sir. No, sir. Three bags full, sir.*

And so on. Oh, it's painful to kiss ass.

Especially for those who've never had to do it before.

This is one of the hardest adaptions to the real world, for those dudes who have just left the corporate world, where everything was ego, appearance, image, posture and position. Here, although you're the most important person in the business, nothing matters *but* the business.

Learn to accept it, learn to live with it. It's good for your self-discipline.

Your day will come. Ego doesn't matter. Survival and success do. Grit your teeth and smile sweetly, until you've gotten where you want to go.

Living well is the best revenge. Succeeding is the greater satisfaction.

Don't get mad. Get on with business. And when your day finally comes, if you have a few old scores to settle, get even.

Working Partners

It happens over and over again.

When it happens, it can often pull the fledgling business to pieces.

Here's the scenario:

You have a friend, an acquaintance, a business buddy, a relative, whatever, who also dreams of having their own small business. The idea gets thrown out: *Hey, let's be partners.*

Suddenly, bingo, you've entered into a long-term business marriage, with all its horrendous stresses, strains and anxieties, with less thought than you would give to buying a new car. People get carried away by their initial enthusiasm and anxiety to get started.

Why? Maybe it's the shared enthusiasm. Maybe it's the fear of working alone. Maybe it's a lack of self-confidence. Maybe it's the need for their financial contribution.

Whatever it is, if both of you are going to be full working partners (if one's a sleeping partner, that's much safer), more often than not it won't work out. Because of those family reasons we just mentioned . . . the personal pressures are the same, except that now *two people* have them, instead of just one; statistically, the odds just doubled that one of you will crack. Because of all the business stresses that you and your partner will have to share . . . you've got to get along extraordinarily well, to be able to come through that kind of pressure cooker with your partnership intact. Be-

> In their anxiety to have partners, many entrepreneurs connect with people whose long-term goals may conflict with their own. People say, "I need to have a partner so I can have confirmation every day that I am doing the right thing." Sometimes, of course, these people could fare better on their own.
> —Sara Olkon, *The Wall Street Journal*

cause possibly one of you won't put in the same work, effort and sacrifice as the other, and the resentments and recriminations will start flying.

Plus any number of other reasons that two ordinary, well-meaning people who have little in common find out too late that they cannot get along productively and harmoniously, when working together daily under conditions of pressure and stress, far greater than they could ever experience if working as fellow employees in some corporation. That's one of the more frequent breakup scenarios: two people happily work together as employees and assume it will be the same as business partners.

Bad assumption; it's a whole new pressure cooker.

And never forget the need for trust–mutual trust. Initial trust can quickly turn into distrust. Distrust will finish off any partnership in a flash.

Yes, good working partnerships can and do exist. But it takes two people who not only know each other very well but, more important, know themselves even better. Then, maybe, they have a chance of a successful long-term partnership.

Often, you're better off on your own.

Lonely as that may be. Better to be lonely than in bad company.

Married Partners

Husbands and wives working together in small business?

Yes . . . if it's a perfect marriage; if they not only love each other but, far more important, *like* each other; if they're totally compatible and share the same likes and dislikes; if they know each other's strong points and weak points; if, if, if. Usually, the ifs don't add up.

Otherwise, the same stresses and strains of business partnership can destroy not only the business but the marriage as well. Two explosions instead of one.

Here again, you're probably better off on your own.

Investment Partners

A sleeping partner is easier to get along with than a working partner. They put some money into your small business venture because they trust you and your abilities, they don't interfere with your work and they're just praying for you to succeed. If everything works out, great, everyone's happy.

But nobody likes to lose money. Sleeping partners and investors who have put money into your business and were once your friends will probably not remain your friends if the business gets into trouble. They will wake up from their sleep, in one foul temper.

Instead of shrugging their shoulders, muttering in resignation, "Oh well, you can't win 'em all," taking their lumps philosophically and moving on to better things, some will need to show the world that they were not gullible, stupid investors.

That means, unfortunately, that they will need to show the world that it was you who was either incompetent or dishonest or both. Even if you were neither.

When businesses collapse, often just because of the luck of the draw, those who lost money seldom remember, let alone thank you for, the twenty-hour days, the working weekends, the incredible efforts you put into starting the business and into trying to keep it afloat, right through to the end. They may prefer to bad-mouth you.

When you invite friends to invest in a business that you will be operating personally, there will be more than money at risk. If the money is lost, usually so is the friendship, and it can often be replaced by dislike or hatred.

It's in the nature of the beast.

So give careful thought to where you're raising the money, if you're looking outside your family.

Family may forgive you.

Friends and acquaintances may not.

The Loneliness of the Long-Distance Runner

How to sum it all up?

Probably by reminding you that it sure gets lonely, out there in the cold, and that the personal price can be high.

If you're going to do everything you should do and can do to make certain that your small business is one of those that not only survives but also goes on to succeed, it's going to cost you.

- You may have to act more of an SOB than you really are.
- Your family may suffer. Their fuse may be shorter than yours.
- Your social life may become nonexistent.
- You may become a workaholic, if you aren't one already.
- Your discretionary spending money may dry up.
- You may live in constant fear of things going wrong.
- You may fight with your working partner, if you have one.

- You may fight with your spouse, if he/she is your working partner.
- Your ego may get crushed.
- Let's see now, was there anything we forgot?

If you're still in one piece, after the tough start-up period is over—one year? two years? three years?—and when things start going better for you and your business, that's when you should step back a little, add up the many debts of sacrifice and suffering that you owe to family and friends (and to yourself) and start trying to give something back . . . if you ever can.

So Go for It

In spite of the pain and the cost, with the right focus you can do it.
You can beat the odds in small business.
You can survive.
You can succeed.
So . . .
May your small business achieve the financial success and the personal success you dream of . . .
May the personal costs not be too painful . . .
May the gods of business, economics and finance smile upon you and your venture . . .
May luck smile also . . . it sure helps.
Thanks for listening, thanks for reading.
Hope it's helped you understand what lies ahead.
Hope it hasn't scared you off.
So go for it.

ODDS 'N' ENDS

Appendix

APPENDIX

ODDS 'N' ENDS:

Brief Memos,
Choice Clippings

Small Business Ain't Neat 'n' Tidy

We get to the end and there are still important points left to discuss, which didn't fit into the book's framework. That's because small business ain't neat and tidy, and can't be smoothly packaged into a *How to Succeed in Small Business in 10 Easy Lessons* promotional package.

So here are a bunch of memos, about odds and ends that may (or may not) be helpful to you, which either didn't fit into the flow earlier on, or else needed, in my opinion, a little additional emphasis at the end. Read the ones that interest you. Ignore the rest.

Here's what follows:

<u>Memo #1</u>	**Lawsuits: Job Discrimination**
<u>Memo #2</u>	**Lawsuits: Sexual Harassment in the Workplace**
<u>Memo #3</u>	**Lawsuits: Injuries and Damages, Real or Unreal**
<u>Memo #4</u>	**Jobs and Wages: Trends Affect Your Business**
<u>Memo #5</u>	**Employees: Bad Apples Can Be Rotten**
<u>Memo #6</u>	**Independent Contractor or Employee: A Key Distinction**
<u>Memo #7</u>	**Leaky Payment Systems: Where You Can Lose Your Shirt**

The press clippings that accompany the memos will help, by giving you little slices of reality from the world out there.

<u>Memo #1</u>   Lawsuits: Job Discrimination

ACCUSATIONS OF DISCRIMINATION IN HIRING, FIRING, PROMOTING AND REMUNERATING, BY REASON OF RACE, AGE, GENDER, RELIGION, DISABILITY, NATIONALITY OR WHATEVER (POOR TABLE MANNERS?) CAN RESULT IN DAMAGING LAWSUITS THAT CAN EASILY DESTROY A SMALL BUSINESS.

The clippings that follow illustrate the dangers. Your small business, you personally, even your managers, can find yourselves at the nasty end of lawsuits and complaints that could put you out of business and destroy you, financially. If the monetary damages don't do it, your legal costs certainly will.

Maybe you'll deserve it. Or maybe it will be totally unfair. Either way, that won't matter. The one excuse no judge or jury is going to listen to is, "But it isn't fair."

Most first-time entrepreneurs know that there are a bunch of laws and regulations that require businesses to treat job candidates and employees fairly and equally, regardless of the color of their skin, their language, their looks, their religious beliefs, their gender (there are more than two, these days), their age and so on.

But you naturally assume this will never be a problem for you because:
- *I'm a fair-minded person and would never allow such behavior in my business;*
- *Only large corporations get hit by such lawsuits. I'm too small to be a target.*

Don't count on it.

However fair-minded you may think you are, you will always be tempted to treat employees with whom you feel more comfortable better than those very different from yourself. Without even knowing you're doing it. And even if you are the most enlightened of businesspeople, maybe one of your key managers will break every rule in the book, without your ever hearing it.

And it'll be your business's responsibility.

Yes, the attorneys for disgruntled employees will usually try to hit the big corporations with the deep pockets. But the anti-discrimination laws are pretty common knowledge with everyone these days, and a sufficiently enraged former employee will not hesitate at having a crack at you, for alleged discrimination, even if only to have the satisfaction of trying to put you out of business.

My advice: take it all seriously; you'll never know when an apparently petty incident can balloon into a legal action. Understand the spirit of these laws–they're pretty obvious, in their basic intent. Watch yourself. Watch your managers. Bend over backward to be fair and considerate to job candidates and employees. Handle all seriously disgruntled employees personally. Work out fair solutions, quickly and reasonably.

By doing this, you may never have to face a discrimination problem or bias lawsuit. And if it does happen, you can at least blame bad luck or greedy lawyers, rather than your own negligence.

EX-COKE AIDE, DISABLED BY ALCOHOLISM, WINS CASE

A former executive of Coca-Cola Co., fired while being treated for alcoholism, won a $7.1 million jury award against the company, for alleged discrimination under the Americans with Disabilities Act. . . . A jury in U.S. District Court in Dallas decided that Robert Burch's rights under the ADA were violated when he was fired by Coca-Cola in 1993. Coca-Cola fired Mr. Burch, 48 years old, a month after he informed his boss that he had been diagnosed an alcoholic and was undergoing treatment. The company alleged Mr. Burch was fired for "violent and threatening behavior."

Alcoholism is considered a disability under the ADA. And alcoholics are protected from discrimination if their illness doesn't interfere with their work.

The jury awarded Mr. Burch back pay of $109,000, front pay of $700,000, additional compensatory damages of $300,000 for mental anguish, and punitive damages of $6 million. . . . Disability-law specialists said the decision demonstrates that employers must show discretion with employees suffering from alcohol abuse.   —Robert Frank and Alex Markels, *The Wall Street Journal*

BRUTAL FIRINGS CAN BACKFIRE, ENDING IN COURT

After seven years of service, Helen Barrett, then 57 years old and a social-work manager at Yale–New Haven Hospital, was forced to leave her personal belongings in a plastic bag and was escorted out the door by security guards, in full view of gaping co-workers. A supervisor told her that she would be arrested for trespassing if she returned, even though there had been no allegations of criminal wrongdoing or any indications of disloyalty.

The incident caused "utter humiliation," says [her attorney]. The jury awarded Ms. Barrett $105,000 for the negligent infliction of emotional distress in its handling of her firing. . . .

Lawyers say they expect to see more courts recognizing claims related to cruel dismissals. "There's no reason for an employer to destroy a person in the process of firing them," says [the attorney]. "They'll be rid of them soon enough anyway."   —Margaret A. Jacobs, *The Wall Street Journal*

HAPPY MOTHER'S DAY? Pregnancy Discrimination Complaints Are Up

Pregnancy discrimination complaints keep rising. . . . A pregnant single woman in Tampa, Fla., had a supervisor place a basket of pennies on her desk and announce it was "an abortion fund." She lost her job as an apartment manager, sued and won nearly $85,000 last year. . . . One woman won more than $1.8 million after she lost her job at California Casualty Insurance Co. Her boss had threatened to fire her, she said, if she returned from her honeymoon pregnant.

—"Work Week" column, *The Wall Street Journal*

SENIORS CHALLENGING EMPLOYERS OVER AGE DISCRIMINATION

When Norman Ross, 68, applied for a job at Brentano's bookstore in Boca Raton several years ago, he considered it a lock. An Ivy League Ph.D. in English and years of college teaching were unbeatable qualifications, he thought. Not so. Instead, the store manager hired a 16-year-old high school sophomore who listed her last job as "counselor, day camp." . . . Like an increasing number of older workers, Ross filed an age discrimination complaint with the E.E.O.C. Brentano's has denied the allegation. . . .

Lawyers credit the rise in discrimination claims to the increased knowledge of the age act, which was passed in 1967, the graying of the work force and corporate downsizing, which has disproportionately affected the oldest part of the work force. . . . Brentano's denies discriminating. . . . The company also holds that Ross hadn't worked in a bookstore and that "familiarity with books was not a requirement for the position." The court still has not decided the case.   —Charles Strouse, *The Miami Herald*

Memo #2   Lawsuits: Sexual Harassment in the Workplace

SEXUAL HARASSMENT OF EMPLOYEES IS NEVER ACCEPTABLE OR EXCUSABLE. THE LEGAL CONSEQUENCES CAN BE EVEN MORE DEVASTATING TO A SMALL BUSINESS THAN JOB DISCRIMINATION BY GENDER.

Here again, the clippings tell the story. Read them carefully . . . very carefully.

The previous memo was about the problems women (and other groups or minorities) can face, in receiving fair and equal treatment in being hired, fired and remunerated. Such complaints and disputes are usually (but not always) based on facts and evidence that can at least be weighed and examined, by both sides.

Charges of sexual harassment are a new and different ball game. This area primarily affects women, it is much harder to prove or to disprove, and it is emotionally explosive. Although, as you might expect, charges of sexual harassment are more often aimed at large corporations with deep pockets, it can affect any business, however small.

As owner-manager of your own small business, you can perceive and prevent sexual harassment in your workplace–more so than in a large corporation. First, by policing your own attitudes and behavior. Second, by watching what goes on among the employees. Third, by making it clear that you won't tolerate such behavior and that you want to hear about complaints personally.

In this modern day and age, we all know what kinds of behavior can be considered as sexual harassment. If it happens in your business, nine times out of ten you could have seen it or heard about it and stopped it before the lawyers turned up and your business headed for destruction.

Take it seriously and it will probably never happen in your business. Turn a blind eye, adopt the "boys will be boys" attitude and you are asking for trouble, sooner or later.

> A [wiseguy] whose name we cannot recall once observed of sexual harassment that it was a crime so horrible even innocence was no defense.
>
> —Daniel Seligman, "Keeping Up," *Fortune*

THREE WOMEN SUE BROKERAGE FIRM IN HARASSMENT CASE

Three women filed a sexual-harassment suit against a New York brokerage firm and its officers, the latest in a string of complaints alleging that securities firms create a hostile work environment. The suit alleges that officers of a small brokerage and investment banking firm brought strippers into its Garden City office, hired "wow" girls solely for their appearance, routinely fondled female employees and verbally abused them as they walked past the trading area.

One plaintiff . . . alleges that she was required to watch an explicit late-afternoon strip show in the office to celebrate the birthday of one of the brokers. When she asked why, the firm's chief financial officer replied "because I said so." . . . An operations assistant alleges that a national sales manager unzipped his trousers in his office and asked her to perform oral sex.

—Dean Starkman, *The Wall Street Journal*

TALES FROM THE ELEVATOR
Two Women Fill In Details of Sexual-Harassment Allegations Against J. P. Bolduc, the Former Head of W. R. Grace & Co.

Bolduc [the former CEO of W. R. Grace], who is married and has four children, had a reputation for crude behaviour and lewd come-ons with female colleagues. . . .

Two women employees spoke to Time. Both insisted on remaining anonymous for fear, they said, that by coming forward they would damage their career prospects and be stigmatized as troublemakers. One remarked, "The good-ole-boy world is still the good-ole-boy world.". . . They both drew a picture of Bolduc as an executive lech. . . .

One of the women, a manager, says she had her first experience with Bolduc's style in an elevator. "He paid me a compliment, then reached over and put his right hand on my left butt cheek. Fortunately, the elevator had reached our floor. . . ." [She described] a scene after a business meeting. "On the way out of the building, as he was saying goodbyes, Bolduc turned to one woman employee and instead of shaking her hand, pulled her toward him and stuck his tongue in her ear. She was startled, but laughed it off. When he did the same thing to a second employee, it was no longer funny."

The second woman, an administrative assistant, recalled the morning that Bolduc popped into her office unexpectedly. "When I bent down to put the cup of coffee on the credenza for him, he reached over and ran his hand up my leg." This was no accident, she says. "He traditionally wears a Cheshire-cat grin on his face, and he was grinning then." In shock, she stalked out of the room and did nothing. . . . It seemed to her that Bolduc was too far up the corporate hierarchy to challenge through normal channels. She later told [the judge], "The big question mark for all the women he approaches is: What will happen if I don't play along? Will I lose my job? . . . I could not believe he could be in the position he was, with a personality like his."

—Richard Lacayo, *Time*

WAL-MART WORKER WINS $50 MILLION

A woman who accused her supervisor at Wal-Mart of sexually harassing her was awarded more than $50 million. Peggy Kimzey, 47, testified that [the supervisor] made numerous crude sexual remarks to her and other female employees about female anatomy and tight clothing. A U.S. District Court jury awarded Kimzey $50 million in punitive damages, $35,000 for humiliation and mental anguish and $1 in lost wages. Wal-Mart said it will appeal the ruling.

—*The Miami Herald*

LAW FIRMS SLOW TO RESOLVE GENDER PROBLEMS

A third of Florida's women lawyers reported in a Florida Bar survey that they had been sexually harassed at work. Sixteen percent said they had quit jobs because of harassment or bias.

What these stories illustrate is that, despite a presumed awareness of the law, men in the legal profession continue to subject their female colleagues—maybe more than in any other business—to harassment that starts in law school and extends to the bench. . . .

What is different about harassment experienced by some women in law is how much of it comes from clients—and is known about and tolerated by male associates. . . .

[A female lawyer] says stiff punitive awards [like a recent record award of $6.9 million in punitive damages against Baker & McKenzie, the world's largest law firm] will probably change conditions faster. "You need harsh consequences to send a clear message," she says.

—S. L. Wykes, *The Miami Herald*

<u>Memo #3</u>   Lawsuits: Injuries and Damages, Real or Unreal

ANY BUSINESS, HOWEVER SMALL, IS A POTENTIAL TARGET FOR LAWSUITS BY CUSTOMERS, THE PUBLIC OR OTHER BUSINESSES. FRIVOLOUS CLAIMS ARE AS FREQUENT AS GENUINE ONES; THE LOSS OF TIME AND MONEY IS THE SAME.

I've already dealt with lawyers and what you should know about them, in Chapter 13. Not the prettiest picture.

Always remember that lawsuits can be brought against you and your business, for injuries and damages, real or imagined. If it ever happens, it'll be no consolation to know that there's some lawyer behind it, instigating the plaintiff to bring the lawsuit, regardless of right or wrong.

There's no perfect advice to give you. Some lawsuits are so unfair and unbelievable that there is no way you could predict them or prevent them. There are businesses that collapse because of lawsuits, simply because they were in the wrong place at the wrong time . . . like being hit by lightning. That said, here's some advice:

- Take a few hours for some "what if" self-analysis. Look carefully at everything that goes on in your business. Think of anything that might generate a lawsuit. See what you can do to reduce the risks of something dangerous happening. Nonslip floor coverings, restricted access to dangerous work areas . . . that sort of thing.
- Liability insurance is the most expensive insurance around. For good reason. However, if you can afford the premiums and feel you may be vulnerable, go for the highest limits you can afford. If you're going to pay for it, you might as well buy yourself tranquillity.
- On the other hand, if the premiums are going to kill you, think about going entirely without liability insurance. Going naked, as they say . . . a case of nothing being better than something. Instead, set aside regular monthly payments into a separate "self-insurance" bank account. It's a form of savings for the unexpected and will give you a small source of "blackmail" funds to pay off any lawyers who come knocking. Once they discover that there's no insurance company with deep pockets to hit up on, and that your assets are worth zilch, they'll often take what they can grab and go looking for the next victim.
- Always react promptly, constructively and generously to any legitimate complaints from injured parties . . . without admitting responsibility, of course. Many people, if treated politely and considerately, will not even think of lawsuits and lawyers. There are more decent people in this world than you might imagine.

VALUE PAYS FAMILY OF GIRL WHO DIED IN CRASH

Ten people pack into a rented van. The driver loses control on Florida's Turnpike and the van flips over, killing a 10-year-old passenger. The Highway Patrol cites the driver for careless driving.

Who pays damages to the victim's survivors?

The rental car company. . . .

Her parents' attorneys . . . announced they had accepted a $1.3 million settlement from the van owner, Value Rent-A-Car of Boca Raton.

Value paid up because under a Florida law known as the dangerous instrumentality statute, the owner of a vehicle is responsible for the actions of whoever is driving it.

"It was a very tragic case," said Value's president. "Value had no fault in the matter, but under Florida's liability laws, we were responsible for the accident."

–James McNair, *The Miami Herald*

ONLY IN AMERICA

Camden, New Jersey: The family of an accused killer who plunged to his death while trying to escape from the Camden County Jail has filed a lawsuit seeking damages. The lawsuit filed on behalf of the estate of Giovanni Almovodar, 18, charges jail officials failed to maintain a "reasonably safe facility." . . .

Almovodar was in jail awaiting trial in the 1992 shooting death of a shopkeeper. Officials said he was the first of five inmates who climbed through a hole in the jail wall. . . . He climbed out headfirst, falling . . . to his death. The other four escaped.

–From an article in the *Legal Intelligencer*,
quoted by Daniel Seligman, "Keeping Up," *Fortune*

ONLY IN AMERICA (Cont'd)

It may look like a sidewalk with a slight incline, but for personal injury lawyers, it's a gold mine.

[New York City] has been sued at least 11 times by people falling on the sidewalk in front of 319 Fifth Avenue. The city has settled seven of the cases–dishing out nearly $300,000. The other four are still in the courts.

The sloping sidewalk has been especially lucrative for . . . lawyers who worked at the building. . . . Four of the suits were filed by people connected to two law firms at 319 Fifth Avenue.

–From a news report in the *New York Post*,
quoted by Daniel Seligman, "Keeping Up," *Fortune*

Memo #4   Jobs and Wages: Trends Affect Your Business

**IN SPITE OF THE BOOMING ECONOMY, THE AVERAGE AMERICAN WORKER HAS
SUFFERED A DECLINE IN EARNING POWER AND LOST CONFIDENCE IN HIS/HER
ECONOMIC SECURITY. YOUR EMPLOYEES WILL BE ONE OF YOUR GREATEST
ASSETS, IF YOU CAN RESTORE SOME OF THIS LOSS.**

I won't take you on a socioeconomic tour of what's been happening to jobs, wages and employee attitudes in America in recent years. Just browse through these clippings and they'll tell you all you need to know.

It's a pretty dismal picture. But it has an upside for any small business, with a small number of employees.

The upside is that, if an owner-operator of any small business takes a strong personal interest in each and every employee, and does what they can to improve their employees' lives and livelihoods, they will be rewarded in terms of loyalty, dedication and productivity. What you give may not be much, but it will be noticed and appreciated by those who have suffered all the effects described in these clippings.

By and large, Big Business has blown it with its workers.

You don't need to follow their example in your small business.

There are many ways you can give your employees a better break, which might increase your payroll costs slightly, but which will be repaid many times over, in improved performance.

It can be any combination of different benefits: better pay, bonuses, minimum take-home guarantee, health care, child care, flexible hours, pension schemes, sense of job security, training and so on.

You have to be creative and you have to measure the cost consequences. But any improvements you can afford will put you ahead of Big Business, in the support you receive from the people you employ. Try it . . . it works.

THE ISSUE IS JOBS
Why Can't We Focus on the Downsizing Buzzsaw?

Thanks to the downsizing phenomenon, a . . . fear exists now in both the corporate and government workplace. As the ruthless combination of corporate power and conservative politics increases its dominance over American life, legions of faithful and mostly middle-class American employees are tormented by the fear that they will be the next to walk the employment plank. . . .

Top corporate executives and rabid conservatives see the forced expulsion of workers from the workplace as a good thing. It is an extremely efficient way to suck money up from the middle classes to the elite. The lead headline in the *Wall Street Journal* said: "'Amid Record Profits, Companies Continue to Lay Off Employees." . . .

Americans are angry and anxiety-ridden because tens of millions are already unemployed or temporarily employed or employed only part of the time. Millions are working without benefits or working two or three lousy jobs because one just doesn't pay enough. And millions more who are employed can hear the downsizing buzzsaw coming ever closer.

[A poll] showed that one in three Americans have had trouble meeting their monthly expenses for housing, and a similar number were financially pressed when medical attention was needed.

—Bob Herbert, "In America," *The New York Times*

PLUMPER PROFITS, SKIMPIER PAYCHECKS

A new *Business Week* analysis of national income generated by the corporate sector . . . shows that workers are getting the short end of the stick. Over the last two years, the share going to labor has dropped sharply. . . .

The numbers confirm what many Americans feel in their bones: Workers have not yet seen big gains from rising productivity and the strong economy.   *—Business Week*

WHERE HAVE ALL THE GOOD JOBS GONE?

The economy is generating jobs . . . but too few good ones.

If anything, the trends have intensified: astronomical earnings gains for the economy's superstars. In the middle: relentless downsizing, with new pressures on once-secure professionals as well as depletion of solid blue-collar jobs. At the bottom: growing part-time and temporary hires, low-wage jobs in services, especially retailing, and dismal starting wages.

—Robert Kuttner, "Economic Viewpoint," *Business Week*

ECONOMIC GROWTH . . . SHRINKING PAYCHECKS

The Collapse of the Relationship Between Economic Growth and Increasing Prosperity for the Average Family May Be the Most Important Political Event of the Last Generation in American Life

Prosperity isn't what it used to be. . . . What's wrong? It probably isn't the President. It's something different—and more alarming. . . .

The trouble is that rising GDP [Gross Domestic Product] no longer means a higher standard of living for the majority of American households. . . . From 1947 to 1973 real, inflation-adjusted wages almost doubled in 25 years. But real hourly wages started to fall in 1973. . . . This trend continues. Expansion or no expansion, most people's paychecks aren't rising as fast as their bills—and they know it .

—Walter Russell Mead for the *Los Angeles Times,* in *The Miami Herald*

The millions of white-collar and blue-collar workers who suffered through wave after wave of layoffs in the last decade are still paying the price for Corporate America's hard-won financial rigor. They represent the human side of today's obsession with profits and efficiency. . . .

The [corporate] successes have come at a high price in terms of careers shattered and communities disrupted. And for all the traumas of the recent past, the experts concede that there is still more pain to come.   —James Sterngold, *The New York Times*

. . . AND IT HURTS

The U.S. Outruns the World, but Some Workers Are Left Behind

The price of beating overseas competition has been bitterly high: wave after wave of downsizing layoffs, wage increases limited or forgone, replacement of full-time workers by part-time or temporary hired hands. Even those who have hung on to regular jobs are often too exhausted by long hours of overtime and weekend work to enjoy the extra money they are earning. . . .

In the long run, continually cutting back is no way to grow. Even in the short run, downsizing carried to an extreme can reduce the very productivity it first enhances. . . . Even professionals and middle managers, coping with the pervasive insecurity generated by wave after wave of cutbacks, may respond not by working harder but by adopting a to-hell-with-this-company attitude.

—Time

<u>Memo #5</u>   Employees: Bad Apples Can Be Rotten

IT'S NOT A PERFECT WORLD. THERE WILL ALWAYS BE "BAD APPLES"–
DISHONEST, INCOMPETENT OR PLAIN NEGLIGENT EMPLOYEES–WHO CAN
DAMAGE OR DESTROY A SMALL BUSINESS. THERE'S ONLY ONE SOLUTION: GET
THEM BEFORE THEY GET YOU.

However enlightened or well-meaning you may be, in dealing with your employees your good intentions can never save you from the damages and losses you can suffer from employees who are just plain rotten to the core–those who are dishonest or grossly incompetent or just don't give a damn. They can do far more damage to a vulnerable small business than to a large corporation. They can destroy your business.

However careful you are in hiring, sooner or later one of these "bad apples" will slip through. You'll never change them, you'll never improve them. All you can do is be constantly aware that this can happen, and maintain efficient controls that allow you to detect early that some form of monkey business is going on and move very fast in getting rid of a "bad apple" when you find it.

Here are some clippings from the dark side.

SMALL BUSINESS IS THE BIGGEST VICTIM OF THEFT BY EMPLOYEES, SURVEY SHOWS

When it comes to employee theft, small business is a big target.

That is the principal message of a major new study of occupational crime by the Association of Certified Fraud Examiners. . . .

Businesses with fewer than 100 employees "were the most vulnerable to fraud and abuse" by employees, the association reported. These companies were victimized more frequently than large companies, and commonly sustained very large losses proportionate to their resources.

–John Emshwiller, *The Wall Street Journal*

RETAILERS TRACK WORKERS ACCUSED OF THEFT, USING NATIONAL DATABASE

Stores lose an estimated $10 billion annually to employee thievery, the largest single factor contributing to retailers' $27 billion inventory shrinkage problem, which also includes shoplifting.

But retailers say the prosecution rate of employee-theft suspects is low. . . . Apprehended suspects are often fired without further legal consequences and move on to other retail jobs.

To screen candidates, [a group of retailers] are using a database dubbed TheftNet.

–"Business Bulletin," *The Wall Street Journal*

BAD CHECKS PROBED

The bank accounts of an ice cream company were frozen by an Orlando judge while AT&T Corp. tries to learn who wrote 13 checks to the firm totaling $750,000, even though AT&T didn't buy any ice cream, its attorneys say.

–*The Miami Herald*

COPS POSING AS DINERS BUST AIRPORT THEFT RING
Agents Say Cashiers Have Pocketed Millions in Receipts from Restaurants at Miami International Airport

When police swooped in on the cashiers at MIA, they say [one cashier] had already stuffed $250 into her pockets in less than an hour on the job. Agents arrested [her] and six others, charging them with being part of a network of thieves who may have stolen as much as $5 million from airport tills in the past year.

[She] and another cashier were cuffed by police right in front of the registers as dozens of stunned airport patrons watched in amazement. . . .

The bust came about after a monthlong surveillance of the American Buffet, a bustling cafe in the heart of the terminal. Police used cameras hidden in the ceiling above the cashiers to record their movements. Undercover agents posing as travelers bought sandwiches, desserts and coffee with marked currency—some of which, they said, turned up in the cashiers' pockets.

"Some of these people are so fast you can hardly tell," said [a policeman], "And some of them start the minute they sit down." Police suspect cashiers pulled off the scam by simply not ringing up sales and pocketing the cash. . . . Police suspect cashiers have been stealing for a long time.

—Dexter Filkins, *The Miami Herald*

RISKY BUSINESS
Trusting a Security Guard Can Be Hazardous

Last weekend's arrest of a security supervisor and a guard in the $1.9 million robbery of Tiffany & Co. in New York City was no fluke. Guards employed by the 25 top security companies committed 261 serious crimes last year, including 36 murders, 29 assaults, 27 thefts and 63 sex-related offenses, a survey . . . shows. Lax screening causes many problems, allowing people with criminal backgrounds to get hired for sensitive jobs.
—*The Wall Street Journal*

DEALS ON THE SIDE
How a J.C. Penney Buyer Made up to $1.5 Million on Vendors' Kickbacks

Dallas: A buyer for J.C. Penney earned $56,000 a year. But he controlled the spending of millions of dollars a year, and he started peddling that influence.

He admits he sold to some suppliers and manufacturers' representatives crucial information, such as the amount of their competitors' bids. To others, he flat-out sold the promise of large orders. In exchange, some vendors handed him cash; others wrote checks to front companies he set up. Over four years, he supplemented his salary with as much as $1.5 million in bribes and kickbacks.

Corruption among retail buyers isn't so rare. . . .

Retail experts say temptations and opportunities for scams are inevitable, with big retail chains' buyers deciding how to spend millions of dollars and thus able to make or break a supplier or manufacturer's representative. And if the buyer does cross the line, catching him or her can be difficult. Often, the racket is detected only when someone tattles. "One guy who worked for me went through a divorce, and his wounded wife turned him in. She'd built a file on all the gifts he'd taken that he shouldn't have," says a retail consultant.

—Andrea Gerlin, *The Wall Street Journal*

<u>Memo #6</u>   Independent Contractor or Employee: A Key Distinction

YOUR STATUS AS AN INDEPENDENT CONTRACTOR (OR NOT), AND/OR THE STATUS OF YOUR WORKERS AS EMPLOYEES (OR NOT), IS OF KEY IMPORTANCE FOR INCOME TAXES, WITHHOLDING TAXES AND PAYROLL TAXES.

In theory, it should be simple. We all know what an employee is. And an "independent contractor" should be what the word indicates: someone who works independently, under some form of agreement or contract with clients.

But there are advantages and disadvantages to one position or the other, and thus the IRS gets involved in defining who is what, when and where. Thus the confusion starts.

For small businesspeople, there are two key aspects:

- If you have a small business where you are the single, main revenue earner with only a handfull of clients, you will want your earnings to be received as an independent contractor, with no deductions, and you will want to classify all your business expenses as tax deductible. However, the IRS may want to say that you are actually a form of employee of one or more of your clients and should thus make standard payroll deductions, at source . . . plus lose the tax deductibility of your expenses.
- If you need to use outside workers, sporadically, you may want to pay each of them as independent contractors, and avoid payroll taxes and other obligations. Here again, the IRS may disagree.

If your business faces these issues (not all do), you will need to talk to your accountant. Logic and common sense have little to do with this; it's all about bureaucratic language and technical interpretations. This memo is only to alert you that this distinction can be of major importance in money terms. The quicker you get yourself organized, to prove your status if the IRS questions it, the better.

Take a look at these clippings, to get a feel for the problem. Then put the matter high on your priority list for discussion with your accountant.

IRS INQUIRY: IS IBM WORKER A CONTRACTOR?

The Internal Revenue Service is auditing IBM to determine if it improperly paid thousands of workers as independent contractors, instead of as employees. Income and Social Security taxes must be withheld from employees' paychecks, but not from payments to independent contractors.

Worker classification audits have taken added importance because a growing number of independent contractors, in filing their income tax returns, report their payments as wages, so that they are liable for only the employee's share of Social Security and Medicare taxes.

Independent contractors, who are self-employed people in occupations as diverse as plumbers, doctors and artists, must pay both the employee's and employer's shares of those taxes. The IRS has a number of tests for determining who is legitimately an independent contractor.

–David Cay Johnston, *The New York Times*

ARE YOU YOUR OWN BOSS? ONLY IF THE IRS SAYS SO
Outdated Laws and Worker Dismay, with Sizable Tax Dollars at Stake

It's a question, it might seem, that only an accounting professor could love: when is a job a job, and when is it a business deal? But for five million Americans who consider themselves their own boss, the issue is much more than an academic curiosity. It's a matter of money.

For the past 10 years, the IRS has been busily stripping away tax advantages that have been enjoyed by more than a million doctors, computer programmers and others who sell their services as independent contractors. The IRS has decided that these contractors are actually employees of the hospitals and businesses for which they work. And employees can't deduct most business expenses and travel costs, or shelter serious money for retirement, as contractors can. All of which translates into many more tax dollars for the agency. . . .

But there is another group of contractors who would like nothing better than to be employees–the poor ones like farm workers, janitors and seamstresses toiling in Brooklyn sweatshops. Many of these workers want to be employees just to be covered by the minimum wage laws. As employees, they would have taxes withheld, making them eligible for jobless, disability and old-age benefits. . . .

In other words, there are five million people whose job status may be in question. Some want to remain as independent contractors; the IRS is turning them into employees. Some want to become employees; the agency is continuing to call them independent contractors. This leaves virtually everyone angry. . . . Laws that no one likes remain on the books. Business owners are distracted from their jobs by time-consuming tax intricacies. Workers and bosses cross swords over who wants which job classification. The IRS uses a 20-part test to see if a person is an independent contractor or an employee. Here are some of the elements.

Whose Rules?

If a worker must follow rules about the manner of work–the how, when and where–that's a sign of an employee. But an independent contractor can proceed as he wishes, as long as the job gets done.

Ending It

Most employees can be fired or can quit without reason or notice. But with independent contractors, both the worker and the company must follow their agreement's rules about when and why they can part ways.

Other Gigs

You are more likely to be considered an independent contractor if you are able to work for more than one business at a time, the IRS says. But an employee often works full time, or must be available to do so.

Whose Tools?

Do you furnish your own tools and materials for your work? Then the IRS hears "independent contractor."

Risky Business

Independent contractors may make money or lose money on a job. But employees will get their paychecks however a project turns out.

–David Cay Johnston, *The New York Times*

<u>Memo #7</u>   Leaky Payment Systems: Where You Can Lose Your Shirt

---

ALL PAYMENTS, WHETHER BY CHECK, CASH OR CREDIT CARD, NEED TIGHT CONTROL, PROPER DOCUMENTATION AND SYSTEMATIC FILING. OR YOU CAN LOSE IT ALL TO DISHONEST EMPLOYEES OR OUTSIDERS.

When asked why he robbed banks, Willie Sutton replied, most logically, "Because that's where the money is!" For exactly the same reason, dishonest employees will concentrate on finding any holes in your payment systems.

One of the most universal failings of small business newcomers is to make business payments about as casually and hurriedly as they handle their personal money–scribbling out a check, pulling cash out of a wallet or slapping down a credit card.

That's okay with your own money. You're in total control of your personal bank account, cash funds and credit card balances. How sloppy or undisciplined you are is your own problem, and the payments you need to document, for your personal tax returns, are few and easy to pull together at year end.

You can never afford to be that casual with your business's payments.

- Remember the "bad apples" in Memo 5? Misusing company checks is one of the prime methods of serious employee theft. There are hundreds of different ways of playing check games.

- So you have a "petty cash" fund, with $50 or $100 sitting in it for small payments? "Petty cash" can easily lead to "petty theft," unless it is tightly controlled. An employee who daily slips ten or twenty bucks into their pocket will be costing you hundreds of dollars by the end of each month, and thousands annually.

- Every legitimate disbursement in a business is tax deductible. But only if disbursements are properly documented in some reasonable way. By year end, you could pay thousands of dollars in extra taxes, just because you couldn't be bothered to keep your payments organized and documented. Remember, ten cab fares a month at $10 a ride would be $1,200 in tax deductible expenses at year end. Not to be sneezed at.

- If money is paid out by the business, without explanation or documentation, the IRS is going to assume you put those funds into your own pocket, and you'll get socked for income tax ... or worse. Still want to keep writing out checks to "cash"?

This is not nitpicking; this problem can ultimately destroy your small business. Laziness or sloppiness is not an acceptable excuse.

<u>Memo #8</u>   Business Insurance: Essential Protection

BUSINESS INSURANCE IS VITAL, BUT PREMIUMS CAN BE COSTLY. SMALL BUSINESS OWNERS OFTEN WON'T TAKE THE TIME TO UNDERSTAND IT, SO THAT THEY CAN BUY THE RIGHT INSURANCE AT THE LOWEST COST.

Insurance is another area where small business newcomers will often act as they do in their private lives. Buy a prepackaged homeowner's policy or a standard auto policy, pay the premiums and forget about it.

The problem is that businesses are far more vulnerable to a wider variety of risks and catastrophes, any one of which has the potential for destroying a business. If you go out and buy every conceivable type of policy and coverage, you'll probably go bankrupt, just trying to pay the premiums. If you don't buy essential coverage, you can throw away years of work and your livelihood, when a serious loss occurs, just because you tried to save a few hundred bucks in annual premiums.

The different kinds of insurance are not difficult to understand. You can easily pull together a balanced program that gives your small business the essential protection it needs, at a premium cost you can afford. The trouble is that doing this is tedious work, which most people will keep putting off, because there are always more urgent matters to worry about.

What's more urgent than a catastrophic fire?

Don't put off this essential task. First sit down and think through all the risks and damages your business might suffer. Then call in a reputable insurance agent, talk and question carefully, and then decide on the final "insurance program" you will adopt. If you have any doubts, put it in writing. It'll help you if you ever have a claim.

Do this work properly and thoroughly, and it will take no more than a couple of days of your time, annually, to set up your complete program and then adjust it periodically.

You'll sleep better at night.

TAKING CONTROL OF YOUR WORKER'S COMP COSTS
Expensive Injuries Don't Have to Happen
You Can Save Plenty by Rooting Out Hidden Hazards

At a time when managers are doggedly driving out every excess cost, some executives still view worker's compensation insurance as an intractable cost of doing business. But an increasing number are discovering the truth: Worker's comp is a manageable expense. . . .

Comp is a state-mandated program. Employers are required to pay all the medical bills and a portion of lost wages to workers hurt on the job. Large employers that self-insure pay these claims out of the corporate kitty, while smaller concerns typically purchase insurance, with premiums based in part on their claims experience.

–Mark D. Fefer, "The Workplace," *Fortune*

DOES THE COVERAGE MATCH THE CALAMITY?

The fire that destroyed Sport-O-Rama health club in Monsey, N.Y., generated enough heat to melt the building's steel beams. Owner Mark Goldstein believes he and his partner got burned again a few weeks later, when they assembled their insurance claim. The insurer refused to reimburse Sport-O-Rama for the hundreds of thousands of dollars of prepaid membership fees it must return. Instead, the insurer informed Goldstein it would pay only for the net income the club would have made during the months of rebuilding. "It's a big thing for people who collect money up front. That was one large gap we didn't foresee," he says.

To survive a disaster, small-business owners need to match their insurance to the financial crisis that could occur. That often means asking insurers questions that make them squirm, about exactly how they settle specific types of claims. In Goldstein's case, he needed to clarify whether he could get reimbursed for refunded membership fees—before he purchased a policy. Had he pressed the point, he may have learned that he needed a special rider to cover that type of loss. Or he might have chosen to search for a company with a more favorable policy.

Keep Track. Standard small-business owner policies provide insurance against business interruption, or lost income, in addition to property and liability coverage. They pay for fixed expenses such as payroll, debt, and taxes that continue even though business has ground to a halt. . . . To collect for business-interruption losses, you must be able to document your cash flow and expenses. Be prepared to hand over past tax returns, receipts, and records of continuing expenses, such as salaries or rent. . . . And remember: Keep copies of all records off the premises.

Reality Check. Pay close attention to the kinds of losses you may sustain that require special coverage. . . . You may be better off devising a disaster-recovery plan rather than buying extra coverage to insure every risk, however. . . . Still, matching your coverage to forecasts of your cash needs is a must. In an emergency, that reality check could mean the difference between a temporary closing and a going-out-of-business sale.

—Richard Korman, "Personal Business," *Business Week*

DON'T LET A SUIT RUIN YOU

Equal and fair pay, on-the-job discrimination, workplace safety, product safety, securities law. There's no end to the grounds on which employees, customers, creditors, stockholders—even the government—can sue a business. And the cost, not only in damages and lawyers' fees but in management time and focus, can ruin a firm. . . . It pays to think ahead about the lawsuits that could hurt a business—and how to insure against them. . . .

Some examples of [liability] insurance coverage you can buy:

- Product liability protects manufacturers and distributors, who could be sued for injury and property damage caused by the use of a product.
- Completed operations insurance would pay for injury or damage that follows a service. This would protect a company that, for example, installed a chandelier that falls on someone's head.
- Premises and operations coverage protects you if an injury or damage occurs on your premises as a result of your business operations. Paying damages after a slip and fall in a restaurant, for example, or for the fur coat ruined by soup the waiter dropped.
- Directors and officers liability insurance covers those officials if negligent acts or statements lead to libel or other suits.
- Professional liability insurance covers specialists—such as accountants, lawyers and doctors—in case of negligence or errors that injure clients.
- You can also get broad coverage from a comprehensive general liability policy.

—Susana Barciela, *The Miami Herald*

<u>Memo #9</u>   Health Insurance and Benefits: You, Your Employees

NEW OWNERS OF SMALL BUSINESSES ARE OFTEN SURPRISED TO DISCOVER THAT THE HEALTH INSURANCE AND BENEFITS THEY ENJOYED AS CORPORATE EMPLOYEES ARE NOT PART OF THEIR NEW LIFE. SO ARE THEIR EMPLOYEES.

New owner-operators of small businesses are often unpleasantly surprised to discover that the health insurance, pension plans and other benefits that they and their families enjoyed, when part of the corporate world, are going to cost their business money they may not be able to afford in the start-up period. Or, even if the business can afford it, that they can't find the right kinds of plans for their needs.

They may also discover that the business can't afford to offer such benefits to its employees, and that this can be a serious obstacle to recruiting and retaining good employees.

There are no magic answers. However, things have got better recently; with persistent legwork and local contacts, most new entrepreneurs can ultimately find adequate (if not ideal) plans.

Whether they can afford them or not is a different matter.

SLIM PICKINGS
Health Insurance? Retirement Plans? Good Luck.

It's one of the hard truths of small business: More often than not, the benefits stink. . . .

Only 62% of small company employees–compared with 82% of those at big firms–have any health insurance benefits, the Department of Labor reports. Moreover, many of these plans are bare-bones. . . And when it comes to retirement benefits, a slim 9% of small businesses offer pension plans, compared with 56% of big companies.

Some employers skimp on benefits simply because they're stingy. Others can't afford the cost, or find the red tape too daunting. . . . Even when small firms offer health benefits, they often don't pay for coverage of employees' children and spouses.

–Elizabeth MacDonald, *The Wall Street Journal*

SMALL CHANGE
Competitive Pressures Are Forcing Some Small Firms to Improve Their Benefits

Marissa Vernon, owner of Interactive Public Relations Inc. in San Francisco, kept losing her employees to larger rivals. Frustrated, she revamped her benefits package to include more vacation time for her 25 employees, a profit-sharing program and even weekly shiatsu massages. She says the result has been a sharp improvement in the employee-retention rate of the company. . . .

How are small companies paying for all these perks? Many are joining so-called professional employer organizations, which allow businesses to pool their purchasing power and save money on health-care coverage.

–Rodney Ho, *The Wall Street Journal*

Memo #10 Market Research, Trade Shows: Do Your Own Legwork

MARKET RESEARCH SERVICES CAN SELDOM HELP SMALL BUSINESSES IN THEIR START-UP PHASE AND ARE USUALLY TOO EXPENSIVE. USE PERSONAL LEGWORK IN GATHERING INFORMATION AND STUDYING COMPETITORS.

New small businesses, trying to work out their initial marketing plans, will sometimes turn to outside market research consultants. My advice: don't. You won't want the bad ones, and the good ones will always charge you far more in fees than their advice is going to be worth to you in improved sales. It may even be great advice, but your limited resources will mean you can only take minimal advantage of their recommendations.

Use your best asset for market research: *yourself*. You know your business and you know where you want to go. Get out, do detective work, do legwork, study competitors, examine how unrelated businesses do things, watch customers in malls, drive around neighborhoods, make cold phone calls and so on. It's amazing how many valuable insights and ideas you will pick up, just by spending a few days out and about, checking, looking, sniffing around, talking and listening.

This won't happen if you sit in your office, staring at the wall, waiting for inspiration to strike.

Never underestimate the value of trade shows. They are one of the most useful and economical marketing research tools for many small business operators. There are trade shows for every category of product or service you can imagine. You can use them either for specific details on your type of business or to gather ideas from totally unrelated fields. A couple of days spent prowling around every booth in a trade show can be immensely productive in generating ideas.

OOPS! NEVER MIND. . . .
Consumer research can be downright misleading. Just because customers say they want something doesn't mean they'll buy it.
—Fortune

<u>Memo #11</u> Advertising and Marketing: Start Slow and Cautious

NEW BUSINESS OWNERS OFTEN EXPECT THEIR FIRST INVESTMENTS IN ADVERTISING AND MARKETING TO PRODUCE IMMEDIATE RESULTS. THAT ALMOST NEVER HAPPENS. THE LOSS OF TIME AND MONEY CAN BE PAINFUL.

Many newcomers to small business have had some prior experience or exposure to marketing techniques and advertising campaigns, often with larger companies or major corporations. All too often, they make the classic mistake of assuming that what worked in their previous experiences will work in their new small business. It almost never does.

The reason is obvious. Most established marketing or advertising programs are for products or services that have been around for some time, have already established a reasonable level of customer awareness, and are building on the successes of prior campaigns. Thus there is a reasonably good sales "payoff," because a base has already been established, and continuing marketing efforts steadily produce better and better results.

None of that applies to new businesses, new products and new services. Thus, any marketing effort that starts from ground zero, with a big bang and big bucks, will nine times out of ten produce dismal results. I won't get into all the technical reasons that this happens, but it does. And if the new entrepreneur has gambled all the business's start-up chips on obtaining one huge customer response to that first advertising or marketing campaign, that may well spell the end, not only of the campaign, but of the small business.

Never gamble on getting great results from big spending on marketing and advertising, at the start. It will probably break you.

Start slow, start cautious. Rely principally on your own personal efforts in being your business's most effective salesperson. If you decide you must advertise, make small investments in different approaches and check the results carefully. Gradually repeat and reinforce the things that seem to work, and discard those that don't.

Slowly, without breaking your piggy bank, you will start building a marketing "base" that will one day allow you to invest in ambitious campaigns that are much more likely to produce the results you dream of.

<u>Memo #12</u> Export Sales, Foreign Sourcing: Risky Business

---

DEALING WITH CUSTOMERS OR SUPPLIERS IN FOREIGN COUNTRIES IS MUCH RISKIER THAN DOING BUSINESS DOMESTICALLY. SMALL BUSINESSES CAN GET WIPED OUT BY NONPAYMENT OR NONDELIVERY.

Yes, there are many excellent opportunities around the world, to make profitable export sales or to purchase low-cost foreign goods and parts. Trouble is, these opportunities come with a high risk of serious problems developing. If this happens, small businesses usually do not have the knowledge, management and money to weather the storm.

Here are a few typical problems that can happen:

- Customers don't pay up.
- The legal systems in other countries are different from the U.S., and it is often impossible to force payment.
- Even if it is possible, the expenses of using foreign lawyers and representatives to recover are prohibitive.
- Foreign suppliers don't deliver on time or ship products that are not satisfactory or don't ship at all.
- There is little possibility of solutions or indemnity, when that happens.
- Many foreign economies go through violent ups and downs, making it impossible to develop steady customers or regular suppliers.

So be extremely careful, if you are thinking of taking advantage of foreign markets or suppliers. This is one area where the services of specialized export trading companies can be invaluable. But check first what their services are going to cost you. The additional cost may wipe out any profit you may be expecting.

When you do business outside the borders of the U.S., be careful, be careful and be careful.

EXPORTS ARE NICE, BUT COLLECTING ON LATE PAYMENTS CAN GET DICEY

Exports represent a growing share of sales for many U.S. companies, but some are finding that it takes longer to get paid by overseas customers, says Dun & Bradstreet.

—*The Wall Street Journal*

GRAPEFRUIT SALES: IN THE PINK

Selling fresh fruit half a world away has always been a tough proposition. . . . [One] problem is getting paid, as [an exporter] found out in dealing with Russians two years ago. "After I shipped the fruit over there, they told me I'd have to go to Russia to get paid," he said. "They also insinuated that I could end up in the Volga River.

"They don't have any money and they don't have any distribution system or sense of marketing."

—James McNair, *The Miami Herald*

SMALL MIAMI EXPORTERS TREAD MURKY WATERS IN VENEZUELAN MARKET

When Venezuela was Miami's hungriest export market, Miami Springs–based Agrilife Corp. happily fed its appetite. . . . But when Venezuela's economic crisis took hold and foreign exchange controls were implemented, sales dropped almost 90%. Many small Miami-based exporters that were concentrating on Venezuela have really suffered a lot and some have gone out of business.

–Ina Paiva Cordle, *Miami Today*

TRADERS: HOLD THE GLAMOUR
Going Global Takes Plenty of Sweat

Trade. Trade. Trade. Listen to the business chatter . . . and you're likely to hear that the best opportunities are international.

But for entrepreneurs-to-be, going global may involve less glamour–and more sweat–than you think. A consultant with years of international experience, often talks with business people with multinational aspirations. He's heard plenty of disaster stories. Ambitious exporters quote products or volumes that they later can't deliver or finance. Or they forget to include shipping and insurance costs. Then their price quote is so low they couldn't possibly profit. . . .

International traders who started at zero will tell you it takes patience, flexibility, learning and contacts.

–Susana Barciela, *The Miami Herald*

<u>Memo #13</u> Foreign Ventures: Even Riskier Business

FOREIGN VENTURES, INVESTMENTS AND OPERATIONS CAN BE EVEN RISKIER THAN SIMPLE EXPORT SALES, AND THE POTENTIAL LOSSES GREATER. THIS IS NOT A GAME FOR BEGINNERS.

If things go sour with a simple export sale or a single purchase order for foreign goods or parts, the most you have at risk is the deal itself. If the profit potential is high enough, you may be able to afford to run some risk and even incur a loss, without damaging your small business irreparably.

However, if your small business has actually progressed to the point that you have some permanent presence and investment in a foreign country–a manufacturing plant, partnership, joint venture, branch office, representation agreement, whatever–your risks will be far greater. If you ever want to extricate yourself, you may well lose everything you have invested in that country. Or you may find you have to keep pumping in money just to keep your foreign venture alive.

Unless small business owners are seasoned experts in such foreign ventures, the potential risks and problems are usually far too great to make sense for any small business. Sure, there are potential rewards in such cases, but usually nothing that justifies such life-or-death business risks.

I won't bother to list all the potential dangers and risks. Either you're an expert, and already know all about them, or you shouldn't even be thinking of embarking on such foreign ventures.

<u>Memo #14</u> Customer Bankruptcies: Don't Get Caught Unawares

LARGE CORPORATIONS DO IT. SMALL BUSINESSES DO IT. INDIVIDUALS DO IT. BANKRUPTCY CAN BE AN ESCAPE ROUTE FROM YOUR CREDITORS. JUST PRAY THAT YOUR OWN BUSINESS IS NOT ONE OF THOSE CREDITORS.

The theory behind the bankruptcy process is a good one. Simply put, if a business is in trouble but has a decent prospect of recuperation, it is better for everyone that it be given a chance to recover, rather than closing it down completely and destroying it forever. So, if the judge approves a bankruptcy petition, the business is protected from its creditors, while it tries to reorganize itself, cut deals with creditors and finally get financially healthy enough to resume normal operations.

That's the theory. The practice is that all too often we see executives or shareholders take grossly unfair advantage of the bankruptcy process, to make creditors pay for their management mistakes and bad judgment.

But forget about the rights or wrongs of each bankruptcy case; you're not going to change the world. Just remember that, if your small business is owed money by a customer who files for bankruptcy, you can probably kiss the debt good-bye.

Your best protection against being caught unawares is to know as much as you can about your bigger clients, i.e., those who owe you the most. If you keep your ear to the ground, go visit them frequently, talk to the employees, talk to other suppliers, you'll soon smell the fishy whiff of an impending bankruptcy filing.

At that point, kiss the company good-bye as a customer and become thoroughly, vociferously, scandalously objectionable in pressing for payment. You are not allowed to harass creditors who are individuals, but companies are companies and business is business. Most companies planning to jump their creditors with a bankruptcy filing want to keep their plans quiet until they're ready. They will tend to divert the little cash they still have, to paying off the smaller creditors who are kicking up a fuss. Shout, yell, scream, camp out in their reception room and make their business lives hell. They will probably pay your bill, just to get you to shut up and go away quietly.

This isn't the way you should ever treat your good customers but at this point you could care less. It won't always work but it's certainly better than sitting back, waiting for the bullet.

DRY CLEANING DEPOT FILES FOR BANKRUPTCY

Dry Cleaning Depot, a small dry cleaning company with big expansion plans, filed for Chapter 11 bankruptcy protection. "The company just got into too much debt," said a vice-president. "We reorganized to help with the vendors and our cash flow." He said the reorganization won't affect the jobs . . . or operations at its 43 stores.

–Don Finefrock, *The Miami Herald*

HOUSE OF FABRICS FILES TO REORGANIZE UNDER CHAPTER 11

After struggling for more than a year to stem losses and redefine its niche, House of Fabrics Inc. filed to reorganize its 472-store chain under Chapter 11 of the federal Bankruptcy Code. The Sherman Oaks, Calif., company, with one-third of its outlets in California, appears to be a victim of both lingering economic weakness there and lifestyle changes that have left women with a waning interest in sewing their own clothes.

—Andy Pasztor, *The Wall Street Journal*

MAGIC RESTAURANTS
Company Files for Protection under the Bankruptcy Code

Magic Restaurants Inc. said it filed for protection under Chapter 11. . . . The Yonkers, N.Y., company, which owns and operates the Red Robin and American Cafe restaurant chains, filed . . . citing a declining market share, undercapitalization and delays in closing unprofitable locations.

—*The Wall Street Journal*

WEINER'S STORES FILES FOR BANKRUPTCY PROTECTION

Weiner's Stores Inc., a 69-year-old retail chain in Houston, filed for protection from creditors yesterday under federal bankruptcy law in Delaware. . . . [It] listed assets of $96.7 million and liabilities of $70.4 million. A company in Chapter 11 is protected from creditors while it tries to work out a plan to pay its debts. Weiner's operates 158 retail clothing stores in Texas and Louisiana.

—*The New York Times*

<u>Memo #15</u> The Unexpected: It Can Happen

SMALL BUSINESSES ARE ESPECIALLY VULNERABLE TO UNPREDICTABLE EVENTS IN THE OUTSIDE WORLD, FOR WHICH IT IS DIFFICULT TO PREPARE DEFENSES OR ARRANGE INSURANCE PROTECTION.

Ultimately, all businesses are totally dependent on the outside world. Good things can happen. So can bad things.

As always, small businesses are far more vulnerable than larger companies when damaging or catastrophic events take place. They have less flexibility, little cash and few human resources, to be able to ride with the punches.

I'm not being needlessly pessimistic. Just realistic. Just reminding you of this vulnerability. Awareness may just help you to recognize bad news when it's about to happen, which may just give you an edge in moving fast enough to protect yourself, before the tidal wave hits.

Illustrations:

BUSINESS DISRUPTION FROM BOMBING

Many people who work in downtown Oklahoma City are grateful to have escaped with their lives but are wondering about their livelihoods. Major corporations had enough alternative sites to shift to, but many restaurants, garages and other small businesses might well be out of business, having served a neighborhood that has been blasted from the Earth.

—The New York Times

ORANGE COUNTY LOSS

Costa Mesa, Calif: Things are suddenly looking up at the H. W. Wright Hardware Company, a small, family-owned enterprise that buys the inventories of companies that go out of business.

"I think this [county] bankruptcy is going to wipe out a lot of small-businesses in Orange County—the people who would supply oil for the county's trucks and toilet paper for the bathrooms," said the owner. "They will be the very last to be paid by the county, and a lot of these are small-business men who can't afford that kind of delay."

—The New York Times

<u>Memo #16</u> Home Office: Start-up Weapon for Newcomers

MANY SMALL BUSINESSES ARE NOW RUN FROM HOME OFFICES, SUCCESSFULLY AND ECONOMICALLY. BUT IT STILL REQUIRES CAREFUL PLANNING AND FULL AWARENESS OF THE PROBLEMS INHERENT IN OPERATING FROM HOME.

I am a great believer in and enthusiast of the many advantages of operating a home office, using modern office technology. The home office is what makes many small businesses, which could never have survived only a few short years ago, financial and business successes in the '90s.

The home office is the secret weapon of the modern small entrepreneur.

However, as usual there's no free lunch. It's not just a matter of waking up one morning, strolling over to the kitchen table and starting work as a small businessperson. As with anything in business, studying the details, thinking things out and planning each step in setting up is vitally important.

Home offices are a "hot" subject these days. So you will find many useful self-help books, plus articles in the papers, giving out tips, ideas and suggestions. Some of it is silly stuff, but a lot of it will help you as a memory jogger, to make sure you have thought of everything and have prepared yourself properly. So check out the offerings in your local bookstore and follow the business section in your daily paper. It's all basic stuff and you'll pick up on it quickly and easily.

We can't go through all such details here, but the following cuttings contain valuable advice and insights.

KEEPING YOUR HOME AND OFFICE SEPARATE
Home Is Home. Work Is Work.
Even Though You Work at Home, It's Important to Maintain That Distinction.
1. Clearly demarcate your work space by using a separate room or partition.
2. Set definite work hours.
3. Have a signal that makes it clear when you don't want to be disturbed.
4. Set boundaries. Learn to say, *"No, I'm working now."*
5. Maintain a separate business phone line and use an answering machine or service.
6. Dress in a particular way when you are working, though you may not put on a suit and tie or heels.
7. Organize your office to keep work materials, paper, and equipment in clearly defined office spaces.
8. If possible, have a separate outside entrance.

—From *Working from Home* by Paul and Sarah Edwards, quoted by Amy Dunkin, "Personal Business," *Business Week*

WHAT YOU NEED

Sam Albert, a computer-industry veteran, now works from home as a computer-business consultant. Despite his high-tech expertise, he's proof that home offices can get by without lots of specialized gadgets. "I have a personal computer, a fax machine, an answering machine and a two-line telephone," says Mr. Albert, who has run Sam Albert Associates from his Scarsdale, N.Y., home for six years. "That's all I need."

Many home-business consultants endorse Mr. Albert's approach. They say most home-based businesses—especially start-ups—can stick to the basics and equip themselves for $3,000 to $5,000. Keep things simple in the beginning, they advise, and see whether you really need any extras in terms of equipment, software or phone service.

—Stephanie N. Mehta, *The Wall Street Journal*

HOME ALONE
For Many Home-Based Entrepreneurs, the Biggest Obstacle May Be Overcoming the Feeling of Isolation

Working alone in a home office, without the chance for water-cooler gatherings or hallway conversations, can create such a strong sense of isolation that it impairs an entrepreneur's effectiveness. Especially in the early days of a home-based business, specialists say, before a clientele is established, the owner's ability to combat the isolation may mean the difference between success and failure.

"We need a pat on the back sometimes, a word of encouragement or a kick in the butt," says [a consultant]. "It's a very unusual person who can supply all that for themselves."

Those who can handle the isolation of working from home often are outgoing self-promoters. . . . People who simply like being alone also thrive in home-based settings. . . . But for many others the isolation of a home-based business can mean big trouble. Perhaps the most susceptible are those working at home out of necessity rather than choice, typically after losing their jobs. . . . Another group that can have trouble adapting: those who lack the self-discipline to work effectively without the structure provided by having colleagues around. . . .

Because of the potential for trouble, "it's very important to analyze your temperament and know how much working alone you can stand," [says a consultant]. A dose of self-awareness also is needed to recognize the symptoms of loneliness. . . .

[An author] says the best way to battle these problems is to structure your behavior so you're working *from* home rather than *at* home. In other words, get out of the house. Joining chambers of commerce or other groups can provide links to other business owners, specialists say. Planning meetings or lunches with friends, colleagues or clients also helps to break up the monotony of sitting at a desk in a quiet house, they say. Sometimes all that's needed is a bit of human contact during business hours. . . .

Another strategy is to organize daily activities so there is little time to think about being alone. . . . Especially for people who live alone, simply getting dressed and going out to get coffee or a newspaper before starting the workday can provide enough contact to combat the sense of isolation. . . . Taking up aerobics classes and getting a pet are also common remedies. . . .

In the end, though, not everyone can hack working at home.

—Calmetta Coleman, *The Wall Street Journal*

<u>Memo #17</u> Multilevel Marketing: It Ain't Small Business

MANY PEOPLE WANTING TO START A SMALL HOME BUSINESS ARE ENTICED BY THE PROMISES OF SO-CALLED "MULTILEVEL MARKETING" ORGANIZATIONS. MOST OF THEM END UP BITTERLY DISAPPOINTED.

You've seen the TV pitches, the direct mail literature and the "free seminar" come-ons, with their stories of successful participants who have become millionaires by selling vitamins, beauty products and similar stuff to their friends and family. If you really believe them, I still have that previously owned bridge in Brooklyn to sell you, at a most attractive price; I'll even throw in the Island of Manhattan, as a bonus.

Those millionaire stories are true, but the very, very few who actually made the millions didn't make them by selling Vitamin C to their Auntie Agnes. They made it by recruiting thousands on thousands of successive, descending layers of friends, family and coworkers, as "members," and raking in a percentage of everything they bought (and probably never managed to resell).

The best that can be said about the few professional, ethical multilevel marketing organizations that exist is that they provide an easy, totally rigid, tightly organized system, for home-based people who want to pick up a little extra pocket money every month, by selling odds and ends to their family, friends and coworkers. On the other hand:

- Most participants give up quickly . . . too much effort, too little reward.
- Participants are *not* entrepreneurs. They are just captive sales reps.
- The investment is small, but more often than not, it's lost.
- Your family, friends and coworkers end up fleeing from your pitches.
- This is not small business, and you gain no useful business experience.
- There is a nasty undertone of quasi-religious hype to most schemes.

WATCH OUT! AS MORE ENTREPRENEURS TRY TO WORK FROM HOME, MORE SCAM ARTISTS TRY TO RIP THEM OFF

With millions of Americans looking for ways to make a living from home, scam artists are finding growth opportunities of their own. Fraud and deceptive practices are moving into new areas, including 900-number ventures and seminars on home-based business opportunities. And older scams involving work-at-home opportunities, such as envelope stuffing, assembly kits and so-called multi-level-marketing companies, are cropping up with increasing frequency. . . .

Close scrutiny and a healthy dose of common sense may be the only protection. . . .

Critics say that television infomercials have often been used to peddle fraudulent opportunities. . . . Many participants, even those who ordinarily would know better, get sucked in.

"The people who tend to answer ads for seminars that are frauds are often vulnerable, because they have to stay at home and they need the income," says [a director of a home-business association]. "They're willing to believe anything is possible, because they're slightly desperate.

"Fast, easy and free just doesn't exist. That's the reality."

—Timothy L. O'Brien, *The Wall Street Journal*

<u>Memo #18</u> Preprepared Documents: Ready in Advance

SMALL BUSINESSES SELDOM HAVE POLISHED DOCUMENTS READY AT KEY MOMENTS. THEY SCRAMBLE, IMPROVISE AND MAKE THEMSELVES LOOK BAD. PREPREPARATION SOLVES THE PROBLEM AND BUILDS YOUR IMAGE.

Small business owners are always busy handling urgent problems and priorities. When they suddenly need a well-crafted document or presentation materials about themselves and their activities, they scramble, they improvise and they usually end up doing a lousy job of selling and presenting themselves. They make themselves look bad, needlessly.

Right from the start, I suggest you get in the habit of setting aside a day or two, say, every six months or so, to prepare, polish and update certain documents and materials, which you will always have "on standby," when the need arises. Specifically:

• **Credit & Business Info:**

Over and over again, you are going to be asked to fill in credit and other applications for suppliers, banks, even clients. Every time this happens, you will find yourself scrambling through files to find bits and pieces of information. Done in a hurry, this will at least make you look bad and at worst help your application to be rejected.

Instead, check out all the information that is usually requested, *plus* information *you* want to present. Create a polished two- or three-page document, containing *everything* that may be needed, and entitle it something like: "Financial & Operational Information on XYZ Company, Owners & Managers." Date it. Then, any time you are asked to fill in some form of this nature, just write across it "See Attached" and staple *your* document to it. Done this way, you're communicating on your own terms. It projects an image of efficiency, and will save you an awful lot of time.

• **Public Relations Handouts:**

Few small businesses can afford or should use PR agencies. However, there will always be moments when you will desperately want to have something in writing, explaining in glowing terms who you are and what you do. This requires careful thought and polished preparation. Right from the start, prepare a two-page "blurb" and have it ready for use. Whatever you do, it will always be far better than having *nothing*.

• **Presentation Materials:**

This won't apply to all small businesses, but if your business is the kind that will sooner or later require you to have good presentation materials (photographs, slides, transparencies, video, etc.), *don't leave this to the last moment.* Think ahead. Think when you might need this kind of material, think out what it should look like and start working on it way ahead of time. Done well, it takes considerable time, and if you have to rush it at the last moment, before some key meeting, you may blow an important opportunity, just because you weren't prepared.

<u>Memo #19</u> Patents and Trademarks: Too Often Neglected

TOO OFTEN, PATENTS AND TRADEMARKS ARE NOT TAKEN SERIOUSLY ENOUGH BY SMALL BUSINESSES, BOTH IN PROTECTING THEIR OWN RIGHTS, OR IN INFRINGING ON THE RIGHTS OF OTHERS.

If your small business has inventions or trademarks that you believe to be unique and potentially valuable, and you want to protect them, it is well worth the time, work and small cost involved, to prepare and file the necessary petitions. What seems to have little value today, may be invaluable ten years from now.

Conversely, if you have the slightest suspicion you may be treading on the toes of another company's patents or trademarks, it is also worth paying for a search, to check out the situation. Being forced to change your name and logo, years later, or even pay damages, could be a most painful experience, after so much work in building up your business, image and name.

These clippings give you an idea of some of the dangers.

PICASSO'S HEIRS FIGHT TO CONTROL USE OF HIS NAME

At Cafe Picasso in New York's Greenwich Village, reproductions of Pablo Picasso's works line the walls, and a pizza named after him (garnished with zucchini) is on the menu for $6.50.

Now the artist's heirs want a slice of the pie. Earlier this month, they filed suits in federal courts in Florida, New York and California seeking all profits derived from what they contend is the unauthorized use of both the Picasso name and masterpieces. The dozen-plus defendants include the cafe, as well as the purveyors of ties, tote bags and scarves. . . . A New York lawyer for the heirs in the U.S. estimates that tens of millions of dollars in licensing fees are at stake.

—Frances A. McMorris, *The Wall Street Journal*

BIG DOG BITES BIG DOG IN DISPUTE OVER WHO GETS THE BIG DOG NAME

Glenn Robinson, the Milwaukee Bucks' $68 million rookie, signed a licensing agreement with Roadmaster, an Illinois sporting-goods manufacturer, to sell a line of basketballs bearing his nickname, Big Dog. But Big Dog Sportswear says he's barking up the wrong tree.

Andrew Feshbach, co-owner of Big Dog, a sporting-goods and apparel company based in Santa Barbara, Calif., says his company has been using the Big Dog brand on items ranging from T-shirts to ski jackets to golf balls since 1984 and currently owns the trademark.

—Sana Butler, *The Wall Street Journal*

J. BAKER ORDERED TO PAY $7 MILLION IN DAMAGES

J. Baker Inc. said Susan Maxwell, an inventor of a plastic device used to join pairs of shoes, won a $7 million judgment in damages, attorney's fees and injunctive relief from the footwear and apparel retailer. The company said it would appeal. Ms. Maxwell, owner of Max Merchandising Inc., a Tucson, Ariz., import-export firm, called the judgment "sweet justice."

—*The Wall Street Journal*

Memo #20 E-mail: Benefit or Nuisance in Small Business?

E(ELECTRONIC)-MAIL IS EFFICIENT AND FEASIBLE, WITHIN A BUSINESS OR WITH THE OUTSIDE WORLD. BUT FOR MANY SMALL BUSINESSES IT CAN HAVE MORE MINUSES THAN PLUSES, IN THEIR BEGINNING YEARS.

For certain types of small business, E-mail can be a valuable tool. But for most, especially in the start-up years, it can be an expensive luxury that reduces rather than improves the close communication between coworkers, which is one of the strengths of any small business. Some feel positively:

WITH E-MAIL, YOU'LL GET THE MESSAGE WITHOUT THE HANG-UPS

Electronic mail is a very quick way to exchange personal messages or important documents with others when you can't, or would rather not, get together in person or over the phone. . . . In the minute or so it takes to hem and haw your way through a complicated voice-mail message, you could transmit over the same phone line a much longer, better-organized written message. . . .

E-mail is, in effect, a revival of the lost art of letter-writing, with all its benefits for completeness and context, but with almost instant delivery to one or multiple recipients, and no need for paper and stamps. Some of this is possible with faxing, of course, but faxes usually take longer to send and chew up paper. In addition, with E-mail you can usually reply more quickly by simply clicking a reply button on the screen.

–Walter S. Mossberg, "Personal Technology," *The Wall Street Journal*

Others don't:

From EXECUTIVE SUMMARY by Stanley Bing:

The claims for E-mail as a revolutionary upgrade in human interaction are grandiose. The facts are these: (1) People who hate talking to people love E-mail and burble on about it all the time; (2) People who under all other circumstances hate computers love E-mail, because it elevates idiot note-writing into the cybersphere; (3) E-mail is a notoriously horrible means of communicating any idea more complex than, "Don't cash your paycheck. I'll be by later to explain," tending to transmit a tone of anger and coldness when none was intended; and (4) by creating the illusion that messages have been successfully transmitted, E-mailcentric companies generally stink at communications.

Messages sent aren't always messages received, numbnuts!

–Stanley Bing, *Esquire*

COMPUTER NETWORKS ARE PROFOUNDLY CHANGING THE WORKPLACE. IT'S GOING TO TAKE A LOT OF GETTING USED TO

The impersonal nature of on-screen communication can foster ruthlessness. Computers may feel cool, detached and expressionless. What's more, networks let people indulge in cyberspace snooping and electronic eavesdropping, and enourage micro-management, disloyalty and information hoarding. . . .

It's precisely this lack of human contact that makes networks so potentially disruptive in the workplace. When people stop talking, communication breaks down. With nothing but computer messages to sustain them, employees can become demoralized and inefficient. Loyalty to the employer suffers.

–Laurie Hays, *The Wall Street Journal*

<u>Memo #21</u> Surfing the Net: Only Fun and Games?

GO CRUISE THE "INFORMATION HIGHWAY" ON YOUR OWN TIME, IF YOU WANT TO PLAY, BROWSE, CHAT OR WHATEVER. BUT THE NET OFFERS LITTLE CONCRETE BENEFIT TO MOST START-UP SMALL BUSINESSES.

In Chapter 12, I discussed how critically, vitally important a good PC, with good software, will be as a management tool in your small business.

However, because of the relentless hype and absurd hoopla in the media about the Internet, some businesspeople are starting to believe that the only reason to become computer literate is to "surf the Net."

Get serious. For the moment, there continue to be few good reasons for a new small business to waste time and money with Internet-related PC activities. Check back in a couple of years.

TAKE THIS REVOLUTION . . .

Why is my ancient modem switched off most of the time, when it could be patching me into the Internet? Basically because there is only so much time in the day, and there are a lot of things I would rather be doing . . . than exchanging ephemeral gossip with faceless strangers over the electronic equivalent of the backyard fence. . . . [Some] Americans . . . spend up to 25 hours a week on the Net, goggling at [a screen], and call it community empowerment. To them, one is tempted to say, *Get a life!*

—Robert Hughes, *Time*

A DISILLUSIONED DEVOTEE SAYS THE INTERNET IS WEARING NO CLOTHES

Clifford Stoll, a 44-year-old author, astronomer and computer security expert . . . in his book, "Silicon Snake Oil" complains that the computer revolution has no clothes, despite what he calls the "technoburbling" of laudatory journalists. . . . "Computer networks don't just get in the way of work. They also separate us from the pleasures of life," he writes. . . .

"The information highway is being sold to us as delivering information, but what it's really delivering is data. Numbers, bits, bytes, but damned little information. Unlike data, information has utility, timeliness, accuracy, a pedigree. Information, I can trust. But the data coming across America Online, or CompuServe or whatever, nobody stands behind it. Is the author a medical doctor or some bozo? I don't know, and they're behind a screen anyway. It might be an 11-year-old girl, or a 70-year-old wizened philosopher. What's missing is anyone who will say hey, this is no good. . . . Computers can get just as addictive as television, and as fascinating. . . . Why is it both drug addicts and computer aficionados are called users?"

—Matthew L. Wald, *The New York Times*

Even in a computer industry that seems to specialize in simultaneous hype and obfuscation, the breathless promotion of on-line services has been a spectacle to behold. . . . The P.R. and media machine promoting the trend has wildly exaggerated its benefits, overstated its pervasiveness and understated the costs and difficulty involved.

The results have been confusion and misunderstanding.

—Walter Mossberg, "Personal Technology," *The Wall Street Journal*

<u>Memo #22</u> Web Sites: Do They Really Help You Sell Stuff?

FROM THE MEDIA HYPE, EVERY BUSINESS SHOULD HAVE ITS OWN INTERNET WEB SITE, AND THE NET IS ALREADY A VITAL MARKETING AND SELLING TOOL FOR ANY SMALL BUSINESS. NO WAY. NOT SO. NOT YET. MAYBE NEVER.

Here's the best "take" I can give you, at this point in time, on the use of "Web sites" for marketing and selling the products and services of new, small businesses:

- The hype is outrageous. Don't believe 95 percent of the glowing stories you hear, on the marvels of Web sites, for selling your products.
- If you want to know what's really going on, look for impartial news stories in the business press (check out the clippings that follow).
- There are a small number of specialized businesses and activities that can benefit from a Web site. If you're one of them, you'll already know it. If you don't already know it, then you're not one of them.
- Some well-established small businesses, can sometimes generate additional sales through a Web site. But that's an "add-on," never a substitute for their main selling activity. But, since new small businesses are by definition not well established . . .
- Unless you can clearly see major and immediate advantages to your particular business, don't do it. You'll throw away your money and waste your time.

Trying to generate business on the Internet has been likened to dropping your business cards on a Manhattan sidewalk during rush hour. Almost no one knows you exist, and the few who stumble upon your card are unlikely to be the kind of business prospects you were looking for.

–Sreenath Sreenivasan, *The New York Times*

"How do you make $1 million on the Internet? Invest $10 million." Comment by agent Deborah Levin, who with cartoonist John Callahan, invested $10,000 in a Web site and made $200.

–I. Jeanne Dugan, "In Box," *Business Week/Enterprise*

The companies that control much of the World Wide Web, or wish to do so, aren't very happy. Oh, sure, they're promoting the Web like crazy. But privately, the computer software and hardware companies, the electronic publishers and the advertisers are getting grumpy.

So far, it has proved fiendishly hard to make money on the Web. The total audience is far smaller than the audience for a real mass medium like television, and at any one moment it is spread among vastly more sites than television has channels. As a result, drawing a respectable concentration of "eyeballs" to a company's on-line news or ads is very tough. Even worse, the Web is truly interactive, with users in control. So people call up only the information they want, flit from one publisher's content to another via built-in links that send them elsewhere at the click of a mouse, and find it easy to ignore ads.

–Walter S. Mossberg, "Personal Technology," *The Wall Street Journal*

DON'T GET TRAPPED IN THE WORLD WIDE COBWEB
Too Often, Opening a Site Leads Only to Vast Disappointment–Not Vast Sales

Lured by hype about cheap, swift exposure to 30 million people around the world, 24 hours a day, as many as 400,000 businesses have opened their digital doors . . . but everybody–from the dry cleaner with the low-budget site featuring grainy shots of pressed shirts, to the nation's most powerful realtors' group that gambled $12 million–is reaping the same bounty: vast disappointment.

"They gave a great party, and nobody showed up," says [an Internet expert]. . . . In a recent poll, 90% of small-business respondents said the Net has had little or no impact on their businesses. . . . Most have not gotten back what they invested.

Ghost Towns: Disillusion is running so deep that many are pulling the plug on their sites or letting them become badly outdated, giving rise to "cyberblight."

–I. Jeanne Dugan, *Business Week/Enterprise*

WEB PUBLISHERS START TO FEEL LACK OF ADVERTISING

The Great Web Shakeout, as some in the industry fear it might become, has been gathering momentum for at least a year, as Internet advertising has failed to grow quickly enough to support all would-be Web publishers, and as users continue to balk at paying for much on-line material beside pornography.

"I became increasingly concerned that the resources we were putting into the Web product could have been better devoted to our core product, which is our magazine," [a publisher] said. "Having a Web site is no longer a sign of being on the cutting edge. It might be a sign of not doing much original thinking."

–Seth Schiesel, *The New York Times*

WHO USES THE INTERNET AND HOW?
WE'LL GET BACK TO YOU ON THAT IF SOMEONE FIGURES IT OUT.

More than two years after the Web burst into the limelight as the next great commercial medium, it is remarkable how little is still known about who is using it and how. . . .

Most Web sites still operate on the principle: If we build it, they will come. These sites, whether proferring information or pitching products, are like cut-rate discount stores where mounds of merchandise are piled on tables. The most hardy shoppers eager for a bargain may sift through piles until they come across the gem they were seeking. But the rest of us, who have little time or patience, simply give up and walk out.

–Laurence Zuckerman, "Technology," *The New York Times*

"DIGERATI" SAY ON-LINE MARKETPLACE WON'T MAUL ANY MALLS
FOR A WHILE

The future turns out to be far, far away.

The Internet and on-line services have lured hundreds of companies eager to set up shop. But some experts say it could take a decade, or two, for full-blown electronic commerce to migrate to the desktop computers of American consumers. Most users aren't on-line at all, much of the technology isn't yet up to snuff, and the specter of government regulation looms.

The highest hurdle, however, seems to be consumers themselves. Unnerved by computer bugs and fearless hackers, they don't yet trust the notion of ordering products and paying their bills on-line, and they haven't found software easy enough to make the practice painless.

–Jared Sanberg, *The Wall Street Journal*

IN CYBERSPACE THE WEB DELIVERS JUNK MAIL

It's the hottest destination in cyberspace. The Internet's World Wide Web has attracted companies—from car makers to movie studios—intent on using snazzy graphics and color photos to parade their wares before millions of computer users. Yet look beyond the glossy surface, and things aren't nearly as slick. Many of these corporate outposts—"home pages" in Web parlance—serve up little but the on-line equivalent of junk mail. . . .

Why are so many corporate Web sites so dull? Many companies, in their race to appear hip by erecting a Web storefront, simply dump on-line whatever text-based marketing materials are at hand. Since establishing a Web site costs as little as a few thousand dollars, they don't have to put much thought into the undertaking.

"So many people trying to do business on the Internet think all they have to do is scan in their print advertising or their annual reports. It's hideous," says an executive of MCI.

—Bart Ziegler, *The Wall Street Journal*

INDEX